Praise For

RUMINATIONS & REFLECTIONS
THE MUSICAL JOURNEY OF DAVE LIEBMAN AND RICHIE BEIRACH

We really don't have an exact name for musicians like Dave and Richie. Across decades of recordings and concerts, their aspirations obliterate the definitions of any single genre. This volume reveals the deep insight and wisdom required to resolve their shared quest for meaning in music. Both are master players who continue to strive for what goes beyond and what lies beneath. Reading their words and following their stories in this wonderful book affirms the feeling that they share on the bandstand as one of the great long term partnerships in this music.

—Pat Metheny

Eavesdropping on these two giants and lifelong pals as they spin streams of consciousness, reminiscing about everything from stickball and Chinese handball while growing up in Brooklyn, to vivid tales of working with Miles Davis, Chet Baker, Stan Getz and Elvin Jones offers jazz fans a vicarious thrill. Liebman and Beirach sprinkle so many gems in these intimate conversations about the late '60s – early '70s NYC loft scene, the Greenwich Village club scene, the nature of improvisation, their respective approaches to preparing for concerts and recordings, and a myriad of other topics across the expanse of their 50-plus-year careers makes Ruminations and Reflections a compelling page-turner.

Letters to Our Masters, in which they address what they would say now to the likes of Elvin, Miles, Chet, Getz, Pete LaRoca, and Bill Evans, is particularly fascinating. As Beirach explained of these fictional missives, "Now that we are senior citizens ourselves this gives us a chance to say things to them that we could not speak about to them at the time because we were either too young, didn't know enough to ask the right questions, or were too shy."

Along with the colorful, free-flowing conversation, it contains a comprehensive and annotated list of their favorite recordings together from 1970 to 2020 along with a list of essential jazz and classical recordings. A veritable treasure trove of information interspersed with insightful, often humorous repartee from these two guys from Brooklyn.

—Bill Milkowski, author of *Ode to a Tenor Titan: The Life and Times and Music of Michael Brecker*

A great document from two insightful and knowledgeable artists, my mentors and colleagues. I am thankful for their wisdom.

—Adam Nussbaum, drums

In *Ruminations and Reflections*, two astute musical minds share their insights, perspectives, and memories of the New York jazz scene and the music that defined it. Their comments take me back to that special period during the '70s (my twenties) when I played with them. The city was wild and alive with creativity, camaraderie, and everyone giving it their all.

—John Scofield, guitar

Dave Liebman and Richie Beirach, extraordinary musicians and educators, also happen to be great raconteurs. Their conversations on just about everything are enlightening and very vivid. For example, when they talk about their early professional years in Manhattan in the late '60s and early '70s, I felt like I was stepping into a time machine. From formative Brooklyn memories to more than five decades as hungry students and master practitioners in the jazz world, their individual careers and sporadic partnership have flourished and evolved. These conversations are a must for anyone who loves the music.

—Michael Cuscuna, music producer

This is a masterfully articulated documentation of the very essence of the life and music I've had the privilege of sharing with Dave and Richie since 1979. Considering my conservative New England WASP upbringing, I was initially frightened by the intensity of the way these two Brooklynites related to one another, especially verbally, but also musically. Their symbiotic relationship has been one of the most prolific, courageous, and historic of all time in jazz.

—Ron McClure, bass

Well, in a nutshell this is exactly how it went, in black and "write." Day by day, month to month, tune by tune, gig by gig, opinion upon opinion, and history upon history, definitive and just about all she wrote. If you want to learn about one of the longest & most fruitful jazz partnerships of all time—Liebman & Beirach, then this is the book for you ... an amazingly detailed work of expansive interviews, conversations, and information.

—Randy Brecker, trumpet

On and off the bandstand Dave and Richie's stories are a gift for all of us to embrace. This honest, conversational duet is an insightful look into the relationship of two of the most visionary universal New York jazz masters in the history of the music. Words about their personal life experiences, the music and musicians they've encountered, along with the brotherly love and respect they have for each other. Highly recommended!

—Joe Lovano, saxophone

Ruminations and Reflections paints a vivid picture of two lives brought inseparably together by music. Dave and Richie have each produced a stream of valuable instruction books, but this is something different ... an eloquent conversation about the lives that led to the music—about how (and why) to leap headlong into the jazz community, and then make a lasting contribution to it. This book documents an inspiring journey taken by two warm-hearted and prodigiously talented musicians.

—Steve Swallow, bass

Ruminations and Reflections is expansive in scope and intimate in detail. The free and easy conversations between Dave and Richie are illuminating and fun … some real time travel stuff. But perhaps most remarkable are the series of letters that each veteran has written to a collection of jazz heroes who are no longer with us. Not surprisingly, these homages are thoughtful as well as moving. The incredible effect—the remarkable I mention—is that, by grace of Liebman's and Beirach's words, the likes of Elvin "Emperor" Jones, John Coltrane, Stan Getz, Chet Baker, and Miles Davis are brought back to life—like heaven we can touch. If music is your thing, then this book is astonishingly essential.

—Peter Erskine, drums

Something special happens when musicians talk among themselves. Their stories are more than stories—they become deep dives into the nuts-and-bolts of music, detailed memories of timeless scenes, and life lessons learned from the masters they met and made music with. Richie and Dave are veterans who came of age in the vibrant, DIY New York City of the late '60s when social and musical rules were being rewritten, two like-minded souls on a journey they've been sharing for more than fifty years. This book is a truly rare treat, like sitting in on a late-night conversation, proof that great music relies on shared experiences and a sense of community. That we should never lose the hunger to hear and to learn. Pull up a seat, fill your glass, and listen…

—Ashley Kahn, author of *A Love Supreme: The Story of John Coltrane's Signature Album*

Dave Liebman and Richie Beirach are musical explorers, thinkers, and dreamers. Their insight into jazz innovation is unparalleled! This book is a monumental work and an achievement of love, with an amazing sense of intellectual cognition and passion. It is a kind of "call and response" travelogue through the creative processes of jazz.

It is a stream of flowing thoughts, ideas, and original thinking by two musical jazz giants, discussing their personal "points of departure." This is unprecedented in jazz, where scholarship, knowledge, research, pedagogy, writings, and critical thinking have rarely been written about in this way. They have shed new revelatory light, while maintaining the soulfulness and the essence of the meaning of their music. This book has both a real artistic and educational approach, which is clear, concise, and to the point. It is a portrait of their lives in music and in jazz.

—Justin DiCioccio, performer, conductor, pedagogue (Manhattan School of Music)

RUMINATIONS

&

REFLECTIONS

THE MUSICAL JOURNEY OF
DAVE LIEBMAN AND RICHIE BEIRACH

WITH KURT RENKER

CYMBAL PRESS

Ruminations & Reflections: The Musical Journey of Dave Liebman and Richie Beirach
© 2022 Dave Liebman, Richie Beirach, Kurt Renker
All rights reserved.

Published by Cymbal Press, Torrance, CA USA
cymbalpress.com

No portion of this book may be reproduced in any form, physical or electronic without the written permission of the publisher. This and other Cymbal Press books may be purchased at cymbalpress.com. Volume and education discounts are available.

ISBNs
Paperback: 978-1-955604-10-9
Hardcover: 978-1-955604-11-6

MUS025000   MUSIC / Genres & Styles / Jazz
MUS050000   MUSIC / Individual Composer & Musician
BIO004000   BIOGRAPHY & AUTOBIOGRAPHY / Music

All marks are the property of their respective owners.

Publisher: Gary S. Stager
Editor: Sylvia Martinez
Cover: Yvonne Martinez

While every precaution has been taken, the publisher and authors assume no responsibility for errors, omissions, changed information or URLs, or for damages resulting from the use of the information herein.

Contents

Foreword 1

Musical Lives
Making the Scene 5
Lookout Farm – ECM 15
The India Tour 23
Forgotten Fantasies – A&M Horizon 27
The Pendulum Recording and the Village Vanguard ... 31
The 1970s in New York City 35
Drugs, Alcohol, and Late Night Hanging 37

Our Views On
Classical Music History 43
Jazz History 49
Playing Free 51
Jazz Education Today 57
Bill Evans 65
McCoy Tyner 69
Herbie Hancock 71
Chick Corea 73
John Coltrane 79
Wynton Marsalis 81
Jack DeJohnette 83
Wayne Shorter and the 1987 Tribute Concert to John Coltrane ... 87

Personal Perspectives
Surviving the Music Business 93
How Do We Feel about Our Past Playing Today? 97
Our Legacy 101

Road Trip Through Our Past
Brooklyn Born 107
Games We Played 110
Family 114
School Days 116
Coney Island 126

Back to Manhattan	134
Lower Manhattan	138
Greenwich Village	147

Letters to Our Masters

Dave's Letters	155
Pete La Roca	155
Elvin Jones	158
Miles Davis	160
Wheel of Life	163
Richie's Letters	165
Stan Getz	165
Chet Baker	167
Miles Davis	170
Bill Evans	172
John Coltrane	174

Preparation & Performance

A Jazz Lecture for the Interested Listener	179
The Challenge of Jazz	179
Preparing for Performances	184
The Five Elements of Learning Jazz	186
Ten Thousand Ways	193
Our Approach to Preparing for Concerts and Recordings	197
Choosing Players and Instruments	197
Concert vs. Recording	200
Piano and Guitar Accompanists	202
All Piano Players are Geniuses	205
Comping	208
The Masters	210

A Listener's Guide

A Short Introduction to a Band Called Quest	217
Richie's Tour of Our Favorite Recordings from 1970 to 2021	221
The Complete Liebman-Beirach Discography	281
Our List of Essential Jazz and Classical Recordings	288

Addresses in New York	291
Glossary	293
Dedications	295
Image Credits	295
About the Authors	305
Index	307
Also from Cymbal Press	304

Foreword

While working with Dave and Richie for over 40 years we have had many very interesting discussions in the recording studio, backstage at concerts, in restaurants, and while traveling together. Their clear memories and articulation brings so much life into these talks that we decided to write down some of those stories. Over the last couple of years we added more material and realized that this would make an interesting book.

So here it is, a wild journey with Dave and Richie telling their stories, starting with their first meeting in 1967, and ending with discussing their latest duo recording *Empathy* released in 2021. There is a chapter on how they approach preparing their music for concerts and recordings, their views on the history of jazz and classical music, on other musicians, on teaching, the music business, and an amazing car trip going back to the past, talking about growing up in Brooklyn in the 1950s and about being a young jazz musician in Manhattan in the 1960s and '70s.

Enjoy.

Kurt Renker

Dave, Richie, & Kurt

MUSICAL LIVES

Making the Scene

Dave: So when did we first meet?

Richie: We met at a jam session in 1967 at Queens College, where you were a student. I don't remember the playing, but I do remember that you were very pissed off at me.

Dave: Yes, a room in Queens College with David Roitman, playing standards.

Richie: David Roitman on drums, Warren Citron on alto sax, who was not very good, but everybody was better than me. You were the king, of course, you look exactly the same, dark glasses, very intense. You were way ahead of me because you were already playing with Larry Coryell, Bob Moses, and many others. And you had the yellow jazz fake book.

Dave: Yes, modern jazz, yellow book.

Richie: I knew like one and a half tunes but somehow we played together and I remember we had an instant communication. I think you saw a willingness in me. So after the session, we went outside to the parking lot. I remember you had a Chevrolet Bel Air ... big as a house!

Dave: A Chevrolet Bel Air.

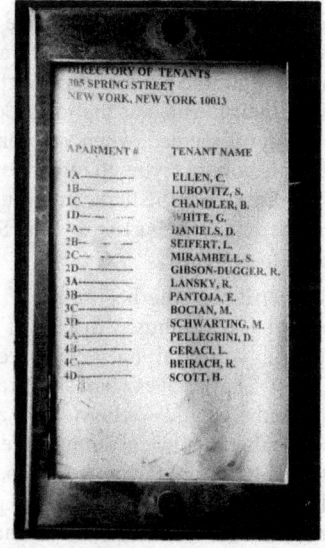

Richie: It was summer and on the hood of the car you took out the yellow jazz fake book, the original bebop fake book. I asked, so which tunes should I learn? You said you have to learn this tune, and you got to learn this this this this this this this, and I said okay. You were very nice, but you were obviously in shock and it was right because you had more experience than me. 1967, Queens College, jam session, parking lot, that was the beginning.

Dave: You moved to 305 Spring Street, and I got the loft on 19th Street.

Richie: I did not see you for a while and then you found the loft on West 19th Street. We discovered that we both had some basic skills and were at the very beginning of the development of our own personal styles. We were kind of looking for our own personal identity and we found that since there was very little jazz education available and it was difficult to get information, we kind of did it together. We learned together ... we helped each other. I helped you with the harmony; you helped me with the melody. You were always an excellent sight reader and we would go through the tunes. Then we played free for hours and hours in the loft. And we also tried to write our own tunes individually.

I would come to the loft every Sunday and sometimes during the week, just to hang out, listen to music, listen to John Coltrane, etc.. Your loft had a tie-dyed cloth ceiling. We had no money, so we needed cheap food, luckily Chinese restaurants were close and were very cheap.

We developed a relationship and a way to play together. You had this old brown German piano, a George Steck. We would play free, we listened to Miles Davis and John Coltrane's music, sometimes trying to transcribe tunes. You would be at that record player and I would sit at the piano and you would say did you get it and I would say no. We had to buy three copies of *Impressions* in order to transcribe the music. We learned Wayne Shorter's tune "Pinocchio" and we tried to play a piece from McCoy Tyner titled "Contemplation" and also McCoy's "Passion Dance," all of which were on the iconic *The Real McCoy* record. I wasn't very good. I was talented but inexperienced, but I was willing. You played drums with me, which was great. It is very difficult to follow you when you play drums. You had the energy and the sound.

Dave: We were, of course, both completely enamored by John Coltrane, at least in my case, big time ... McCoy Tyner and Herbie Hancock on piano ... the Miles Davis Quintet of the 1960s.

Richie:...the Bill Evans Trio...

Dave: And Paul Bley of course. Plus, we both studied with Lennie Tristano for a moment at different times, so we were sort of in love with the roots of jazz, but we were of a different era. This was the late '60s, and we were not immune to the hippie stuff, the psychedelics, Vietnam, etc. We were aware of the Beatles and we liked their music, but the John Coltrane Quartet was my main inspiration. And in a way, it seemed, when we look back in retrospect, we found that we were on the forefront of trying to integrate the variety of musical styles that we were being exposed to. For the first time, you could get records of all styles easily, from Jimi Hendrix to Béla Bartók to Ravi Shankar and, of course, Coltrane, Bird, and so forth in one store.

Richie: It was the beginning of what became known as ethno-musicology ... basically world music. In 1968, I was going to the Manhattan School of Music, studying classical music and composition, not jazz. I was discovering the greats: Charles Ives, Bartók, Stravinsky, Prokofiev, Shostakovich, Alban Berg, Schoenberg, and Webern, and all the great pieces of the so-called modern classical contemporary music literature. So I was learning it and then showing it to you. I would say, "Hey Lieb, look at that chord!" I was trying for my own development to integrate contemporary classical harmony into the fabric of the jazz tradition, which was a real challenge. It was easier to write your own tunes in that contemporary style, but to do it within "Stella By Starlight" or an F blues was a real challenge, somewhat new and personal.

Dave: And we badly wanted to do it together.

Richie: We were groping at the beginning. We didn't really know what we were doing, but always two heads are better than one and we had the ability to play all the time in your loft. In those days, you could never play in your own apartment because you caught hell from your neighbors or the landlord. It was impossible because New York is the city of small apartments unless you have a lot of money. So you had to have a loft to work on the music at any time with anybody.

Dave: That was the beginning of January, 1969 ... 138 West 19th Street between Sixth and Seventh Avenue. I was the first in that building. By complete luck, the landlord's name was amazingly Saul Lieberman ... a complete coincidence. In those days, there was a kind of formula to finding housing of any sort, let alone so specific. You went to Sheridan Square to get the new edition of the Village Voice at the newsstand to check the first listings every Wednesday at 7 a.m. If the description of the apartment or loft was close to what you needed (as well as the price), you made the call and hustled to check it out. This 19th Street loft used to be a tie-dye shirt factory, which is why I had those materials strewn across the floor when I moved in. To liven up the place, I stapled the colorful material left by the former tenants on the ceiling. It was kind of hip and a conversation piece.

Richie: What was your rent?

Dave: $125 a month and I had to pay a fixture fee. The fixture fee was basically a ripoff. You pay the guy who rented the loft before me and had to pay supposedly for what we called the key money or a fixtures fee which meant that they had put in a sink, maybe a bathroom, maybe a refrigerator, maybe a stove which in this case was not true because these tie-dye folks did not live there. They really only did work there. My key money was $1,200.

But the first clause of most leases for lofts said, "Thou shall not live here!" But of course, that meant you could have a hot plate and a little mattress on the floor in case you got tired. You were allowed to lay down! The building inspectors were all paid off, of course. Though that was a bit of money, it made me appear independent and that further enabled me to go to Saul Lieberman answering the expected questions, "Do you have a job, do you work?" I said I have a license to be a teacher in the school system, which was how I made money. So he said, "Okay, you can afford $125 and your last name is Liebman, so I guess it is alright." He was an old school landlord, his office, the smell, it was like a picture out of an old movie. I moved in to the 3rd floor while they hoisted the grand piano up from the roof. I was shaking, thinking, is the building going to collapse? You should've been there.

Richie: How did Dave Holland end up living there?

Dave: I had met him when I first went to Europe in 1967 ... the first time on my own. My parents gave me $1,000, and a book called *Europe On $5 A Day*. I started in London. My mother was very smart. She booked me a hotel for the first night and an open return ticket to New York, instructing me to use the guidebook, see the culture, go to Paris, and so on. I started in London and, of course, as I rested from my first big flight, I contacted some musician names that bassist Cameron Brown had given me. The first call I made was answered by a guy who said there was a session at the famous Ronnie Scott's club that night ... all the young bloods would be there. So come down, we would love to meet you. At this period, a young New York musician was exotic even though I could hardly play. After a horrible dinner, I made my way to the club and was met by great guys who were nice, fun, and could play. I had my tenor with me just in case. So my first night in London was a lesson in itself. I'm really jet-lagged ... lonely and scared. When I got out of Victoria Station in downtown London, I got to tell you ... people running around me as I carried a valise and my tenor ... I almost broke down. Here I was across the ocean for the first time in my life at 20 years old. But again that night, everybody was beautiful to me. Future famous guys were there: Alan Skidmore, John Surman, and especially bassist Dave Holland, who said get out of the hotel and stay with me and Surman, which I did for three weeks!

In 1968, living in the loft, Dave Holland calls me: "I'm in New York playing with Miles Davis!" I said, "What?" So I went to the Blue Coronet club in Brooklyn that night and I saw Dave playing with Tony Williams, Chick Corea, Wayne Shorter, and Miles. I said "Dave, you know I would like to return the favor since you let me stay with you for three weeks. Have you got a place to live?"

He said, "Well, we're looking for something. I'm with my wife Claire and daughter Louise who is two years old." Meanwhile, I am living in a building with the second and first floor empty, so let me talk to the landlord. I went to Saul, who says, "Can he pay the rent?" I said, "He is playing with the most famous jazz musician in the world. I think he can pay the rent." OKAY!

So that's how Dave and I got to live on the second and third floor of 138 West 19th Street between Sixth and Seventh Avenues. A few months later, Dave says Chick Corea is getting divorced and is looking for a place to live. Dave said let's drive over to hang out with Chick. So one day we went out to Queens and ended up listening to his recent mixes of *Now He Sings, Now He Sobs*. I will never forget this because it was the first time I met Chick. His house was in the middle of Queens Village. They were living on a normal street ... middle class. I remember thinking to myself, this Chick guy sounds a lot like McCoy Tyner. "Is there any chance of getting in on the first floor in your building since you seem to know the landlord?" says Chick. Of course, Saul was happy and so forth. That's how Chick got into the building with us.

So now we had Chick on the first floor, Dave Holland with Louise and Claire on the second floor, and myself on the third floor. This was basically a jazz building ... and the beginning a lot of free jazz being played. There could be three sessions going on at once.

Richie: There were!

138 West 19th Street

Dave: Chick downstairs with Anthony Braxton, Dave Holland, and Barry Altschul doing something. Then upstairs with you, myself, Steve Grossman, Michael Brecker, Randy Brecker, etc. Anybody could come at any hour. The house key was in a sock that I threw down three floors. I had a brown five foot six grand piano, a drum set, eventually a set of vibes ended up there. We would play all night and then go to Chinatown to a restaurant called Wo Hop ... open all night with a lot of "fringe" artists hanging out waiting for the egg rolls.

Richie: 17 Mott Street, the best Chinese food in Chinatown, New York.

Dave: That would be enough food for the whole day. Then we went back to the loft and started all over again. I taped a lot of it.

Richie: Do you remember our Wake Up 6 routine? After a full day and night of playing, talking, hanging, and usually going out to eat some cheap but good food, we would come back to your 19th Street loft to sleep for a few hours. I slept on the couch, you in your bed.

Sometimes we would have to wake up early because you might have a sub teaching job in Harlem to make a living, or I had classes at the Manhattan School of Music. So we basically tumbled out of our beds and immediately you sat down behind your drums and I sat at the piano. We started playing and fell into a very relaxed, slowish 6/4 feel, usually trying to copy the great McCoy Tyner tune "Contemplation" from his *The Real McCoy* record. This slow and relaxed swinging 6/4 feel helped us to wake up gradually. This tempo was better than a ballad, because a ballad is too stationary, we would fall right back to sleep! And we were not awake enough to play a fast up tempo tune. So this feel became our way of coming out of a dead sleep, sometimes with some kind of a group hangover.

The Wake Up 6 became part of our duo routine and we sometimes actually used this feel as a viable setting for our music.

So the loft was the beginning of our relationship and the beginning of our contacts with a lot of other musicians, some of whom are still active.

Dave: You were schooled, but in my case, I knew that to get better, I had to play a lot. I wasn't a natural like Steve Grossman, who was playing great very early. To play a lot meant I had to have a loft. I knew about lofts through drummer Bob Moses, who I met in 1962. He was living in lofts since he was sixteen. Moses was my guide to the music.

Richie: Moses was the same age as you?

Dave: He was one year younger ... he was way more advanced than me because his father and mother were involved in jazz. His godmother was Abbey Lincoln, the singer. He lived in the building where Elvin Jones lived, 101st Street and Central Park West, so he was very involved, very early. He introduced me to the Bulgarian Women's choir, James Brown, Ravi Shankar, a lot of music in all styles, which was a trademark of the 1960s generation. We went to see John Coltrane together. I knew a little bit already about the jazz scene when you met me ... that was my cachet. I had been around a bit because of Moses, absolutely through Moses.

Richie: So I got to benefit from your thing with Moses?

Dave: Yep. So I had the loft and then you started coming around. How did we organize the music ... you and I?

Richie: Everything starts at 19th Street with the duo, us going into different musical directions. First playing free, just without any predetermined idea, as we do now. By the way, let's get this thing straight about free playing ... a matter at times of misinformation. Nobody plays "free." It has nothing to do with money! Playing free means freely, without a predetermined sense of structure or harmony or form. Playing completely free of any spoken musical matters means you just start to play. For us, it is like a duo stream of consciousness. It's a great way to play and if you've got good ears, know how to listen, and accompany, and interact, it is one of the best ways to play and if it works it produces the freshest sounds. Of course, you could play "free" solo, but it is a lot more challenging and intense with other people.

Dave: In the 1960s in my loft, you could have ten guys playing free for hours. Sometimes it sounds like a barnyard or a pet store on fire, while sometimes it was amazing. The whole point is you don't know what's coming, and that's fantastic and scary.

Richie: Scary, yes. Also in the contemporary classical music world, going on at the same time or even before, were such composers such as Pierre Boulez, Karlheinz Stockhausen, Ligeti, Luigi Nono ... all these guys basically notating the kind of music that we were improvising. Frederic Rzewski had this amazing group in Rome, Italy, called Musica Elettronica Viva. Boulez built the IRCAM studio in Paris, the music studio at Pompidou Center in Paris. Also in Germany, the government gave Stockhausen millions to build an electronic studio at WDR Radio in Cologne. In Germany and France, they respect culture.

Dave: Those were the places to develop electronic music.

Richie: The point is that the stuff that we were playing in the duo on 19th Street, playing free, was part of a larger musical movement of the day, even in 20th century written music. I don't remember a music stand in the room.

Dave: As you described, we played a lot. Our model was basically *Ascension*, John Coltrane's recording from 1966, which features six or seven horns playing what is categorized as Energy Free Jazz ... all playing together with solos in between ensemble passages. This was for a few years a kind of modus operandi for us. But there was change, as always, in the air. I'll never forget it. Lanny Fields, a bass player one day came into the loft and said, "Do you know this record?" and he put on Wayne Shorter's great recording *Speak, No Evil* from 1964, with some of the greatest tunes of all time and it was like a revelation. I wasn't really that exposed to what Miles Davis's group was doing at that time ... I was so Coltrane'd out. I really didn't understand the tunes on Wayne's record. I remember we sat down to transcribe the tunes from that record. We did that for the next day or two with the phonograph needle absolutely destroying the vinyl. I realized I could not really play that great on advanced chord changes. I needed more work. In any case, this free jazz thing had reached its peak in the late 1960s and early 70s for the guys coming to play and hang out in my loft.

We believed so strongly in free jazz that we formed an organization, Free Life Communication, of which I was the president, and you were the vice-president ... that's a whole story in itself. Free Life Communication was a co-op of musicians that was basically formed because of the necessity for us to finally go out and play in public instead of just in the loft for each other.

Musical Lives

Richie & Dave. Late 1960s at Dave's 19th Street loft

Richie: We weren't good enough to play in the Village Vanguard or other clubs at that time.

Dave: We were young, 21, 22, and also that was historically the lowest point in jazz. I can remember Woodstock in 1969, Jimi Hendrix, etc. Rock music was ascending while jazz was completely forgotten. Even the Village Vanguard was closed for a couple of months in the winter. So things weren't that great for the jazz community anyway. But in any case, we were playing free jazz and felt the need to go out and play this wild music in public. The first meeting of Free Life Communication in my loft was historical.

Richie: Yes.

Dave: I can't remember the exact dates, but definitely 1969–1970. We had 20 guys in my loft. Bob Moses was deep into it at that point. We invited Anthony Braxton and Leroy Jenkins as guests since they had experience as part of the AACM in Chicago and another group in St. Louis. They each spoke to us. Leroy basically said if you don't have a reason and you are not Black, forget it! This is talking to a room full of mostly young white musicians. You must remember that during this time, it was quite a historic period as far as race relations go in the United States, especially in New York City. A couple hours later Anthony spoke and his message was "peace and love, do your thing, etc." He was extremely supportive. It was a really dramatic moment in the loft. We then decided to form an association. Next order of business that night was the need for a meaningful name. Bob Berg was sitting on the floor next to the bed that Dave Holland and his wife slept in. There was Bob with his hippie hairdo, "Lets call it free life communication. It's about our lives and we want to communicate." We voted and agreed to name it Free Life Communication. You came right in there being my lieutenant with me as president. Long story short, through connections to a lawyer and accountant, we received the 501c3 designation for non-profit organizations. Shortly after, we were awarded a grant from the New York State Council on the Arts ... amazing!

Richie: What about the Samuel Rubin Foundation?

Dave: New York State gave us $5,000. Then our accountant found out that the Samuel Rubin Foundation was looking for artists to populate a building called the Space for Innovative Development on West 36th Street. They financed the renovation of an old church, located midtown at the cost of one million dollars. The well known Murray Louis and Nikolais dance companies were resident as was an organization called Open Theatre led by Joe Chaikin. The Rubins were looking for a music group and came to the loft to hear us play ... pretty heavy!

I will never forget it when Mr. and Mrs. Samuel Rubin came to the 19th Street loft. They came in a limousine, both very well dressed and elegant. They sat on the floor in the middle of the room where I had drums, vibes, and a grand piano. By then, we knew pretty much how to build a set of music and keep some attention, using musical devices that we were experimenting with. If I remember it was you, me, Nancy Janoson on flute, Bob Moses on drums, Frank Tusa on bass, and percussionist Armen Halburian might've been there also.

Richie: Mrs. Rubin started singing with us in the middle of the free set.

Dave: After we played, I offered them some Mu tea. Remember, some of us were strict with a macrobiotic diet (including me). I also gave them a pancake that I used to make for us. They loved us. After all, here were true Bohemians, young and hungry for the music and its offshoots at that time in history. They decided to give us one whole floor in the church, 3,000 square feet with a Steinway piano, a pristine wood floor and a few dozen pillows for folks to sit and get comfortable. All for a required $1 a year because you legally had to have a lease. So now Free Life Communication had all the fixings that corporations do, except being run by a bunch of hairy hippies! That first year we had several hundred concerts, playing mostly our versions of post-Coltrane *Ascension*. For me I learned about holding meetings, making a budget, upkeep, etc..

But as mentioned earlier, we started to recognize that we had to get closer to the tradition in order to understand jazz better. So we started working individually and together on the more traditional side of jazz with chord changes, swinging time, etc. Eventually a few of us got lucky and became sidemen to the masters ... me with Elvin Jones and a little later Miles Davis ... you got the gig with Stan Getz and later Chet Baker and others. Our time was coming!

Richie: Here's the thing. The trajectory of the duo and Quest began on 19th Street ... free, duo, un-predetermined, and then you were saying we realized that we really couldn't play the jazz literature as well as we should. We could kind of get by, but we didn't want to do it like that. So we got down on it, two white Jewish intellectual kids looking for answers and ways of growing. Now the guys that were already doing it really well around that time were not that much older than us. They were less than one generation older. Chick Corea is six years older than me, Wayne was five years older, Miles was 20 years older, John Coltrane was dead, etc.

Dave: Herbie Hancock, McCoy Tyner, and Keith Jarrett are only five to seven years older than us.

Richie: So here we are in the loft on 19th Street in 1969 listening to the Wayne Shorter recording *Speak No Evil*. What were they doing? We were trying to figure out what chords they were playing. We were trying to transcribe the chords and melodies that they improvised. We called the record shop and asked, "Did you get the new Miles Davis record *Miles Smiles* yet? Yes, you got it? Hold it for me, I'm coming over right now to buy it."

So we bought the record and got into it. We would play the record over and over again. Dave asked me, "did you get that phrase?" And I'd say "no ... shit," go back, listen again, destroying the typical LP physically. Records were 3 dollars and 33 cents, which was pretty cheap. Transcribing the music together was not easy for us since we did not have perfect pitch. We did not have fantastic instant ears like Steve Grossman and Mitch Kerper ... remember that guy?

Dave: Yes, he had perfect pitch.

Richie: We had good ears, and we were fairly talented, but we were not geniuses. We had to work hard, intellectually, hours and hours.

Dave: We really wanted it.

Richie: Our first record was recorded in 1970 and titled *Night Scapes*. It featured poet Carvel Six reading plus us improvising, and was followed in 1973 by *First Visit* with Dave Holland and Jack DeJohnette, recorded in Japan.

Lookout Farm - ECM

Dave: The next main happening was an offer for me from ECM Records, which was a growing new label that had just released *Facing You* by Keith Jarrett and two solo piano records by Chick Corea.

In essence, we had our first record deal, which included promotion and some tour support. There was a feeling that this new "fusion" element could be useful. Polydor was representing ECM, meaning they had good distribution and a certain allure as a new hot little label from Europe that everybody eventually knew about. They also had exciting European groups with Jan Garbarek, Terje Rypdal, Bobo Stenson, and Jon Christensen, etc. By the early 1970s, ECM had released about 20 to 30 records. Producer Manfred Eicher offered me a deal to record the first time in 1972 at the Berlin Jazz Festival when I played there with Elvin Jones. He didn't follow through until the next year when I played the festival in Berlin again, this time with Miles Davis. He asked me if I had any music in mind? I told him that I had a rhythm section in New York ... a quartet with Richie Beirach on piano, Frank Tusa on bass, and Jeff Williams on drums. I would like to add percussion and a guitar player, John Abercrombie. He said okay, let's do it. And that's how the first Lookout Farm record came out which is probably still my most well-known recording.

Now I had to finish my gig with Miles ... I mean, how do you "leave" Miles Davis? Here's a short story I remember very well. We were on tour in Brazil. One night, I asked him if we could meet in the hotel room. He knew I was giving notice. "What will you do?" I said I got guys for a group and I don't want to wait. He said, "You gonna play those eight-bar forms?" Insinuating I'm going to be a corny bro. I said, "What did you do for forty years?"

Richie: Good answer!

Dave: "If I pass through and don't play the language which YOU WERE PART OF DEFINING, wouldn't that be a drag?" He growled, "yeahhhhh." Whenever Miles didn't want to acknowledge that you were right about something, he would go "yeahhhhh." This followed by a hand movement dismissing whomever was conclusive!

We started Lookout Farm in May 1974. On our first gig we opened for Larry Coryell's Eleventh House in Westport, Connecticut, in a theater. I will never forget that first gig and I will tell you why. When we got on the bandstand, I realized I couldn't look at Elvin or Miles anymore for leadership. I saw you guys looking at me and I realized, holy shit, I have to come up with the real deal all the time since I am the leader now.

Richie: You were the man then!

Dave: I'll tell you, man, I had that lonely feeling in the pit of my stomach, gotta say it was the first time it really hit me, you know? And then the next gig that was notable was at this Irish bar Debbie's in Boston. Basically, a college beer hang, TV and billiards operated by Irish cats ... typical Boston deal. The gig was happening the night Nixon resigned.

Richie: That's right, it was on TV.

Dave: When we walked in Nixon was giving the resignation speech ... this was August '74. I of course, think I'm Miles, wearing scarves, treating everybody like a piece of shit cause I had a job to do!

Richie: Attitude!

Dave: Attitude with a capital A, bro.

Richie: You had a chip on your shoulder like the size of the Empire State Building.

Dave: Well, I was king for a minute with a hot new band featuring great young cats. Plus, equipment-wise, we had a Fender electric piano with Altec Lansing speakers, and I had an echoplex and chorus box for my saxophones. We were taking no prisoners!

Richie: Also you have to remember Chick Corea had a fusion band ... John McLaughlin had the Mahavishnu Orchestra ... and there was Weather Report and Dreams with Michael and Randy Brecker, John Abercrombie, etc. Those fusion groups were around and that's why we had to have the electric piano and all that gear. We went with the contemporary flow ... the language of the day.

A Fender Rhodes with 88 keys which was a drag to haul around, and especially our sound system with two gigantic speakers ... the fusion days! That's how I hurt my back! And remember the Mutron III effect for the electric piano?

Dave: We had equipment like a rock band. This was the height of fusion and, after all, in our mind WE WERE FUSION!

Richie: Contemporary Fusion.

Dave: So we play the first set and before the second set, the owner comes over to me. We're outside, probably smoking or whatever and he says, "It's time to play!" And I said "I don't feel like playing yet."

Richie: Yeah, Miles shit!

Dave: I wasn't "inspired" enough to play. He took me by the shirt and put me against the wall, not violently, but enough to make the point. He said, "I tell you when to play. This is my place!" That was a lesson which was getting along with the people you work with and work for ... don't be an a-hole.

Richie: You could not pull off that Miles shit then ... you couldn't do it.

Dave: No way. If something happened with Miles like that, he would leave the gig and the hell with it. In any case, that was actually the beginning of our thing.

Richie: It comes down to how much you want it. So in 1973, we recorded the *Lookout Farm* album for ECM, a very important record for us. And then a year later we recorded *Drum Ode*, again for ECM. The music came out great but the recording session was a complete scandal.

ECM was funded by Elektro-Egger in Munich, remember Mr. Egger? Manfred was this skinny guy who loved music and who had already by 1973 produced some amazing records with Chick Corea, Paul Bley, and others. That was the beginning of a kind of German Blue Note in the sense of a lot of product in the early days, always with Manfred as the producer. He was a classical bass player who had very specific taste.

Dave: ... concerning repertoire and sound.

Richie: He knew he wanted to sign young and upcoming musicians, some of who played in various Miles Davis bands. What he really wanted was Herbie Hancock, he loved Herbie. But he got Chick Corea, Steve Kuhn, and of course Keith Jarrett. I'm not sure why our music appealed to him, we were a burnout band.

Dave: We were some of the young and upcoming cats in New York City.

Richie: Lookout Farm was a half acoustic and half electric band.

Dave: Nobody was immune to this fusion onslaught: Mahavishnu, Weather Report, Chick's various bands, and of course Herbie Hancock ... I'm missing some groups, but you get the point. By 1980 basically fusion was over.

Richie: ...Keith was immune to fusion...

Lookout Farm 1974: Jeff Williams, Richie, Frank Tusa, Dave

Dave: ... and except for that European thing which Manfred exemplified and it became a thing of its own. He had Jan Garbarek, Terje Rypdal, he had Keith, he made albums that were selling, packaged beautifully with great sound. He had a vision ... that's the way he conducted himself and therefore all the records had a lot in common, more so than most other labels.

Richie: Just like Blue Note, a vision! We really wanted this recording deal with ECM but sometimes you have to be careful what you wish for because you might get it. For a while we had it, then we lost it. Through no fault of our own. The thing about Manfred was that he was a wonderful producer, one of the best, very creative, as long as you played the music that he liked—ballads, free things, rubato, no hard edges. But he would accept some harder stuff in order to get the freer stuff. So we had some issues with him. You had some problems with him on the *Drum Ode* record.

Dave: Let me go back to the beginnings. We have to give credit to producer Manfred Eicher and his record label ECM for coming up to me. He pursued me and finally we came together to do a project which would end up being the Lookout Farm recording. That first project still sells. We did four tunes. Remember, at that time, LPs were more or less 20 minutes per side, so let's say ten minutes per tune. If I think about it, my whole artistic life, musically and stylistically, was on that first record. A Latin crossover tune called "Pablo's Story," an odd meter rockish tune called "Sam's Float," a rubato 20th century tune called "MD" for Miles, and a complete post-Coltrane burn titled "Lookout Farm." In the end, those four tunes made up the record.

Richie: Yeah, those four tunes represent of a lot of our musical direction until now.

Dave: In the end, you are who you are. Lookout Farm had a good two-year run and we have live tapes that represent some of those gigs. The electric piano was a big part of our repertoire and as I had mentioned, I had certain pedals, echoplex, chorus, etc. Frank Tusa played electric and acoustic bass, Jeff Williams on drums ,and for a time we had Badal Roy on tablas along with Don Alias on congas. The music was truly multi-directional.

Richie: The electric piano was a combination of choice and self defense. Because we were a young band, these were our first tours, including Europe. We did a gigantic American tour in a van, swung all the way around Vancouver, with stops in Denver, Philly, Boston ... we went everywhere. Those tours don't exist anymore for jazz groups. A lot of the places we played had pianos that sounded like firewood, or did not have an acoustic piano at all. So we carried a special electric piano that was made for me with an 88 key keyboard build by Harold Rhodes, made specially for us. It had two 12 inch Altec Lansing speakers in the bottom. It weighed a ton and destroyed everybody's backs from carrying it. When you are young you have tremendous energy, you sleep on the floor, you sleep in the van—it doesn't matter—you don't sleep that much, you don't eat that much with the music really keeping us going. The main thing about Lookout Farm was the incredible collective energy that all of us had.

Dave: I always thought we were a kind of a rock band in jazz with the vibe like in a rock band. With rock bands, the guys often lived and played together all the time, which is kind of what we did. It was not a jazz band like Miles, who hired guys that you would see only at the gig. We wrote a book together called *Small Group Improvisation*. This is considered a classic now and re-released.

Richie: We were smart not to try to be a bebop band. We didn't get stuck in a stylistic trap. This way, we had at least a chance to expand. Plus, there was a lot of other music going on at the same time. Fusion was at its height and spawned good and not so good bands. An album like Herbie Hancock's *Headhunters* got killed at first from the jazz prunes. They said it was a sacrilege ... Herbie is a great jazz pianist ... this is a commercial record ... blah, blah, blah! Actually, there are long improvisations all over these records, chromatic solos over vamps. On occasion, a beautiful ballad enhanced by pedals and effects could be heard on these LPs. Commercial record ... not really!

Dave: It is the beat that made it commercial.

Richie: The beat, right, critics didn't get it.

Richie: So *Lookout Farm* was your hit record.

Dave: Yes, *Lookout Farm* was my best-selling record—25,000 plus.

Lookout Farm 1975: Jeff Williams, Frank Tusa, Dave, Richie, Badal Roy

Richie: *Drum Ode* is a sad story and a funny story. Looking back, it was funny, but it wasn't funny at that time. Manfred was very happy with *Lookout Farm*. He was cool ... we did tours with a great guy who worked for ECM in the beginning before he went on his own ... like us! His name was Thomas Stöwsand. We were young cats ... we were on the road, feeling good. We knew we were not Wayne Shorter or Herbie Hancock or McCoy Tyner or John Coltrane, but we were working. We were working all the time, going out for six-week tours, coming back home to chill, then we'd go out again ... it was not just a weekend thing. There were gigs ... there was a circuit. In the 1990s, the circuit died with too many festivals and musicians asking for too much money.

Dave: By the way, Lookout Farm is where Eugene Gregan, a painter and good friend, lived. He had a big influence on us. We spent many days with him and learned how to look at art and absorb other things besides music.

Richie: Well said ... a great master ... a very nice and down-to-earth guy.

Dave: So our next recording was *Drum Ode* and is about me loving drummers. Drummers, the joy of my life ... we had a whole bunch of them on this record: Don Alias, Patato Valdés, Jeff Williams, Bob Moses, Collin Walcott, Ray Armando, Badal Roy, so at times all six or seven drummers played together.

Richie: Plus Gene Perla on electric bass and me on electric piano only, my souped up 88 Fender Rhodes. This record was not European…it was an American recording. Like *Lookout Farm*, which was recorded in New York City, something Manfred only did on rare occasions. The music was interesting. "Loft Dance" really popping, great energy with the drummers. "Oasis" with Eleana singing, etc.

Dave: The main tune on this record was "Loft Dance."

Richie: How many guys arrange this tune for a big band?

Dave: It is played everywhere.

Richie: "Satya Dywani" with Badal and John Abercrombie.

Dave: John Abercrombie played on *Lookout Farm* and *Drum Ode* and then went on to be one of Manfred's main guys.

Richie: After the *Lookout Farm* recording ECM signed me and Abercrombie to the label as solo artists and our next record was *Drum Ode*.

Unfortunately, the record date with drums left Manfred feeling upset ... shall we say appalled? We were in New York with seven drummers, mostly Latin guys, loud guys, wonderful guys, drummers. Drummers are not bass players, they are not hiding.

Dave: You know what I'm saying!

Richie: They are out there with a lot of macho shit ... I love that, I can't help it. Plus, I love drummers.

Dave: This is New York, 1974, my second record. Manfred is in the studio. Tony May is the recording engineer. We had recorded *Lookout Farm* with Tony, so we got along very well. We had done our first European tour, booked by Thomas Stöwsand who represented ECM.

Richie: And I had recorded *EON*, my first record for ECM.

Dave: We were on a roll and I was feeling no pain. *Drum Ode* was a burning record because each tune featured a different group of drummers with me. Jeff Williams played drums on the record; my tunes "Iguana's Ritual" featured the congas, "Satya Dywani" highlighted Collin Walcott and Badal Roy on tabla with me on flute, and so on.

Now we are in the studio ... it's all drummers ... we are in New York City. Needless to say, anybody in that day and age is going to be smoking marijuana—giant splifs everywhere. So it's us plus drummers. Our friend Eugene Gregan, the artist described above, lived with Beverly. He grew the best smoke. The drugs were ample, and it seemed everyone was high ... but a nice high ... big fun!

Of course, Eugene was there in the studio with us for *Drum Ode*. He was our patron saint ... the Godfather. There was so much smoke in the vocal booth you couldn't see anything. Of course, smoking was illegal, but Eugene always grew the best stuff. Manfred is very quiet. We are recording the second tune. I am surrounded by drummers who are yelling and screaming ... New York high energy. It is not at all like a normal ECM record date. I mean, we are burning.

I am in the hallway and suddenly Manfred jumps up, comes running out of the control room, he is red in the face, "I can't take it, I cannot work like this! My sessions are like laboratories, even the wives don't come." He is really flipping out.

Richie: He was hyperventilating, completely losing it.

Dave: So I said, "Manfred, this is New York City ... drummers ... this is the whole point to get energy and the synergy of the brothers playing because that is what I am looking for."

And of course, that was the end of my relationship with him and ECM!

Richie: The record did very well, but he never talked to you again.

Dave: I saw Manfred at Abercrombie's funeral and he was very friendly.

Richie: Yes, 45 years later, thank you very much. Here is something I found out later, he loved the record.

Dave: Everybody loved *Drum Ode*. *Lookout Farm* and *Drum Ode* did very well and were very different in his catalog. Because he had mostly quiet European music and we were burning out.

Richie: And the covers with Eugene's paintings were very different from the normal ECM cover. He loved the records, he made money from them. Manfred just didn't want you anymore as a leader.

Dave: He had Jan Garbarek ... he did not need me.

Richie: A lot of people left ECM, Chick Corea, Jack DeJohnette, Pat Metheny. Only Keith Jarrett, Jan Garbarek, Ralph Towner, and John Abercrombie stayed.

Manfred is kind of a vendetta guy. Either you are with me or you are up against me.

Dave: Had I stayed with ECM, my life would have been very different. On the other hand, I can't take orders from anybody.

Richie: Absolutely, me neither. I also had my little fight with him. But Manfred is a great producer.

I did three records as a leader for ECM. The label was really taking off, Keith Jarrett's *Köln Concert* sold five million copies over a short period. Five million copies of a solo piano double LP, improvised music, most of it very good and some of it not. This was amazing. It was like *George Benson on Broadway* ... it was a mistake, a wonderful mistake. It is Ligeti's groundbreaking composition "Atmosphères" prominently featured in Kubrick's film *2001: A Space Odyssey* and everyone knows this film music. It happens sometimes when a genius and great musician becomes very popular. For example, Coltrane with *My Favorite Things* or with *A Love Supreme* which sold 500,000 copies of some of the heaviest music in the world. This is a very happy coincidence, what do they call it in science, a singularity? ECM was now very well distributed by Polygram Records. Besides Keith's sales was the success of Chick Corea's *Return To Forever*. Unfortunately the music on that record in my opinion was like baby food. It was a complete turnaround for Chick from his early music which was fantastically creative in my opinion. But Chick started to make a lot of money.

Dave: So really, our debt is to Manfred.

Richie: Totally. It ended in a catastrophe but we were lucky that out of that crash came John Snyder and Horizon, so another lease on life took place after the Manfred episode.

The India Tour

Dave: India!

Richie: On this tour I personally became an adult and stopped being a child.

Dave: In 1975 we went with Lookout Farm on a tour to India, sponsored by the US State Department (USIS, the United States Information Service). We played in Japan first, stopping off for a day in Hong Kong and then flew on to India.

We were the first American group maybe since Benny Goodman or Duke Ellington, to tour India for the State Department. Also, we had Badal Roy, the Indian tabla player in the group which was a bit controversial.

We landed in Calcutta past midnight. It was very humid and hot. Badal Roy's parents lived in Calcutta. He brought them a big TV that he had purchased in Japan. He had problems getting it into India and had to pay a lot for taxes and so forth. Once we cleared customs we were taken by separate cars to the US Embassy and then to our hotel. We had one car each. I asked why we had separate cars and the guy from the embassy said because you have to get used to what is going on here, just look around you. This sounds like a cliche but people were dying outside, bodies getting picked up off the ground. There must have been a slum outside of the airport. We were very tired.

Richie: The ride from Calcutta airport at 3 o'clock in the morning to the hotel was very sobering. For the first time in my life I really experienced the third world. It was dark, there was an overwhelming smell in the heavy moist night air. What we saw was like going back in time to the 12th century. Dead animals lay on the side of the road, everything in a horrendous state of disrepair, neglect, and general post-apocalyptic trauma. The people, the poor humans that lived in the street "greeted" us in front of the hotel which was by the way the best in the city, but in a terrible state. Literally starving and begging, with their scrawny arms and hands out, wearing rags, they were not scary or aggressive, just too weak of course. We soon learned the difference between them and the professional and more aggressive beggars.

Dave: We stayed at the King George Hotel, which was supposedly the best hotel in town ... it was on the main street ... an old English building with beggars everywhere surrounding the hotel.

Richie: The hotel was a holdover from the colonial British empire, shabby and scary but at least serviceable. We were told repeatedly not to give the beggars any money. It would not help them and would cause us to be inundated and mobbed every time we came out of the hotel. We were all in a state of shock and of course on that first occasion in the middle of the night gave the folks whatever change we had on us. We could not help it.

Musical Lives

Dave: Yes, the advice we got was to ignore them because if you give them something they will never leave you alone. The streets were covered by these people ... as soon as you stepped out of the hotel they were everywhere.

Next morning we went down to have breakfast. We couldn't eat the shit. The eggs were green. We looked at each other and could not believe it. There was so much shock between the five of us that we couldn't talk.

Richie: I slept with my switchblade knife in my hand because I thought if these guys were so desperate they could kill you, but of course it was not like that. It was obvious that there was no food in the country and we were like complete aliens to these people.

This tour happened before India became a great economic power, this was at the time when people were dying of starvation. They wouldn't eat the cows, because they were considered holy by the Hindus. It was a really awful time.

Lookout Farm, Calcutta 1975

Dave: Plus Badal is coming back to his country and him seeing this stuff ... he was crying.

Richie: The State Department guys were very official. They were immune to the level of poverty but we could not believe it.

Dave: You know, one of my most important musical experiences was our first concert in Calcutta. We rehearsed in the afternoon and played the concert that night. I will never forget the reaction, how we felt and how the audience felt that first night in Calcutta. The people were hungry for the music ... more like starving for it!

Richie: Yes, it was very moving and we played for four hours. The next day we traveled to Bombay and did a record date for Badal.

Dave: The name of Badal's record was *Passing Dreams*. I remember, we had to walk up the stairs to a small recording studio. There were about 50 people waiting for us. They had a Tascam four-track tape recorder.

Richie: The weather in Bombay was beautiful and I remember the big arch. We played a great concert and then there was this recording date set up by Badal with Indian masters. It was 12 o'clock at night and we had to climb up six flights of stairs in the dark. We get into the studio and it was a very unusual scene. Normally when you get to the studio guys are hanging out, drinking coffee, etc. But here the Indian guys were sitting in the studio, behind their instruments, ready to play. We walk in, nobody is talking. But the vibe is great, very warm, lots of smiles all around. Badal introduces us, this is the sitar player, this is the gatham player and the most impressive was Sultan Khan, the sarangi player. A big guy, like a wrestler.

Dave: My instruction was: just watch me and when I point to you ... play. Badal was translating.

Richie: There was an upright piano and I started improvising in a C minor/Rachmaninov vibe. Then Sultan Khan on sarangi comes in, just perfectly, as if we rehearsed it. It was totally spontaneous, everyone smiling all around. And then you played your first solo on the alto flute, killing. Jeff and Frank played amazing stuff, and we recorded four or five tunes. This was different from anything else we had ever done.

And here you did this political thing. We played one concert for the US Embassy in Bombay and only diplomats and their wives or whomever were allowed in to that concert. But there were about 100 guys outside, begging to get in, including all our new musician friends. So you said for the second set we will open the doors and let people in, otherwise we are not going to play. And we got what we wanted.

Also I got sick as a dog. Stupidly, it was my fault. We went to Moti Mahal, a great open air restaurant serving roasted chicken tandoori with a live band playing. But I was stupid and ordered a Coca Cola with ice. I forgot that you should never have ice in India because it is water after all coming from the tap. No bottled water in those days! We had a great time at the restaurant. But a little later I got deadly sick. On this tour we are playing these long concerts and as you know when nature calls you, you have to go. So all of the sudden there is no piano player ... where is Richie? I had to go to the bathroom several times during the concert to check on my dysentery.

Dave: You were getting up after every solo to go to the bathroom and you had it for six weeks even when you arrived Stateside going home.

Lookout Farm, India 1975

Richie: Yes, but I made it through the tour and then I lost my bag with my beautiful knife in it. Actually I became more of an adult on that tour. The last gig was in Goa.

Dave: At the end of the tour we went to Goa for the final show and some rest and recreation. Goa at that time was a big hippie hangout. We stayed at the Taj Hotel, all black glass, in the middle of Goa, looking over the beach. There was a lot of jungle around but everything was clean and very beautiful. I looked out the window and five guys were carrying a piano on their heads to the gymnasium where we were playing. It was so hot ... I was sweating my ass off. Meanwhile the people were talking and laughing throughout the concert for which I tried to quiet them ... good luck! People were not listening. They were just hanging out. It was hot ... the warm Indian Ocean. This was a great ending for the tour.

Richie: Goa was hippie heaven. It was a wonderful, eye-opening experience. Then we flew back to New York City the next day.

This tour in India was total culture shock. All these very diverse and complex, horrible and beautiful experiences have stayed with me since then, vividly etched on my memory and soul. We certainly lost a lot of our young innocence about the way other parts of the world operate. It was uplifting, heartbreaking, sobering, and inspiring.

Forgotten Fantasies – A&M Horizon

Dave: Our first duo recording is called *Forgotten Fantasies*. I got a major break with a label. This was the period when labels were looking to record fusion jazz and A&M was a heavy label at that time.

Richie: The label was named after Herb Alpert and Jerry Moss from the Tijuana Brass ... very successful ... they made millions of dollars.

Dave: With that money, they opened an office on Charlie Chaplin's old movie lot ... impressive! They hired John Snyder who used to work for CTI Records which was very successful, created by Creed Taylor who was in charge of the business.

They gave John Snyder a million dollars and told him to do what ever he wanted to as far as projects. George Benson had a giant hit called "This Masquerade" which made a big impression on the record companies, meaning: "Can't we do something like that?" His first call was to Dave Brubeck, his second was to me ... unbelievable. He says: "I know who you are and I know your work with Elvin Jones and Miles Davis. I love your playing. What would you like to do?" He gave me carte blanche meaning I could do whatever I wanted within reason of course!

Richie: The productions were excellent. The name of the label was Horizon. The money was very good and all in all there was a lot going on. He had Charlie Haden, Hampton Hawes, and Chet Baker to name a few artists ... well established compared to us who were young and unproven.

Dave: He recorded Ornette Coleman and the Revolutionary Ensemble, taking the music over the edge. He gave me a great chance. I was going to take this fusion thing all the way. The first album we recorded for Horizon was called *Sweet Hands* expressing my admiration for Indian music represented on the recording by Badal Roy playing tablas. This was an augmented version of the Lookout Farm band which included Charlie Haden, John Abercrombie, and Don Alias. I first met Badal when I played on John McLaughlin's record *My Goals Beyond* in 1971 and the Miles Davis recording *On The Corner* in 1974. In 1975, for my second record for A&M Horizon, we decided to record a duo album which is called *Forgotten Fantasies*. This record is still known by a lot of people.

Richie: *Forgotten Fantasies* is our second recording for A&M Horizon. This shows what a great guy John Snyder was. We had a successful first record with Lookout Farm, *Sweet Hands*, and you would expect that he would like a follow-up record to be similar to that. But no, we were able to do something completely different, abstract and great, using the contemporary language, all acoustic, with no compromise. This is our first duo recording, 1975, at Electric Lady Studios in New York, Studio B, built by Jimi Hendrix, with a great piano. This was before we played any duo gigs. We were very concentrated and recorded six tunes in two days.

I wrote my piece "October 10" for several reasons. It was the date of the first time I played with Stan Getz in Montreal and I met my first wife there in Montreal. Other things happened to me on October 10, good and bad. It was one of these requiem-like tunes which I still really like.

Dave: It is a beautiful tune which is in our book, *Lookout Farm: A Case Study of Improvisation for Small Group Jazz*. We were among the first to put out a book of that nature ... one of a kind!

Richie: Can you still get it?

Dave: You can buy it as an ebook on Amazon.

Dave & Richie 1975

Richie: *Forgotten Fantasies* was a really good record, capturing the duo and we got it right. Electric Lady Studios was on Eighth Street and Sixth Avenue. When you walk down Eighth Street you got the jewelry and other stores and there this is a giant round brick thing protruding out that obviously doesn't belong there. There was a tremendous amount of rock and roll money in this place. You walk down the stairs which is like a cavern, beautiful, fantastic feeling, a bit like a spaceship. And the studios were great. There was a big one, Studio A that Eddie Kramer used to work in and that's where the big projects were recorded. I did a whole bunch of things in there with flutist Jeremy Steig. Then there was Studio B in the back, just a smaller feeling but still like being in a spaceship. I remember the beautiful Yamaha Grand, a wonderful piano. We had three or four days to record and mix.

Dave: The money was there ... I spent a hundred thousand dollars on three records. I still get royalty statements that I owe A&M ninety-eight thousand dollars. I get royalty statements for three cents a year. But this was a rock-and-roll budget for a jazz musician. Everything was on the plate and I mean everything! Remember when we recorded the *Sweet Hands* album in 1975 out in California, hanging at the hotel, sitting in the sun and at three in the afternoon we would say okay, let's go and record. We flew Don Alias and John Abercrombie in from New York for one tune.

Richie: We were living the rock and roll life for a minute and had a taste of that.

Dave: It was fantastic, limousines, oh, come on man.

Richie: It was great.

Dave: It was great to see a minute of that. A&M Horizon spent a lot of money on my projects. Like I said, the groups at that time had promotion because the record companies saw it as a way to appeal to younger listeners, especially if it had a rock beat. Some of it was very good, some of it was terrible, but as you pointed out by 1980 big money and promotion were pretty much gone for the majority of jazz recordings.

Richie: The reason why fusion was more accessible was because of the obvious beat. With the triplet in jazz you can never quantify it, cause it's amorphous. It is hard to pin down what makes it great, the swing element and the flow of the time. It's like a river, it's fantastic. Funk is about the two and four ... it's a groove and it has to be repetitive. But the jazz beat is not as accessible.

Dave: But there was no interaction in funk. The Miles Davis band I was in had no conversation. Fusion was like a grid ... you're plugged into the elements that were new, electric, synthesizers, triplet feel, even vocals. What happened was that we chose certain elements that seemed to be fresh and new. Not all fusion was bad. It had a short life, but a great life and I think in the end Weather Report exemplifies the success of fusion.

Richie: Weather Report had interaction...

Dave: They had interaction and they were all jazz musicians.

Richie: The first editions of Weather Report had Alphonse Mouzon or Eric Gravatt on drums and Miroslav Vitous on bass. There was tremendous interaction, they interacted like we would. Trading over the time, it was fantastic.

Dave: Yes, and some of it was very successful. They had sales of hundreds of thousands. They had a life ... Weather Report had a life.

The third record I did for A&M was *Light'n Up, Please!* in 1975-6 with former James Brown saxophonist Pee Wee Ellis. When the record was released they got me on the road for a promotion tour. I went to ten cities and did not play one note. I would be picked up at the airport in a white limousine because they were thinking rock and roll. They didn't know me ... they didn't know who I was. The only thing they knew that I was coming from A&M to do promotion and the word got out concerning my M.O. I'd go to a radio station for an interview and asked if there were any jazz clubs around here by any chance? Jazz was not at all in the consciousness of normal people. To them, jazz still felt like a foreign word. These are young promotion guys from Chicago or Detroit. I asked about jazz clubs and they took me to supper joints!

But anyway, that takes us to 1976 musically. Lookout Farm wins the *DownBeat* poll for Group Deserving of Wider Recognition which was a notable thing at that time. I got greedy and started to think musically that I wanted to go further into funk with Pee Wee, a master of that style.

We renewed our relationship, which we had earlier in the late 1960s in a band we named Sawbuck. Musically I wanted Pee Wee to burn on the funk and me to play Coltrane-like. I thought that the fusion style was ready for a new mixture of funk and chromatic jazz. Pee Wee coming from *Cold Sweat and Mother Popcorn* with James Brown and me coming out of ECM and A&M. I moved to California and spent a lot of someone else's money. You are on that record ... remember? We had a great time with this band and I have fond memories of my time with Pee Wee, the funkmeister.

Dave: However in the end a return to jazz was beckoning.

The Pendulum Recording and the Village Vanguard

Dave: In 1976 we broke up for a minute. You toured with John Abercrombie, I lived in California, had the Ellis–Liebman band, and in 1978 I came back to New York and we planned to put a band together. So our next record was *Pendulum*.

Out of nowhere we received an offer to play the Village Vanguard. I worked there a lot in the 1970s and '80s. Max Gordon, the iconic boss, liked me. I used to work there with Pete La Roca and Elvin Jones, you with Chet Baker and others. Bassist Frank Tusa was still in New York, and drummer Al Foster, who had often been to my loft when we both were with Miles. Even though Al played a kind of rock and roll style with Miles he is one of the great jazz drummers, and who was later the first drummer for Quest. So we went into the Vanguard with Randy Brecker, a very old friend to both of us, playing standards, pursuing a "one off" idea which means just one gig with no plans to form a band, which we ended up doing of course.

Can you imagine—we are 30 years old and are playing and recording at the Village Vanguard?

Richie: This is one of the biggest honors of all because of all the great people who have played there and have their pictures on the wall.

Dave: Bill Evans, Sonny Rollins, Miles Davis, John Coltrane, I mean everybody played there. Do you remember what the experience was? This was a one-week gig.

Richie: I will never forget what that was like. When you work the Vanguard for a week it is six nights, three sets a night. Did we do a matinee?

Dave: Possibly.

Dave: "No Greater Love" "Blue Bossa" of course "Impressions"—killing.

Richie: "Solar" "Impressions" "Picadilly Lilly" "Bonnie's Blue" "Footprints" "Night and Day" this was how we played in the late 1970s. Randy was killing on every tune. His solo on "Pendulum" is the classic textbook solo on how to play chromatically and motivically.

Dave: Yes, I use that solo for teaching also.

Richie: It was old friends playing together with a reunion vibe in a way. We were very comfortable with each other. When you play the Vanguard, three sets a night, by the second or third night you are roaring and the music flows like water. Plus every night you have to deal with friends and people coming in because when you work in New York you never know who is going to show up.

That week was amazing because a lot of people came and sat in; Jabali Billy Hart, Pete La Roca, Adam Nussbaum sat in, Woody Shaw played a set, Chet Baker came in and borrowed some money from Randy, which was a sweet kind of thing. And I will never forget the feeling when you walk down the dark stairs in to the Vanguard. It's a basement, like a big New York City E-train subway car. Right near the piano there is picture of Bill Evans and one of John Coltrane. The Vanguard was the center of the jazz world, for decades the most meaningful club in the world and we young bloods recorded there.

Dave: It's the church.

Richie: It is the church, some of the heaviest music ever played was made there. That vibe was ever present with Max Gordon running the club, who was very much like an old garment center salesman sitting there in the front row listening.

And you had a guy cooking, Elton, who made the best hamburgers in the world, very famous. Some people think that he made the hamburgers out of people, that's why they were so good. Remember him? Miles used to come in just to get a hamburger. The kitchen in the Vanguard was also the dressing room, it was a convoluted backstage if you could call it that. It had the back entrance to the stairs, bathrooms, and the bigger kitchen area. Anyway, when you play a club for six nights you really get dug in. You make friends with everyone. Of course Jay, the kitchen helper was there, with Jerry at the front door, Mike the bartender, Mickey the waiter, the guy with no nose, all these guys, and Jane, crazy Jane, the waitress with the glasses. We spend years hanging out there, we knew our way around the Vanguard.

But the most important thing about this week was that engineer David Baker, our dear friend, was in the kitchen of the Vanguard, recording us for three nights, that is nine sets!

Dave: This was for John Snyder's label Artists House and they released it under the title *Pendulum*. *Pendulum* is a famous recording.

Richie: Famous and a very good one. The LP came out, 20 minutes one side, 20 minutes the other with a 17 minute version of "Pendulum" which was a long tune in those days. Michael Cuscuna released the rest of the recording on Mosaic, there for posterity. We were really inspired ... we played our best ... we sounded really good and we were swinging.

Dave: And of course Max Gordon.

Richie: Max would be there for the first set, listen and when he fell asleep it meant you are cool, everything is okay. If he couldn't sleep there was something he didn't like. He was already 75 years old at that time.

We were very lucky to have had that experience, it really established our jazz credentials. The records came out on Artists House Records, extensive notes and photos, a memorable production.

Dave: It was a great honor to record live at the Vanguard ... I mean it didn't get any better than that. I remember thinking what do I do now? I actually thought that in a few years the way things were going maybe I would change life directions. In a certain way I just felt like what more can you do than play live at the Vanguard where Coltrane, Miles, Bill Evans, and Sonny Rollins played. Not that we were on a level with them, master-wise, but we kind of accomplished something already.

The 1970s in New York City

Dave: What was it like in the 1970s with Miles Davis, Chet Baker, Bill Evans, Tony Williams, Herbie Hancock, Elvin Jones, all alive playing their best ... what was the atmosphere like in New York especially?

Richie: We didn't know it but these were the best times. Most of the major masters, the best guys, the big dogs, the tall trees were alive and they were not old, more in their prime. When you are young you think it will go on forever and there is a sense of immortality. It is in your genes, your organism is so strong, you can't imagine being frail or anyone dying. I could not imagine John Coltrane dying. He was so big ... and Sonny Rollins. These cats were like mountains, but they were human.

In this special time in the 1970s there was a feeling like what I imagine what it must've been like in the 1950s on 52nd St. for the older cats. You could go to hear Bird, Coleman Hawkins, Sonny Rollins, Lester Young, Duke Ellington on the same night. In the 1970s all the clubs where there for us within a three mile strip on Seventh Avenue South, downtown in Greenwich Village. Village Vanguard, Sweet Basil, St. James Infirmary, Seventh Avenue South (owned by Mike and Randy Brecker), Ali's Alley, Lush Life, Village Gate, George Braith's Musart, and Cafe Au Go Go. Moving uptown you had Bradley's, Knickerbockers, Fat Tuesdays, Cleopatra's Needle, and the old Birdland. Forget about Brooklyn, nothing existed there then.

Also we were working all the time because Miles and the other big names were not working in clubs very often any more. They played concerts like at Carnegie Hall. Occasionally Herbie or Chick would play the Village Vanguard and that was an unbelievable experience. But we could also play the Village Vanguard for a week, McCoy would play Sweet Basil, Bill Evans would play the Top of the Gate, Chick Corea at the Blue Note, everybody was playing all the time, seven nights a week. Monday night was a special nights ... a lot of big bands played on Monday nights: Thad Jones and Mel Lewis Big Band at the Vanguard, Gil Evans Big Band at Sweet Basil, and guitarist Les Paul at Fat Tuesdays. People went out every night to listen to music, even Tuesday, Wednesday, Thursday, the so called dead nights. During these days some clubs are only open for the weekend which is ridiculous cause as a player you just warming up. In the '70s you could finish playing your last set at the Vanguard, and then go over to Bradley's, one of those duo clubs that could not have drums. Not because they did not want to but because of the stupid club cabaret laws. It was alive, thriving, and an incredibly vibrant and vital time. The music was there, live music, all the time!

Dave: But I must tell you if you now go to the West Village on any given night there is a lot of activity. There are a lot of jazz clubs that come and go. We now have 12 jazz schools within 50 miles around New York. The students come from all over the world and still go to the West Village to hang out and sit in at the clubs. There is a scene. Some places go to five in the morning … they have a two o'clock set. It is not what It used to be, but there are places.

Richie: I am happy to hear that … nature finds a way. I hear that there are a lot of clubs in Brooklyn now.

Dave: Yes, and that is because New York is still the center of the jazz world, no matter what we say, no matter how it compares to 30 or 40 years ago. There have been and are more musicians per square inch than anywhere else in the world and it has been like this since the 1940s.

Drugs, Alcohol, and Late Night Hanging

Richie: A little story about Boomer's and other clubs like Bradley's. Boomer's was this lovely little club on Bleecker Street. But it was a den of iniquity. There were always things going on, all the time, in the back, and in the front. People were getting high, both the audience and the musicians.

Dave: That did affect the music, no question.

Richie: For the third set we would not be drinking Coca-Cola. What the drugs gave you was fuel. And of course besides cancer, heart disease, and early death, there is no question about that, it did make you more alert. You start the first set at nine or ten o'clock and you play until two or three in the morning. Most normal people get up early in the morning, have breakfast, go to work, by 10 o'clock in the evening they are tired, since they have been up for 15 hours and are ready to go to sleep. But jazz musicians usually sleep until two or three in the afternoon. You play the gig in the evening and after the gig you hang out ... you have fun. An example, a guy works Wall Street, he gets up early, goes to Wall Street, burns from 9 to 5, at five, you think he goes home? No, he goes to a nice bar, has a drink, then he goes for dinner. This is his hang after his gig. Our gig finishes at three in the morning, so are you going to go home? How could you sleep, the music is in your head, you have met many people, you're still high.

This was the great sense of community and like in the cave with the fire, it goes back to human needs. Then of course if you are just drinking and smoking you go to sleep but the drugs give you a false sense of alertness ... the fuel. Now you can stay up and talk ... sometimes too much of course. But there were certain times when everyone was cool.

Dave: ... on the same page...

Richie: ... on the same page, no loud or violent shit. We would hang with the owners of the clubs, especially with the owner of Bradley's, who was the king of the late night hang scene. We would sit around the table with Red Mitchell, Cecil Taylor, Mulgrew Miller, Tommy Flanagan, Albert Dailey, Kirk Lightsey, Ronnie Matthews, George Mraz, LeeAnn Ledgerwood, Ron McClure, and myself. Those were the regulars ... It was kind of a family, a dysfunctional family. An example ... I would come home from a European tour with the John Abercrombie quartet or Quest with you and instead of going home to my apartment on Spring Street I took a taxi from the airport and went first to Bradley's because it is four the afternoon. They opened at ten in the morning as a restaurant and bar and they officially closed at four in the morning. I would go there directly from the airport, put my bags down, see if there are any messages for me, talk to the waitresses, have a hamburger, decompress, chill, and then I would go home. You know everybody needs that kind of a place. In former times it was called the Elks Club ... it was like a communal meeting place where a certain group of jazz musicians in New York City met, almost nightly.

I learned so many specific musical things by playing, listening, and hanging out at Bradley's. I was able to hang with the masters. For example, one night I saw Tommy Flanagan, Hank Jones, Red Mitchell, and Jimmy Rowles arguing about one note in the tune *Lush Life* and everyone had a different idea what it should be. Don't ever tell these guys about sheet music because they tell you about the assholes that write the sheet music! I sat there and learned. The way everyone talked to each other was not aggressive. It was like: "When I hung out with the Duke two days on the bus he said this and then I talked to Sweet Pea (Billy Strayhorn) and he said this and then Lester Young said no, that's not it." They were talking about the sources of jazz, like classical musicians talk about a Mozart piano concerto. Well that note is not right and he said well, I was with Wolfgang the other day and he said this is this, this is the source, and so on.

Dave: There was that camaraderie, and of course there were casualties of wars. At three or four in the morning, if you were still hanging out, you probably did not want to go home, or couldn't go home. But there is no question that the different drugs fueled extended communication. You talked more, you asked more, you got engaged on the one to one level and where you ordinarily would've said hey, how are you doing. You found another source of communication. This is the positive side of drugs ... it wakes you up ... it gives you energy. At least you're cool for a period of time. If you have a small group of people doing the same drug, and they are all on the same page, it can be a really exciting time to talk about everything. When you've had enough you go home and just say hey, I had such a great time, a great night, it was great to talk to these guys.

Richie: Why can't we talk like that all the time without the drugs? That was the question. Keep in mind that we have been up for a long time, played three sets of music, met many people, had lots of interaction. It is hard to wind down after all these different energies coursing through you.

Dave: That's the truth. Drugs have been around since the beginning of mankind.

Richie: And the attrition rate of drugs is enormous. Let's face it, a lot of our best friends went down in front of us, died, or became dysfunctional. When you play with Chet Baker regularly like I did, he is wonderful to hang out with. And even when he was sick he was okay, but you see him in front of you and when you see what the drugs have done to him, you see it in his face, it's tragic. He looked like James Dean in the 1950s ... he was a handsome boy ... all the girls loved him ... such a good looking guy. But later he looked like death, although he was still playing great. He could not stand up to play. He was the only trumpet player who could play sitting down with the full power. He rarely stood, but he burned.

The drugs can give you a false sense of energy that keeps you awake. Because otherwise you would naturally be going home after playing three sets, hanging out with people, after having a couple of drinks or feeding yourself drugs, etc.

You would be physically and mentally tired. Because all night you have had input, specially when you play in these clubs where there is no bandstand, like the Village Vanguard or Bradley's. The people are right there in your face. This is both great and terrible. When you are an introvert it is torture because you are so exposed but when you are extroverted, like us, it is fun, we like it. If you can excite the audience you know you're going to get great feedback and it feels wonderful. You can have contact with your fans, like the rock people. When you perform a classical concerto you play, go to the dressing room, and then you might go out for a small bite and a drink, and then home.

We all have selective memory but I must say there were a lot of nights where bad things happened with the guys, myself included. And then when you have a wife and kids and you hang out in the clubs until five or six in the morning, you're not going to take Little Johnny to school at 8 o'clock. So a lot of things could fall apart. You don't have the energy over the day because you live for the night.

Dave: Your grandmother is not going to be at Bradley's at three in the morning. It is people doing the business of the night that are hanging out at 3 a.m. Just like chefs meet after their work at their restaurants. You want to talk to your own tribe, you want to be around camaraderie, and rest from your work all night. Because you have to do it again the next night! In the long run drugs are a very destructive force and have messed up more lives than have been saved.

Richie: And that is why most people either stopped taking drugs or alcohol or are dead. We are talking about the main guys like John Coltrane who died when he was 40, which I still can't believe. I still think of Trane being like 80 years old and still creative, since he was so productive during his life.

OUR VIEWS ON

Classical Music History

Jazz History

Playing Free

Jazz Education Today

Bill Evans

McCoy Tyner

Herbie Hancock

Chick Corea

John Coltrane

Wynton Marsalis

Jack DeJohnette

Wayne Shorter and the 1987 Tribute Concert to John Coltrane

Classical Music History

Dave: Since we have recorded our versions of classical themes with improvisations on our CD *Eternal Voices* let's talk a little bit about classical music history and about classical composers, that you are an expert on and what you consider to be essential composers and why. And then we will move on to all direct influences on jazz.

Richie: If you look at the continuum of classical music basically from Bach to Ligeti, of course there were people before, like Monteverdi and there were people after Ligeti. I am talking essential historical composers, not about people who we'd like or love or that are popular. Just for the hindsight of history, to me Bach was the first really major composer. You have to remember, people could not play in every key before Bach, before the well tempered piano. He created the necessity of well tempered tunings which is a big thing. Also Bach was not so much of an innovator but he used everything that was before in a way creative way. His compositions were genius material with heavy doses of humanity, empathy, and he had an enormous creative output. We know that Bach was a great improviser and that a lot of his pieces sound to me like notated improvisations. We know that he dictated parts of his last piece, *The Art Of The Fugue*, to his son while he was dying. Bach was also very practical and pragmatic. He had a gig every Sunday for which he wrote new church music every week for 27 years in Leipzig, Germany. Bach"s music was written for the glory of God and it was exalted. The cantatas ... the air on the G string ... the pieces he wrote had an air of majesty about them with love and goodness, written with clarity and power. As my friend George Mraz said, Bach was the only true composer, everybody after him was only an arranger of his music.

I never heard a piece from Bach that was bad...never! Even the pieces from his book for Anna Magdalena that he composed for his children have an element of genius and beauty in them. He was unbelievably productive ... he had four wives and 23 children.

Dave: How did he find the time to work?

Richie: He made the time. These cats didn't sleep. It was freezing, muddy, no penicillin, no bathroom, no central heating.

Dave: Mostly candlelight to copy the music cause it got dark early in his part of Germany.

Richie: We don't think about the millions of people that died in poverty in the dirt, experiencing tremendous fear. In those days it really made sense to believe in God, because everything outside was so scary. The reason Bach was so productive was that he was in service to God. He felt like it was a commandment from God.

Our Views On

Plus Bach had a way of internally hearing what he wrote every Sunday which is amazing, right? If you want to take the whole continuum, as I said, from Bach to Ligeti, and if you agree that Ligeti is the end of let's say the newness of composed music, then we are not talking about combinations. I am talking about essential composers that if you take one away you have a large hole in the history of music.

After Bach we have Mozart, Händel, Beethoven, Brahms, Chopin, Scriabin ... these are great composers that I love. Some of them I love more than Bach but from a historical perspective it is important to know the absolute sources. After Bach I would say Arnold Schoenberg came next because again he revolutionized the idea of what were the basic components of writing a melody, a chord, rhythm, and addressing the form and instrumentation. History goes from Bach to Schoenberg. You hear the beginnings of Schoenberg in the late music of Wagner. It was the end of the tonal system, the logical death of it because of all the incredible modulations in Wagner's music. Wagner had a way of using diminished chords to avoid the constancy of the tonic. You have to remember for Bach and others for hundreds of years, the system revolved around tonic, dominant, subdominant ... those were the basic chords for years.

The other question is how were the classical composers able to write so much? Scarlatti wrote 500 piano sonatas, Beethoven wrote 32. They were able to write so much because they had something called COMMON PRACTICE. This means that there was an agreement about forms from which they wrote their music. The Sonata Allegro form means you have a main theme, you have an exposition of that theme, you have a transition to a secondary theme, then you have its development. Then you have the second movement. These rules were not set in stone but they were pretty much agreed upon. This means that a composer could sit down and write a sonata in three or seven days because he knew the form he had to fulfill.

All the forms changed with Schoenberg. The forms changed from piece to piece because Schoenberg felt that the content of each piece should determine its own particular form. That's why the number of contemporary pieces is much, much smaller. These are all forms that are loved and agreed upon around the western world for more than 300 years. So then Schoenberg comes along and says no. This is no to the major/minor scale system. He said it's enough, that everything has been done, or so he thinks. Schoenberg was a genius and self-educated. He took a few lessons from Alexander von Zemlinsky, his cousin. Plus he had an unbelievable ear. In my opinion his greatest pieces were written before he developed his 12-tone system. The Five Pieces for Orchestra, the piano pieces ... this was all done by ear. It was called free atonality. He trusted his ear. All the rules, even Wagner's, go out the window. Schoenberg is the one responsible for us to be able to play chromatically. Chromaticism has always been there since Bach. Chromaticism means a note out of the chord. The differences are in the application. The way that Bach used chromaticism was that the chromatic note alway resolved up or down into a chord tone.

But Schoenberg disagreed to the fact that everything had to resolve. He said in the chromatic scale every note should be given equal respect ... every note can be a long duration melodic note without having to resolve. Wagner resolved. Schoenberg was radical at that time, totally radical. When you listen to his Five Pieces for Orchestra especially the one called "Farben" (Colors), even it has some incredible dissonances that are flowing. Schoenberg had a very different flow ... it was not one directional, but more like a river.

You know if you put your foot into a moving river the water under your foot goes right by, you can't get it back. Schoenberg said that contemporary music should be like a river because remember, in the common practice, period things always came back to the melody. Things always came back to an ABA form, even in bebop jazz we do it. Schoenberg said, "No, composition is more like life, more like a river." Beautiful!

His harmonic ideas were not about traditional harmony. They were about intervallic structures. It was a combination of tones that he liked, based on his taste and his incredible ear. It worked for him. He created some of the most beautiful masterpieces from his ear before he developed his 12-tone system. The problem is that a lot of people tried to use this 12-tone system without having this masterful, amazing ear to guide them. When I say ear I don't mean just pitch recognition like what chord is this. I mean his inner ear that was so developed and connected to his inner source of creativity. He also wrote very much from the heart ... his music is very emotional.

But Schoenberg in my opinion had problems in terms of authority and he was under a lot of conservative pressure as the century went on. "They" made more fun of him than of John Coltrane or Albert Ayler and the other free jazz musicians. Critics said those guys couldn't play ... they can't write ... they don't swing. Schoenberg's music was so new that the critics rejected it and put it down because they did not understand it. So instead of saying I don't have an opinion yet, I have to listen more, they just said it sucks or that he was an amateur. Then he found a system called the 12-tone series. He created the tone row, a particular order of the 12-tones from which he drew his melodies. This was instead of the major/minor harmonic system. The row is horizontal but he would take the row and make it vertical to take chords from it ... it was very interesting.

By the way, Schoenberg did not create the 12-tone system. Josef Hauer created the 12-tone system but he was a mediocre composer who came up with the idea and Schoenberg appropriated it. Just like Chopin did not create the nocturne itself, he took it from other people but he developed and perfected the form. Schoenberg had an amazing influence, specially on his students Alban Berg and Anton Webern. Schoenberg ran away from the Nazis. He came to Los Angeles to hang with Stravinsky and a bunch of other guys that fled from Germany. Berg died of a bee sting tragically when he was 40.

Dave: And Webern got shot by an American soldier while standing on his own porch smoking a cigar during one of the many curfews after the war.

Richie: Can you imagine this crazy shit on both sides. Berg was actually much more visionary than Schoenberg, being younger. Schoenberg was very exclusive. This is it, forget about the past ... the past is not usable!

Our Views On

Dave: But Schoenberg did compose in the "old" language from the past.

Richie: Not only that, after he came to America he went back to the tonal system and wrote a string quartet in D minor.

But Berg, as Schoenberg's younger student realized the true implications of the 12-tone system ... it was not exclusionary ... it was inclusive. You could have the 12-tone system ... but you could also have standard, old-fashioned diatonic harmony alongside it. Berg proved it in his most iconic piece, his Violin Concerto which was his last piece written before he died. The original 12-tone row for the Violin Concerto consisted of four major/minor triads! Plus there is some amazing manipulation of the 12-tone techniques because Berg somehow integrates the famous Bach chorale "Es Ist Genug," a very famous one that he somehow manipulated within the 12-tone rules. It actually appears clearly and briefly as itself ... fantastic.

Berg was inclusionary. He saw that the tone row was just another color on the palette, like for a painter. Like we want to use only the colors of blue, green, and yellow. So Berg said no, we will use them all. Berg really wrote fantastic pieces like the operas *Lulu* and *Wozzeck*, the Chamber Concerto, the First Piano Sonata. And remember Chick Corea playing the Berg B Minor Piano Sonata in the loft?

So we have Bach and Schoenberg, who also has a tragic life but changed music across the board. And then we come to Ligeti, with all the wonderful composers in between: Scriabin, Prokofiev, Shostakovich, Takemitsu, Boulez, Charles Ives, Lutoslawski, and Penderecki. All these cats are great and wonderful. I love them. But when did music change again radically from the bottom up? Early Ligeti is like Bartók, who is also Hungarian, running from the Nazis. But he created an entire replacement system for all the elements of music. He went further than Schoenberg still working with melody, harmony, accompaniment, and form.

I am not talking about Stravinsky, whom I love. Stravinsky was very influenced by Schoenberg. It seems Stravinsky said he did not like Arnold and at some point put him down. When Schoenberg died, Stravinsky started using the 12-tone system. This is very funny, right? Stravinsky's pride! Can you imagine the ego that Stravinsky had?

Dave: So would you say that Ligeti is a pivotal composer because he raised the idea of timbre and color becoming elements of music? In the Western diatonic world there was melody, harmony, and rhythm. Now you must say color and timbre. In other words texture for texture's sake. Texture is a byproduct of the chorale from Bach's time. But actually as an element that in itself exists, independent from melody, harmony, and rhythm.

Richie: Texture was the main thing.

Dave: That's the 20th century. Would you say that Ligeti is the foremost composer who emphasized that aspect?

Richie: Yes, he was the composer that emphasized texture as the predominant source material. When you think about Ligeti's "Atmosphères" or "Lux Aeterna" or "Apparitions," these are amazing gigantic choral pieces. The interesting thing is Ligeti used no electronics ... he used a traditional orchestra. It's fantastic that almost the same orchestra which plays Haydn and Beethoven can play Ligeti ... amazing. Ligeti replaced the need for melody with texture.

Everybody had melody, Scriabin, Schoenberg, Takemitsu. Ligeti has very few stand-alone melodies and they are at the top of a giant texture. Ligeti had to have special music paper printed because he had 62 separate parts for the chorus to sing in his astonishing compositions called "Requiem"! Also the level of ear training and intonation that the music demanded from the performers of Ligeti's composition was enormous because of the often used half steps. Ligeti has these amazing clusters in his pieces that would sustain and had to be perfectly in tune. He had C, D flat, D, E flat, E, and F to begin with, very soft, pianissimo, all sounding together. You can hear this in his "Atmosphères." He envisioned the loop effects used in todays music, the ambient stuff.

Dave: What is it about his Études For Piano that is so much spoken about and that Ligeti wrote in the 1970s?

Richie: Ligeti is not all smooth textures or atmosphere ... it is not all orchestral. His works for the piano are very different, especially the Études. They are incredibly complex and technically difficult. Some of them are textural but mostly they have these incredible counterrhythms. I studied some of the Études which are most extraordinary. Ligeti has got three different tempos at the same time up and down the piano plus a lot of scaler stuff. When Steve Reich created his repetitive minimalism concept he was very influenced by Ligeti's Études. But these first piano pieces by Ligeti involve a complete fresh look at the basic elements of composition. Some of them are actually in the key of C major, sometimes F sharp major, but he is not thinking of harmonic blocks ... he is not thinking of resolution of cadences. Motivically they are written like a rock solid mountain. They are études which are only two or three pages long. When you hear the Études you get a sense of form. It is not the ABA form ... none of that. Sometimes he begins in the middle of an idea and then he has like a flashback thing ... it is fantastic. The main thing is that with all the technical stuff going on, when you listen to it you still get that amazing feeling of wonderment, like a miracle. Wow, this is a piano. I never heard the piano sound like this!

I would say that Ligeti's main instrumental delivery system is the orchestra. His early string quartets from 1952, specifically his String Quartet No. 2, is very much influenced by Bartók. It is a continuation of Bartók, like apprentice – master. But Ligeti's effect on the classical world and all contemporary music is far reaching. We say for example: This sounds like Ligeti, this sounds like Schoenberg, this sounds like Bartók. He is an iconic original source. Like we say now this is John Coltrane, or this is Miles Davis, or this sounds totally like Herbie Hancock ... and onward!

He created more than the music. He created a whole new brilliant language using these acoustic instruments with no electronics. Musicians extended the music more after him primarily with electronics. A lot of it is not listenable to me. However, Stockhausen, Luigi Nono, and Mario Davidovsky are three examples of contemporary composers combining electronic tape with live acoustic instruments. What I'm saying is that there is some fantastic music still on the creative cusp from 20th century sources. Early Stockhausen is great ... "Hymnen," "Stimmung," or "Kontakte." We heard "Kontakte" when we were on tour with Lookout Farm in a cave in the mid 1970s and it was amazing. Stockhausen was very influenced by Ligeti, by the way.

In my opinion Ligeti was the summation and the end of a period the same way that Bach was the end of the pre-Bach era. No one has done anything radically new after Ligeti that I have ever heard, similarly after John Coltrane. Takemitsu is fantastic, but it's still a combination of earlier languages. You know what I mean?

To sum up this chapter my main three historically essential composers are Bach, Schoenberg, and Ligeti.

Dave: Yes.

Jazz History

Dave: So let's move to jazz. Before we go to specific guys, the three musicians that are absolutely essential for the development of the art form—Louis Armstrong, Charlie Parker, and John Coltrane. Let me talk a little bit about that.

Louis Armstrong was the first person to record an improvised jazz solo on a record. One can not overemphasize the enormous importance of this fact.

Richie: Duke Ellington in my opinion follows Louis Armstrong in historical jazz importance because Duke was the first real orchestrator of the jazz vocabulary.

Dave: Of course Duke Ellington was one of the other very important guys. Even though I am not an expert on him it does appear that he already did amazing things in the 1920s, pre-bebop. He had his big band for 50-plus years, amazing. And his sacred music was iconic. He also wrote more than 3,000 tunes. He is in the collective consciousness of everybody ... tunes like "Mood Indigo," "Sophisticated Lady," and "Take The A Train," etc.

Duke was definitely the guy after Louis. Every time they ask jazz musicians about the most influential person in jazz history Duke's name is there on top of the list. And then of course there was Charlie Parker (Bird). When I think 20th century it is Charlie Parker and Schoenberg because they both changed the language. They changed the way these 12 notes are organized and eventually everybody had to absorb it.

When Bird found the upper structures that we now call F sharp 7th sharp 5 flat 13 for example, he obviously had an amazing gift. Bird at a certain time of his life practiced daily. Paul Desmond said in an interview that Bird practiced 10 to 12 hours every day during his teenage years in Kansas City, a real blues town. The speed with which he executed his lines was previously unheard of. You hear it now in pop music ... use of the upper structures.

Richie: In double time, he was effortless!

Dave: His speed and sound on the alto saxophone as the purveyor of the new music was revolutionary, after Dixieland, swing, and big bands. Of course he had people around him like Dizzy Gillespie and Bud Powell, but Bird was the genius.

Richie: In my opinion Bud Powell was just as much a genius as Bird. As we can see by his influence on every important pianist that came after him up until today. And what about Miles Davis in terms of influence?

Dave: Miles is a big influence in the collective unconscious of people because he changed the way the language was perceived. He did not change the music like Charlie Parker did, but he did change the way the music was crafted and organized through the incredible series of small groups he led over the decades.

Richie: Would you say his genius was more in assembling these special groups?

Dave: Yes ... his genius was being the leader.

Richie: But he was also a great trumpet player ... he was burning.

Dave: His leadership and trumpet playing complemented each other. He would not have gone such a long distance if he only had one of those aspects. He had his trumpet playing down, contributing a very iconic style that is and has been often copied. So I would say for jazz, Louis Armstrong, Duke Ellington, Charlie Parker, and John Coltrane ... not much in this sense after Coltrane.

Richie: Similar to Duke Ellington, Miles Davis's larger influence was as a creative bandleader and visionary. So nothing new, not even combinations, extensions?

Dave: Combinations maybe.

Richie: So it is Bach, Schoenberg, Ligeti for classical and Louis Armstrong, Charlie Parker, and John Coltrane for jazz.

Playing Free

Richie: Let's talk about some recordings we did together that still stand out over the years.

Dave: *The Duo Live*, recorded in Germany with an amazing transcription of this live concert by Bill Dobbins called *The Duo Live: Transcriptions: Soprano-Saxophone, Flute and Piano*.

Richie: It was a duo concert for our publishing company, Advance Music, produced by Hans and Veronika Gruber in Tübingen, Germany. They had a fantastic Bösendorfer Imperial grand piano there for the recording. We played really well, accurate and relaxed, a great combination by the way. And we had a wonderful time, surrounded by friends. When we listened back to the recording Hans said it should be transcribed. Bill Dobbins happened to be there with the biggest radar ears in the world and said something to the effect of—piece of cake to transcribe it!—unbelievable. He transcribed the whole concert at real speed, not slowing the tape down. Plus he had to create a whole set of new symbols to notate some of the music. I was doing things percussively at the bottom octave of the Bösendorfer, while you played those saxophone flurries. It is an amazing document and a lot of musicians studied and enjoyed the combination of the CD and book.

Richie: Next record, Quest, *Of One Mind*.

Dave: All improvised?

Richie: The Quest recording *Of One Mind* with Ron McClure and Jabali Billy Hart was supposed to be all improvisation. We were staying at the CMP Studio in Zerkall, Germany. In the morning you got up and said I think we need some written sketches.

Dave: Moods and colors.

Richie: And you were right. It was very brief and not on paper.

Dave: Just a general vibe culled from some of the music we played with Quest.

Richie: I thought we were punking out. We should have just gone out and played free or something, but you know what, you were right, and it turned out great. Walter Quintus was engineering, Kurt producing ... the record sounds fresh and was very satisfying to do. We chose four moods that we already used in our written tunes and played that mood without a form or head or whatever.

Dave: *Quest for Freedom*, written and arranged for big band by Jim McNeely who is of course one of us and definitely understands your sense of harmony. Jim did an amazing job arranging some of our tunes for the HR Radio Big Band in Frankfurt.

Richie: The great thing about McNeely is that he knows our music so we were really lucky. His arrangement of "Pendulum" is amazing. He worked for months on all the arrangements and conducted the band for the recording. We had a lot of fun together.

Dave: It was great to hear our tunes arranged for big band.

Richie: Yes, that was a thrill for me too.

Dave: A recent duo double CD is called *Eternal Voices* and it consists of classical themes with improvisations. One CD featured songs from the classical repertoire, while the other CD was drawn from the Bartók string quartets ... a pinnacle of 20th century harmony.

Richie: I have been working for years transforming classical pieces into vehicles for improvisation. Some of the songs and composers were Mompou, a short Beethoven piece, a Chopin Prélude, slow movements from Scriabin, Bach, and Mozart ... all special gems ... slow moving, one or two pages only.

The original plan was to record a historical overview. That took care of those repertoire compositions listed above. The Bartók was the challenge! Our first idea was to record Bartók's string quartets with violinist Gregor Huebner's group, the Sirius String Quartet. Then we decided that this was not practical and we realized that we would not need the strings ... we could do it as a duo. So we outlined those interesting moments of the Bartók slow movements to use for improvisations. So we had definite motives, textures, and chords that we played off of.

The interesting thing is Bartók's music is so similar to our own development. I studied his music with Ludmila Ulehla at Manhattan School of Music from 1968 until 1972 so to me it was a return to my roots. This is where my tune "Pendulum" came from. The intervallic cells in "Pendulum" are similar to the kinds of cells found in the Bartók String Quartets.

After we finished both recordings it made perfect sense to combine them into one double release. CD number one started with Mozart, followed by Beethoven, Bach, etc. and ended with Schoenberg. That led to CD number two with all the slow movements from Bartók's six string quartets ... and that was a great experience ... really amazing.

Dave: So in a way if you took the Bartók string quartets to a desert island you would be cool for the 20th century music, right?

Richie: Absolutely.

Dave: So Bartók did everything?

Richie: He did everything and he did it well. Here is the other thing about Bartók. I am classically trained ... I love classical music, but I have very little use for the normal classical rhythmic style. It's really not me. It's too far away from the jazz feel that I am comfortable with. A lot of the early classical compositions were written for the king, the church/God ... like that. The slow movements are what I really love in all the classical music from the beginning. But Bartók, because he was Hungarian and came from a tradition of folk music, his rhythmic sense was great and not so stiff as the older classical music. In a way it was similar to jazz. Bartók's rhythmic sense is much more indicative of our music. The classical use of rhythm is unusable for us except for the slow movements where the wonderful melodies and harmonies could be delineated.

Then we did the project called *Aftermath* with recording engineer Florian Van Volxem and Kurt producing. They gave us a prepared track ... very dark ... that we could improvise over freely ... something we had never quite done before ... overdubbing over a pre-recorded track. There are a lot of implications ... very interesting.

And that brings us to our most recent duo recording titled *Empathy*. I feel like we now have a new beginning highlighting the way we are playing on this recording. I don't miss having a composition to play ... not even a great tune ... because we create the "tunes" in the moment. Because of all our experience and training, now we can do it. I have done two freely improvised solo piano recordings for Kurt. The first one was *Breathing Of Statues* from 1982 and *Self-Portraits* from 1992, both on CMP Records which were very satisfying ... similar to recording *Empathy* with you from 2018. I felt like superman after recording *Empathy* and I had the foolish feeling like I never want to play tunes again ... we don't need the tunes! That's a little bit stupid, why limit yourself?

There is a certain feeling you get when you improvise EVERYTHING that you don't get from playing even a great song because you are creating the whole thing from nothing.

Dave: That's why there are guys that only do that, like Dave Holland and Sam Rivers in their duo in the 1970s.

Richie: Right, that's what Paul Bley did. The problem with that is that we are human and you have to be inspired for 60 minutes.

Dave: It is a chance you're taking.

Richie: If you improvise live for 60 minutes it exerts great pressure on producing consistent quality, meaning you take big-size risks as far as performance and recording go. I like to play jazz. I am a jazz piano player. I like that word. I'm not afraid of what it means because to me jazz means improvisation meaning everything else is style. Also I must say playing with you, the possibilities are endless. The other important thing about playing free is *who* you play with. I could only play free with very few people for one hour and create music at this level.

Dave: So after more than 50 years, for the first time we recorded in a completely free way.

Richie: Completely free. But you know what? I am glad we waited, because we killed it. I don't think I could have done it as well 10 or 15 years ago. I could have done something good, but it would not have been this consistent. It is so complicated when you represent yourself for an entire 60 minute album playing free, because you have to remember what you played before so you don't duplicate the same phrases ... not so easy.

Dave: But you also have to remember what you played on the blues. Shouldn't you know what you already did?

Richie: Yes, you have to remember what you played on a blues solo but if you play free you have to remember everything you played on all the other pieces also. You stopped me once in the midst of playing and said you already did that ... and you where right! It's different than developing a motive. Even if we are playing free there are still certain consistent ways we play because we are human and we have patterns. The trick is not to duplicate your own patterns too much. To play free you need a lot of experience. I am not talking about talent since everybody is talented. It's a question of discipline and development.

When we were young and we played free, like on the *Night Scapes* CD from 1970 on CBS Sony, you played some fast shit with no development, just boom ... then you went into the piano ... boom ... and then you played another fast solo, boom ... exactly like the first one. That's what I mean. So instead of 50 minutes of variety you only have 20 minutes repeated, because we were limited by what we could do, a result of our young age and experience.

So when we recorded *Empathy* we were aware of what we had played before. We had to be aware so we would not repeat something. Because there is no take two. In a duo it is much easier to play free with a compatible guy like you.

Dave: If you have more people it is hard.

Richie: Two is ideal, three is harder, four is tough.

Dave: I must say in Europe I have done this more than everywhere else and I enjoyed it. There, the guys know how to play free. They know when to stop which is crucial to the success of a performance. It's really not when to start ... it's when to leave it.

Richie: You gave me a free record with Pablo Held ... it's beautiful.

Dave: It was great. I had never met him before the recording.

A few words about *Empathy*. At the moment we both feel that it is a pretty spectacular and unusual recording. Of course we have episodically played free, but never a whole recording.

Richie: We have played free intros on a tune but never have done a whole record with that focus and no musical preparation. The mental mood has to be attended to!

Dave: The good thing about playing free with someone you know is that it is not as free as you might think. It may appear free but I know there are things that you will do. Not the key necessarily, but mood wise. When I hear you start something I pretty much for the most part have an idea of where you will go. Familiarity with your partner's style is absolutely a plus. It is free, but free within a feeling of familiarity.

Richie: Listen to our *Night Scapes* recording, then listen to the *Empathy* duo recording for an interesting comparison.

Dave: I had not listened to *Empathy* for a while so last night after dinner we sat down and listened to it all and I feel it is definitely a classic.

Richie: How did you know what to do when I took a certain direction in the improvisation?

Dave: I have to say when I play free it is usually a nice experience. You can't think because there is nothing to think about. You can't think about a chord because it is not going to work so you trust your ear and your instinct. What I depend on is the color and the mood rather than the specifics.

Richie: And how do you know what to play?

Dave: Because I have been doing it with you for such a long time.

Richie: Can you explain this in words to somebody?

Dave: It is all experience. It's like talking to your best friend or to your wife. You start a sentence and they can finish it.

Richie: Okay, very good.

Dave: I may interrupt you musically because I am finishing what you want to say.

Richie: Good, it saves time and I'm not bothered at all. Here is another question on top of this. Because we know each other so well, musically, socially, our friendship, isn't it hard to do fresh things?

Dave: I don't know? In this case, if we could get away from the page and make a life out of playing free together I would be very happy.

Richie: Me too, because this is pure jazz. To me Paul Bley personified the pure sense of free improvisation and his path of no preparation before a recording. He was a direct influence and inspiration for our *Empathy* recording.

Paul Bley came to my house before I recorded *Hubris* for ECM in 1977. Bley was 10 years older than me and he was already with ECM when I was still a teenager. Bley had been around for a long time. He was an ex-junkie, always asking everyone if they had any tapes they wanted to be released on his label. Unbelievable, blatant, but a wonderful guy and a genius.

We were hanging out in my apartment on Spring Street, and I was talking to him about his *Open, to love* record.

Dave: His first one for ECM?

Richie: Yes, it is an amazing record, completely improvised, beautiful cover.

Dave: But you told me Paul has no left hand ... how can he play solo so successfully?

Richie: Because he had that amazing ringing sound in the right hand. Paul asked me, "So, what are you going to do for your first solo record?" I said I have about ten new tunes. So he said, "Oh, you know what you're going to play?" In other words he is calling me a pussy. Are you an improviser? No! So you know what the tunes are. You are just going to play the tunes? Of course he was implying that I already know what I am going to play. His implication was that he, Paul Bley, does not play tunes and he does not know what he is going to play at all. And that in my opinion is the purest form of jazz improvisation.

Dave: He's got a point.

Richie: He's got a point!

Dave: Big point!

Richie: And that's *Empathy,* brother.

Dave: In this case, yes.

Richie: And I am very proud of our recording because, guess what, not everybody can do this and create an hour of interesting music. Bley could do it and what he was talking about is to play absolutely free. You go in with no agenda, a clean slate. I love it! You need tremendous discipline, training, and experience to make this kind of music.

And look, in the end nobody cares if you play free or written music or if you improvise. They want to hear great music. So the challenge is enormous and we know that we will never be able to perform perfectly.

To the listener, the similar parameters that they listen for are there. There has to be a sense of melody, and there must be a rhythmic sense at some point. There has to be a balance of tension and release, between excitement and calm. Those basic elements pretty much have to be there unless you go for a total ambient atmosphere or a burn. I find this the most challenging music, much more challenging than playing tunes.

2019

Jazz Education Today

Richie: Can you give me your assessment of the jazz scene now because you are on the front lines, working and teaching all the time in terms of gigs and performances plus education, compared to previous years.

Dave: It really is a dichotomy between negative and positive, so let's start with the negative. Getting paid in order to make a decent living is becoming a joke. There used to be several sources of traditional income ... royalties, tour support, and recording fees. The younger generation has accepted that those things are not there anymore so they don't know anything different. My daughter does PR for young jazz musicians in New York who still need and want promotion. If they get a review, especially in *DownBeat*, *JazzTimes*, the *New York Times*, or *Wall Street Journal* it is a victory for them (and my daughter!). It is for them what a gig or another record date was for our generation.

Richie: Does the review lead to anything?

Dave: Not in my opinion ... it never did. It leads to the artist feeling good or not depending on the tone of the review. But not as far as affecting work unless it is the *New York Times* or the *Wall Street Journal* because they are read worldwide. The problem is supply and demand. It always has been the problem for artists. There are many more of us than there is room for. That level used to be proportional but now it is very wide. The one thing that is happening is jazz education, which is still growing. Jazz education in a certain way is still growing and has action and activity. There is great support for education even though it's going down budget-wise but it is still the only game in a lot of cities besides commercial means of making music.

The positive part is, and I put this directly as a part of YouTube, the availability of music at the click of your thumb and how that has changed the scene now among young musicians. It is a complete smorgasbord from left to right, every idiom with the word jazz at least included, also from every historical period. I am hearing more mixtures and interesting things than ever before because they are now playing with their peers and they have the hardware to really sound good ... no cassette machine on the piano! The master-apprentice relationship is pretty much finished because the masters are dead. Young folks play with their peers which is pretty much what rock and roll bands have been doing for years. In a certain way jazz musicians have become that way.

They go to school and get down with somebody, like the way the guy plays, they become social friends, just like we did, and when they get out of school they use each other on gigs. The problem is that these are $50 gigs and the fees have not changed in the last 50 years. So there is a great gap between what is happening musically which I find really challenging and interesting. I see it every year at our annual convention of jazz schools where I interact with 50 students from 20 schools and countries that are doing unbelievably great work. On the other hand the opportunity to make a living and have a career in this music is getting more and more difficult.

Richie: Let's talk about the traditional master-apprentice relationship. You and I learned through this time-worn way of teaching young musicians. We had to climb that ladder working for a bunch of greats who were masters: Art Blakey, Stan Getz, Chet Baker, Freddie Hubbard, Art Farmer, Benny Golson, Elvin Jones. These were the bands, and of course Miles Davis at the top. Ten or fifteen piano players, saxophone players, bass players all rotated around each other and the masters, getting the available gigs. Most of the true masters are dead now or not playing anymore with a few exceptions.

Dave: Some are more active than others depending on their physical health.

Richie: What about the masters of today. Is that us? You hired younger guys with your band Expansions.

Dave: True. But the true masters are the generation that has been around longest and that is becoming us. Of course there are also Herbie, Chick, Wayne, and others that are five to six years older than us. Whatever way you do it you are granted this status of master by the time you get to 70 years old. Somehow the five decades mean that you're in the club of masters now.

Richie: It's really about longevity isn't it?

Dave: In a certain way it's not even about the music so much. The fact that Jon Hendricks still sings at 93 or 94 years old, that's a fact that's respected and which is right. How many clubs have guys like him played in their lifetime? How many buses, trains, and planes were boarded by mostly African-Americans bearing witness to all the well-known bigotry, like having to enter through the back door, smoke everywhere, funny money, the list goes on. The places they worked weren't clubs like we know it ... they were bars like on 52nd Street. These guys came through that period dealing with customers and a lot of negativity from the boss concerning working and living conditions with all kinds of people late at night. It was exciting but on the other hand let's face it, it was a bit tough up there. So you're granted the status of Master kind of when you made it to 70.

Richie: Another important question: Can young musicians really learn enough from schools or YouTube without the masters looking over their shoulder telling them they play too much or whatever? Doesn't that lead to a lesser quality of the music?

Dave: It leads to musical uniformity because everybody gets the same stuff at the same time as far as learning the music. And the jazz school wherever it may be necessitates learning in the middle level, saving the advanced guys for whatever.

Richie: But I'm not here for the middle...

Dave. We make it clear that we only want to talk to advanced students but the truth is there's also the mundane level kind of student that goes to Berklee College of Music in Boston to learn music because they can get a good education. But it does affect the level of the music. The classroom fosters uniformity because of the number of students and other considerations. One on one teaching is my preference cause you can get past the surface and teach more globally and artistically. So is individuality stifled? In a certain way yes ... it is stifled. On the other hand, cream rises to the top and the good students figure the game out. Bottom line is that the general level is higher than it used to be, students *and* most importantly teachers.

Richie: I think it is corrupted in a certain way. We are talking about producing artists. Everything we are came from inspiration. Your whole life came from listening to John Coltrane. I had the same experiences from listening to Bill Evans, Herbie Hancock, and Miles Davis. It's the top of the top sounding elitist and exclusive. Sorry, but I did not come to a school to be good. I wanted to be the best I could be. This is not about competition. We feel that uniformity destroys individuality. So I am trying to say, is there a point to make that a master apprentice relationship is the only way? In a way it is great that there are more and more students. Everybody wants to learn because of the easy access to information. But does it create more artists in your opinion?

Dave: Well, let's put it this way. My students have had a much better education than I had because they are getting the material from A to Z from people like us, who know what they are doing. The teaching level in general has gone way up. Years ago it was that the musicians who taught were considered the guys who could not play. The guys who can play now have to teach because of economics. One side bar—learning jazz is the best way to understand all the styles that are now evidenced by the kids. You learn to read, to hear, to compose, to be in any number of small ensembles, to discover ethics, learn how to do business, etc., etc.

Richie: But also it is accredited. The only jazz school I went to was Berklee and even at that time it was not an accredited college. At the Manhattan School of Music at that time, 1968, there was no jazz courses. It was not even mentioned except as a four letter word!

Dave: That's a good point that the accreditation has become official.

Richie: In other words it means something when you graduate from an accredited music college. You have a diploma and you can go and get a masters at Harvard if you want.

Dave: It used to be when you heard somebody play, the first thing you would say to them is you sound good and who are you playing with? Now you sound good, who do you study with? And that tells you a lot about the school, about the geography of the school, Indiana versus Miami versus the New School in New York, with all the little peculiarities about the place.

Richie: So you are saying, in a nutshell, that the master-apprentice system has been basically replaced by the university.

Dave: Basically yes.

Richie: For better or worse.

Dave: What you get is peer-to-peer contact. You can do that in and out of class. But now it is all formalized; you get a master's degree, then you get a doctorate, and on paper it looks like you did the job which you did. They have great teachers now. A lot of students have a great teacher, there is much less dead meat than there used to be. This is what I meant before when I said that they are better educated today than me.

Richie: We were self educated!

Dave: We picked and chose what we were interested in, skating around the main courses that you have to take. We liked this or that and became good at it. That is how we rose in the ranks. I never learned arranging and you know my penmanship is terrible because nobody ever told me how to write music.

Richie: I know that I tried...

Dave: We learned informally, from observation, from each other, and then hopefully from being with a master. They learn now in a very rigorous and, in some schools challenging curriculum which graduates them with a piece of paper.

Richie: You and I had a very similar background. I started with the classical piano master from the age of five to eighteen, you studied saxophone with Joe Allard, for the instrument, the serious shit. I went to the Manhattan School of Music and did get a degree in theory and composition. You never went to music school and it did not hurt you.

Dave: I was lucky...

Richie: But my experience in the classroom, and I know from teaching fifteen years in Leipzig, Germany which is an amazing school, the level is very high. The whole thing is about the quality of the students. It all comes down to the audition and who the school decides to accept, and that will raise the level of quality of the whole school. If they take everybody, of course they make a lot more money because they are supported by the government. You have 300 or 600 students, great! But there are not 600 great students. The reason they hired me in Leipzig was to bring the level of the school up which was a very big challenge but doable. So I figured out an audition method and therefore we only took one or two of the best students on each instrument instead of all 30. When I first came to teach at the Mendelssohn Hochschule in Leipzig there I was teaching kids that could not read bass clef. This was a problem because the school wanted numbers.

Then we brought the level of the school up, and it was a community of excellence that we tried to install there. I had ten kids, two girls and eight boys, and they were the best piano players from the towns that they came from. The interaction with other talented students really helped them. Besides scholarships and prizes, this interaction gave the school the reputation of excellence and atmosphere of higher learning. Actually it was like a big apprentice–master teaching situation. If schools would be run like that then they can turn out real artists. This is one way of avoiding the problem of uniformity of teaching levels. Many of my students are playing concerts while they are still in the school.

There is only room for a certain number of musicians. We know this from classical schools. Every student wants to be a violin soloist or play in an orchestra. How many of them can do this, two percent out of the thousands? The statistics are much worse for jazz because you have a much higher rate of graduates and a much lower rate of success. Success used to be judged by the recordings you would do. Because you were not able to make recordings yourself in the '70s and '80s unless someone calls you from a record company and says, "Hey Lieb, I want to record you!" There was none of that self-made stuff and if there was it was very funky. Now everyone can make their own recordings. The technology is cheap and wonderful and everything sounds great, pretty much. So it doesn't really mean anything anymore to make a record and of course there are very few gigs. People play for very little money just to get experience or they play in school, but that's not the same at all.

Dave: Here's a story I like to tell. This is the early 1990s at East Stroudsburg University, a small college near where I lived. The teacher there, Pat Dorian, liked to bring in heavy musicians to play with the college kids. The big band was an elective for the kids from the community. Pat invites Freddie Hubbard. Part of the gig is that Freddie has to do a workshop or clinic or whatever it was called in the early '90s. The setting was 3 p.m. in the afternoon with maybe 100 people there because it is Freddie Hubbard. We have a jazz vibe in this area of Pennsylvania, Phil Woods was my neighbor and so on. Freddie comes in ... gets up and begins to talk. Actually he seemed a little nervous. He says I have never done this before ... I am not sure what to talk about but I will tell you my life story. He talked for 40 minutes about the jazz culture where he grew up in Indianapolis. Playing and learning from Wes Montgomery, J.J. Johnson, etc. I go backstage to pay my respects and he asked me what was I doing here? I said, "I live here" and he asked, "Oh, where am I?" He probably slept in the car so I said Stroudsburg, Pennsylvania. He said, "Lieb, I was so nervous, how was I?" "Man, you were great, you were sincere, you were honest, you were real, you were great!"

The point is if Freddie Hubbard had to do a clinic (and make some more money) that was the beginning of a new era of teaching jazz. And the public gets to meet Hubtones (Freddie's nickname) or whomever. More and more artists began to teach and give a personal rap. You had to visit for a few hours, talk to students, and give them something to remember because we are in a situation were it is not only gigs we are concerned about but also teaching jobs. The bottom line is we are getting better and better at it. Our generation was the first to "explain" the music ... rather difficult ... but a far cry from the old days and the belief that jazz cannot be taught. Kenny Werner told me he was teaching in Seattle last week and named the staff. They were all under 35 years old and we didn't know any of them.

Richie: This is very interesting because I think the same thing happened in classical music 30 or 50 years ago because the music is older and established. Jazz is becoming more formalized. What do we want the most from a jazz musician? Individuality, we want to hear his or her view, not a bad copy of someone else. What does uniformity lead to usually by definition? Imitation! This is true for composers too. We don't want to hear rehashed Stravinsky or Boulez.

Dave: All the arts are affected like this.

Richie: So it is an interesting collision of amazing access to information. We used to go to the library, you could get ten books on one subject with ten different opinions. Remember the librarians there? Two lesbians, dressed in men's clothes, rulers of the place. I can still hear them complaining when I dared to reach across the desk to touch a book. Back then, openly gay people were less common, their very existence was eye-opening to an inexperienced twenty-year-old like me.

But today even though there are more books available, students tend to all get the same book from the internet because it is more convenient.

Dave: And then records came out at four dollars an LP.

Richie: We would call the record shop named Everything From Bunk To Monk and tell them to hold two new copies of the *Miles Smiles* LP for us because they only ordered ten copies.

Dave: Accessibility is a big part of the modern world. You can hit the button and hear 10,000 tunes through the internet.

Richie: You can have many of the books in most public libraries in the world in your hand. You don't even have to be at home. You can read on your phone or laptop. It is great but it can be dangerous because it is too easy to get the information. I am conflicted because I am guilty in my own house. I don't even have to stand up to get the CD and put it into my player. I go to YouTube because I have the computer and amazing speakers and almost everything is on YouTube or Spotify, etc..

Dave: In a level playing field more education is positive. People are informed, hopefully informed correctly. With the arts it is a little bit trickier because the goal is not general knowledge. The goal is specific knowledge and there is some strangeness teaching an art form that's a little in a gray area.

Richie: In accounting or law you know—here are the facts. In law, finance, mathematics, science, the basic things are set. It is also true that at the top of those fields there are many creative things happening, just like in music and arts. This is a great time to be a scientist. It is also great to read about all the medical research that's going on.

Dave: A lot of positive stuff!

Richie: But we are talking here about artists ... we are talking about inspiration and it doesn't quantify very easily. Look at Chet Baker. Do you think he went to school and received a masters degree? Our masters did not have so many college degrees.

Dave: But they played 45 or 50 weeks a year. They played three sets at night and then they went to another club for a jam session. They did not have to leave New York the way we do now. Pretty much every month I have to go to Europe because that is where the work is. We don't have the home base like those guys did. They would play the Half Note and two weeks later they would be at the Village Gate. When they worked in New York, they recorded also. It was a great time with lots of opportunities, a lot of stuff going on. The musicians got good. You had to be brain-dead not to get good with all these opportunities, playing 250 nights a year. The vocabulary they were playing was in a certain way a bit limited compared to what we have now. Not everyone was a Coltrane, developing his own language. He was unique in that respect.

Richie: You could be in there because the language was set.

Dave: So they had school without being in school because they played so much. Elvin Jones told me with Trane they played 40 to 45 weeks a year, doing three sets, sometimes four sets a night if there was good business coming through the door for hanging out. The audience could be rough at times, especially on a Saturday night.

The owner comes and says give me just one more short set. These people just came in and we can make some more money. They would play "My Favorite Things" for the second time that night!

Richie: I had breakfast with Herbie Hancock once. He played a concert ... I was opening for him and we had breakfast together the next morning. I didn't want to be a drag asking too many questions because I didn't really know him. He looked at me and said hey Richie, so he knew me. I asked him what it was like to live at that time, when the greats were around in abundance. So he looked at me and said, "Richie, the best cats became the best from playing the most with good people!" He meant you shouldn't play some stupid clubs with dead meat musicians. In the early days I was playing every night with Donald Byrd, Pepper Adams, and many others.

Dave: Knowledge seeped in even if somebody did not say this is the so-and-so chord. It was the environment of learning. There was also a lot of wasted time with foolish pursuits but there was enough time to learn if you concentrated a little bit. If you were playing with Wes Montgomery you are going to walk out with knowledge because it is right in front of your eyes, if you listen and observe.

Richie: Or if you're on the bus with Frank Rehak, the great trombone player. You will hear all the stories but also you could ask what did you play last night in the first bar and he might say I don't know. But you might also get an answer because a lot of these guys were very articulate.

Dave: They were, but a lot of them kept it to themselves.

Richie: Why?

Dave: Mafia, secrecy is better?

Richie: Omerta, the code of silence!

Dave: Why let everybody in? Because they are standing at the door? They got to pass the test. Or you know what, I have nothing really to tell you. Go to Dizzy Gillespie, he is good at this.

Richie: There are two cats, Benny Golson and James Moody. These two Black cats are the kindest, warmest and most articulate guys I ever met. If you ask them a question they would be happy to answer you. Then there were Woody Shaw and

Willbur Ware who couldn't or wouldn't answer. Bill Evans was also amazingly articulate, helpful, and kind.

Dave: So here is the thing. Let's say there is a clinic with John Coltrane, announced worldwide. The rest is history. Now you know what happens. You get a clinic with a well-known guy and you get a few interested students these days.

Richie: Why?

Dave: The kids take it for granted. I see that a lot in the master class wars. Maybe they show up but only if it is a superstar which then becomes a different story. But in general this education thing is becoming like I heard them already, I don't have to go. We always ask why our students are not coming to our gigs ... other priorities... even with discount tickets. Being taken for granted is a sad state of affairs.

Richie: Because they hear us every day!

Walter Quintus, Dave, Richie 2010

Bill Evans

Dave: Okay, let's talk about the individual influences upon us as we perceive them. We take turns here…you start.

Richie: I start with Bill Evans. I have come to some realizations about Bill, some are wonderful and some are a little bit painful. Bill was the first white piano player that brought classical aesthetics into Black culture with the Miles Davis recording of *Kind of Blue*.

Dave: Very good point.

Richie: Very important, and it hurt Bill too when you heard him talking about it. Not so much from the cats in the band but some Black musicians that were around Miles at that time had asked why did you hire this white piano player when there are so many other Black piano players that you could have hired? So Miles replied, "Bill Evans gives me what I want for this recording and I know what I want." Bill was a complete introvert and he looked like a professor at the time. But Miles loved Bill and when you hear interviews with Miles he sometimes sounds race conscious but I don't believe that he was a racist.

Dave: I agree, he was not a racist.

Richie: He was the most un-racist of all … look at the white musicians that he hired: Dave Schildkraut, Gil Evans, Lee Konitz, Dave Holland, you, Keith Jarrett, Steve Grossman, and Chick Corea. But Bill was the first white piano player Miles hired, while taking Wynton Kelly's place. Wynton Kelly was beloved, earning universal acclaim, great swing, tone, and very nice cat as well. Ron McClure, our bass player from Quest, has stories about Wynton. But Miles knew what he was doing and he didn't care who didn't like it. Miles would get together with Bill Evans and Gil Evans, by the way, and they would listen to the Ravel Piano Concerto in G Major and some of the Debussy piano works. Miles loved this music because he was not coming from the ghetto. He was an upper-middle-class son, his father was a dentist in St. Louis. Miles had great taste in clothes and art and he wanted a certain style in his piano player for the *Kind of Blue* record. Miles was tired of bebop, as great as that music was. He wanted something different and *Kind of Blue* is basically a ballad album.

Dave: Basically yes, slow tempos.

Richie: Here is the thing. I think Miles was brilliant in his hiring of Jimmy Cobb instead of Philly Joe Jones for the *Kind of Blue* recording with Bill instead of Wynton Kelly, except for one tune, "Freddy Freeloader."

Dave: I don't understand why Jimmy Cobb instead of Philly Joe?

Richie: Because Philly Joe was much more active and interacting aggressively.

Jimmy was capable of floating around the time and he was not as aggressive as Philly Joe.

Dave: Jimmy Cobb was married to Dinah Washington for many years.

Richie: Thank you, and he accompanied her. Philly Joe was not an accompanist for a singer. He was a real killer with great energy, but not right for that recording which is iconic upon iconic and more ... sorry bro!

Dave: Interesting. I don't know if Miles knew that upfront.

Richie: I think he did 'cause he hired him. Bill brought in the classical aesthetic of touch, tone, and harmony. Because *Kind of Blue* was a very fragile, delicate recording with interaction and Bill was perfect for it, unlike Miles' two previous recordings, *Milestones* and *Round Midnight*. They had other heavy shit on their own.

Dave: How much before *Kind of Blue* did Bill play with Miles? Two months, six months, a couple of gigs?

Richie: A couple of gigs. They recorded K*ind of Blue*, followed by *Jazz at the Plaza*.

Dave: "Green Dolphin Street" and "Stella by Starlight" are on *Jazz at the Plaza*, a live recording from the Plaza Hotel in New York.

Richie: The *Jazz Tracks* recording was another beauty with this band. Bill brought a tremendous amount of raw emotion and humanity into Miles music, because Bill himself was so vulnerable. He was quite insecure for a lot of the reasons. My feeling is that he became a junkie while he was playing with Miles because of the racial resistances coming from outside of the band.

Dave: When did he get into drugs?

Richie: During playing with Miles, and then it became worse after Scott LaFaro died in that terrible car accident. Bill had the ability to take the piano which is not an easy instrument to communicate emotions with. It is a hard instrument. It has keys ... you have no direct contact with the actual sound. The saxophone has the lip of the player on the mouthpiece, the trumpet also has the mouthpiece, the bass, violin, and guitar have the strings with direct finger contact. But on the piano you hit the key, the key moves the hammer, and the hammer hits the string. Your fingers are far away from the actual production of the sound.

Bill had a sound that you could identify on any piano or any record after one chord, that was Bill. He did it on my piano too. He came to my apartment on Spring Street in Soho, Manhattan in 1977 and he said, "Oh Richie, what a nice piano, can I play it?" Of course I said please do. He sat down and only played one chord, B, C and E, C major 7. You know that voicing from "Peace Piece"? And here is the amazing thing ... even though it was my piano, it sounded exactly like Bill with his touch ... unbelievable. But that is the same with every master. They pick up any instrument and it sounds like themselves right away.

Bill was like a vulnerable open wound. The intimacy displayed on a tune like "Blue In Green" always kills me when I listen to it. By the way, Miles at times also had that incredible vulnerability.

Dave: Lonely.

Richie: Lonely, but not like "pity me".

Dave: Not like Chet Baker.

Richie: Chet is like I'm dying, you want to come with me, I don't care, whatever you want, I am sorry, I am finished. Rescue me! Miles had power, but he also has that side that makes him so human. What do people feel when they hear Miles play the melody of "My Funny Valentine" or "Stella by Starlight." It affects them deeply and emotionally because it is real. Miles is not trying to get over to the audience, like Freddie Hubbard sometimes did. When Miles plays there is no show, no bullshit.

So Bill supported Miles 100%, and even on "So What" from *Kind of Blue,* everything Bill plays is really coming from a ballad feeling. That is beautiful, but it can also be a limitation. For example, Bill did not have the rhythmic pop that Wynton Kelly or Red Garland had.

Dave: But Wynton Kelly fit the harmony.

Richie: Right, but when Bill tried to play rhythmic stuff, when he burned, his lines were great but sometimes I am sorry to say, it sounds a little bit stiff.

Dave: On fast tempos, he is not Herbie Hancock or McCoy Tyner or Chick Corea.

Richie: Or Tommy Flanagan. And I have to admit that there are a whole bunch people that don't really believe that Bill was as great as he was. When you listen to Bill, even on "So What" or "All Blues" it is another way to play. He can play the other styles like hard bop and he proved it on his first trio recording *New Jazz Conceptions* from 1956. It was Bill's choice the way he articulated rhythmically on *Kind of Blue*. I got to know him pretty well ... he was ever so kind.

Dave: And very literate. The words he wrote about music are very articulate and logical.

Richie: Just read his liner notes to *Kind of Blue* which are so poetic and beautifully written. When I got to know Bill, we would meet and the first thing he says is hi Richie, how are you doing, got any new records for me? He is asking ME if I have any new records for him! I went to see him at the Village Vanguard and he says oh you have new solo record, so I gave him my solo piano recording on ECM called *Hubris*.

Once Bill was playing trio at the Village Vanguard and some amateur piano player fan that loved him, who had every record he did said, "Hey Bill, can you help me with something." Bill said sure, so the guy asked, "Can I get the changes for "Waltz for Debbie," can you write them out for me?" Bill said sure. He takes a sheet of paper, sits down in the back of the Vanguard and writes out the changes which are long. A lot of people are waiting to talk to Bill but he says no, I'm sorry, I have to do this. That kind of kindness. I mean, would you write out a tune in a situation like this?

Dave: I don't think so.

Richie: He had this sense of kindness and empathy. He was very supportive of young artists including myself. He didn't get negative even though he later talked in interviews about the abuse that got hurled at him by the jazz community.

Dave: He became a wreck.

Richie: He became a wreck, as it was said. Some people have said that his was the longest suicide in jazz history. He wanted to die. He had experienced terrible tragedies. His brother Harry committed suicide ... his wife jumped onto the subway track in front of him ... really awful.

Dave: Depriving the world of beauty, this guy had much more to give.

Richie: I agree.

McCoy Tyner

Richie: In the late 1960s McCoy Tyner was already like Mount Everest. McCoy is the papa, he is the main source of contemporary jazz piano. There's nobody else like McCoy.

In a way he was a throwback to the pre-bebop piano players like Art Tatum, Earl Hines, and Teddy Wilson 'cause like those great players McCoy had awesome command of the entire piano in terms of technique, knowledge of the instrument in the extreme and just a phenomenal grasp of jazz piano history. This was combined with his advanced and comprehensive approach to contemporary harmony. His pioneering use of modes, especially the creation and application of chromaticism, and of course his innovations with John Coltrane demanded the frequent use of the pedal point techniques. McCoy was able to take familiar material like "My Favorite Things" or "Chim Chim Cheree" or parts of "Softly, As In A Morning Sunrise" and transform these standard Broadway show tunes into creative modern vehicles for extended group improvisation.

At a certain point in history McCoy was the only piano player in the world that was able to support John Coltrane in the way that he was looking for. We all have heard Trane on recordings with Tommy Flanagan ... we heard him with Steve Kuhn and Cedar Walton. I mean they were good, playing bebop. But for Trane's ideas about chromaticism, it was *only* McCoy who worked out a way of playing dramatically supporting Trane's other notes in his chromatic scales ... any note could be a pedal point. This is similar to Schoenberg's democracy of chromaticism...the freedom of it ... the unchained ability to have long duration chromatic notes that are outside of the chord while you are blowing. Duke. Ellington, Charlie Parker ... these cats were unbelievable, but they definitely avoided certain notes. With them there were definitely notes that were right or wrong. For example: You do not play a B natural as a long duration on a G minor 7 chord. It sounds wrong. But with the "right" voicing, that intended tension will be alleviated.

McCoy Tyner's chord voicings were rich and with such new intervallic combinations using fourths and fifths, also minor seconds and tritones, they set up a cloud of sound where every note that Trane played sounded fine, again not necessarily matching ... that was the chromatic universe. For example if they were playing on a C pedal Trane could be playing a C sharp and holding it. McCoy could have a B natural in his voicing. This was the bridge from bebop to modal to chromatic and it opened up enormous possibilities to all of us that came after.

Dave: Plus of course McCoy's soloing. His speed, tempos, the left hand drone on the fifths, ... he was one of a kind. His universe was gigantic and you enter it at risk because you must be comfortable to play within his world of chromaticism ... it's not like bebop.

Our Views On

Richie: No, no ... he had his own iconic itinerary.

Dave: McCoy's solo on the second version of Coltrane's *Meditations* recording is like a 20th century sonata. These incredible solo piano interludes sound like they were written out. McCoy was extraordinary. He had an amazing run in the 1960s and '70s. *The Real McCoy* from 1965 is one of the classic albums of all times.

Richie: And in the '70s, *Song of the New World* ... amazing. McCoy had a similar level of technical mastery as Bud Powell and Art Tatum. This is very important. Tatum was an excellent jazz pianist who had a collection of brilliant runs and fantastic ideas but they were very much the same each time.

Bud Powell had classical chops, he studied at the Philadelphia Academy of Music like McCoy. They were classically trained and could play anything. McCoy wasn't one of those technically limited bebop piano players like Horace Silver, Al Haig, or even Tommy Flanagan. They played well but they did not have that fluency of McCoy or Bud and their left hand was not as strong.

Dave: They were like horn players.

Richie: Yes, and let's face it ... bebop was horn music. The front line with Bird and Dizzy of alto sax and trumpet was not originally music for piano. Also the pianos at that time sucked, especially in clubs where they had mostly old uprights and you couldn't hear the bass players. Bud Powell raised the level for all piano players because of his ability to project his sound above the drums. And there is some discussion that it was half of Bud that made Bird. His tune "Glass Enclosure," written in 1952, had this polychord of B flat major 7th sharp 5 in the left hand and D major 7 sharp 5 in the right hand. That's the special chord that Chick Corea used in his amazing composition called "The Brain," originally recorded on Chick's *IS* recording from 1969.

Bud had terrible personal problems ... the cops beat him silly and sprayed him with ammonia at Creedmore Hospital to get him under control.

McCoy Tyner set the bar for contemporary jazz piano and led the way for artists like Chick Corea, Herbie Hancock, Kenny Kirkland, Joey Calderazzo, myself and many more.

He is in my view THE essential modern jazz pianist!

Herbie Hancock

Richie: Herbie Hancock is the Mozart of jazz. He started very young, had all the basic skills. He had an amazing touch, an incredible natural sense of time, great taste, and a great feeling for swing. I mean in terms of just pure swinging there are only three people which I feel are the absolute top: Elvin Jones, Freddie Hubbard, and Herbie Hancock. Do you agree?

Dave: Yes, there are others of course but those three are the most notable with the greatest time feel.

Richie: Great time feel! The kind of time feel that you love and that you always want to hear because it sounds so natural and connects with your basic body rhythm. And those three have demonstrated this consistently over an estimated 3,000 recordings, and countless live performances. Just a deep swinging feel without sacrificing anything. Herbie is a combination of Wynton Kelly, Bobby Timmons, Bill Evans plus Debussy and Ravel, Scriabin and James Brown and Sly Stone. And of course Herbie's own contribution for the jazz vocabulary has been enormous.

Dave: Amazingly no McCoy Tyner, not one iota.

Richie: The influence of McCoy's vocabulary on Herbie was minimal and negligible on Bill Evans too. And that was on purpose because the major piano players in the 1960s were Bill, McCoy, and Herbie. And each one had their own identity. Herbie sometimes used the fourth chords in his left hand, but never percussively like McCoy did. Herbie is actually mostly a right hand piano player, with a very colorful and supportive left hand.

Dave: And he is a great mood painter on the piano.

Richie: He has good technique, but melodically he Is phenomenal. His left hand has great colors but he is not so well equipped as a solo piano player. He only recorded two solo piano records and they're both not exceptional, and he knows this.

Dave: Why, is he not orchestral enough?

Richie: Technically Herbie's left hand is not independent enough for great solo piano playing. Herbie is capable of playing great intros, but so far he has not been able to sustain it for a whole recording. As a matter of fact, in the 1970s George Wein promoted a big solo piano concert in New York. It had Keith Jarrett, McCoy, Chick Corea, and Herbie and I read an interview with Herbie about the concert and he said that he felt really intimidated. Keith is known for his great solo concerts, McCoy is capable of being a monster solo pianist, and Chick did play great solo piano until the early 1970s. In my opinion Herbie is not as equipped as those other guys. But he is really the ideal band piano player.

Herbie is so consistently and relentlessly creative even playing a blues, playing anything, you never know what will happen and he has that same sense of composition that Wayne Shorter has. He creates musical ideas and develops them. His ballad playing is unbelievable, spontaneous reharmonization, and he has a great rich piano sound.

Dave: He wrote one of the greatest tunes of all time, "Dolphin Dance."

Richie: "Dolphin Dance!" Amazing tune, "Maiden Voyage," iconic tune with fantastic chord changes and a great rhythmic vamp. "The Eye Of The Hurricane," a complex and brilliant 12-bar F minor blues. These tunes have all become part of the jazz standard repertoire. He did not write as many tunes as Wayne and his early tunes are mostly all iconic. And Herbie is also very eclectic, like you are. McCoy is just McCoy. Did you ever see him going near an electric piano? No. Keith Jarrett? For a second, and he played some Farfisa organ with Miles Davis in 1970. By the way, Herbie went to Grinnell College and studied engineering.

Dave: Is it true that Herbie was playing classical concerts when he was 11 years old?

Richie: Yes, he studied classical music and played Mozart piano concertos when he was 11. He loves gadgets and he is still a bit of a nerd, he always had the newest tape recorders. I once saw him with Miles at the Village Vanguard in 1965. Herbie was late, Miles was pissed at him, they started the set without him and when Herbie came in the first thing he did was to put a new tape recorder under the piano. He wanted to hear what he played!

Herbie is also a very articulate guy. There is a part of him that is not exactly jive but a bit insincere because he meets so many people.

Dave: He's got the Hollywood vibe, he has to be that way.

Richie: Besides having been a great composer in the 1960s and early '70s he played on an enormous number of records as a sideman and leader, and I never heard him play a bad solo. He is one of the most consistent and creative jazz piano improvisers in the world, and in jazz history. And that is very important to me. When I listen to his music sometimes I have to walk around the room, he swings so much and he is so creative.

Chick Corea

Richie: Chick was not a friend of mine, but I was friendly with him. He lived in your loft building underneath Dave Holland, on 19th Street, in the late 1960s. We were acquaintances, colleagues...we liked each other ... he was about six or seven years older. He had his own group as well as playing with Miles Davis. This was before he joined Scientology ... a little later he became a very different Chick. Before Scientology he was macrobiotic ... getting high ... smoking pot like all of us. He was one of the young piano players on the scene.

And Chick was a great bebop player, he was very familiar with Bud Powell's music and also about McCoy's great creative innovations. When I met him in the late 1960s he was listening intensely to Schoenberg, Berg, Stockhausen, and Ives, starting to incorporate this language into the music. He was much more advanced at the time than me and we loved to discuss this music. He had a group called Circle, originally with Dave Holland and drummer Barry Altschul and later they added saxophonist Anthony Braxton. And of course Chick had just done two iconic records ... one is *Now He Sings, Now He Sobs* with Roy Haynes and Miroslav Vitous for Blue Note and later *The Song Of Singing* with Dave Holland and Barry Altschul. In those days for me it was McCoy, Herbie Hancock, and Chick. They had the linear approach mastered combined with fantastic original harmony, a great sense of swing, "killing" natural time, and a great understanding of the piano. All three were wonderful composers. They were the top of the line. The next record he did was *Sundance* with his amazing tune "The Brain," which by the way is a 12-tone row. It is an incredible piece with great intervallic stuff.

Dave: I wonder if he got that from Coltrane's "Miles Mode," because that was Trane's 12-tone tune.

Richie: Maybe, but I think he got it more from Schoenberg. I know he was working on this. Then he ends the melody of "The Brain" on a G minor pedal so here you have both worlds, the diatonic world of G minor pedal and the 12-tone world of the melody of "The Brain." Chick solos on G minor pedal point with Dave Holland and Jack DeJohnette on bass and drums. It is one of the most iconic and burning solos ever. He utilizes everything McCoy has done and in my opinion even surpasses it in places in terms of pure virtuosity and intensity. Also he had Dave and Jack and those three of course were Miles' rhythm section for couple of years so they worked together all the time. There was a certain synergy in that band because Dave Holland was like the horse. He loved to play time and gave Jack total freedom in a similar way that Ron Carter gave Tony Williams rhythmic freedom. Also Jack expanded the vision of what the drums could do in a small group situation. It was overpowering at times ... it was so intense but it was always musical at the same time. The combination of 4/4 time with Dave and Jack while

Chick played like a contemporary piano concerto greatly expanded the possibility of what was possible, helped by using the entire range of the keyboard. Generally jazz piano players usually don't use whole range of the piano. To me this tune, "The Brain" was the next logical development after McCoy in the history of jazz piano.

Of course it went unnoticed by the jazz public. Remember, Lieb, we went with Randy Brecker to see Chick at the Village Vanguard on a Sunday afternoon matinee. He played with Miroslav Vitous, Jack DeJohnette, Woody Shaw, and Bennie Maupin ... that was the band. Incredible.

Dave: And of course we heard them rehearse downstairs in the loft on 19th Street.

Richie: I do have some criticism for Chick, his life's work. I'm trying not to be judgmental, but just thinking in terms of what history might say. Chick is a great piano player who still sounds fantastic. Because he was not a junkie ... he did not get high ... he was not whoring. He is a good guy. Unfortunately he allowed Scientology to change his artistic vision. You have to remember, he started his career with some fantastic records, *Tones for Joan's Bones, Now He Sings, Now He Sobs, Sundance, The Song of Singing, ARC* and two fantastic solo records for ECM. And then he goes to Manfred Eicher with this *Return to Forever* record, this bossa nova stuff with electric piano and a singer, Flora Purim, Stanley Clarke, Joe Farrell, and Airto Moreira playing drums. Not a bad band but if you heard *The Song of Singing* or *Sundance* or the other early records, burning, and the fantastic free jazz this was very disappointing to say the least.

Dave: Can we say that in the 1970s musicians tried to be successful. Record companies were rather generous with their budgets and we were also beneficiaries of that.

Richie: ... and record companies started to expect sales.

Dave: And there were sales. Just like Miles was called into Clive Davis's office who told him that his sales were not good enough, *Nefertiti* only sold 5,000 copies at the time, do something! So these next records, *Miles in the Sky, In a Silent Way* and of course the iconic *Bitches Brew* set a whole new level.

Do you think that the recording of *Return to Forever* was influenced by Chick joining Scientology around that time?

Richie: Absolutely right, because what Scientology teaches you is to be successful. Success means acceptance ... acceptance means money like you were saying. Chick's *Sundance* record is not for every jazz listener, but it has great musical and historical value. The big lie of Scientology is in this sentence—The quality of the art is in its ability to communicate! This is a terrible subtext ... it says if very few people like it, it sucks.

Dave: It's implied.

Richie: It is very much implied. So Scientology delivers the vision of one weird guy named L. Ron Hubbard, with some other crazy people to enforce his scene. Scientology is another form of commercial therapy. It is supposed to help people that are lost, that are confused. Okay, whatever Scientology is, they got Chick at a weak point when he had seven people in the audience at the Village Vanguard and he had to pay alimony for his children. Scientology said we can help you if you do this and if you do that and of course they were right ... they teach you how to be successful.

And this is what pisses me off about Chick, because he knew better. Who were his heroes? Van Gogh, Claude Monet, Schoenberg, and Bartók...

Dave: ...Ives, Monk, Bud Powell.

Richie: Van Gogh died in poverty. He sold one painting to his brother Theo. Is the art in the communication of how many people buy? No! Bartók died penniless on Riverside Drive in New York. Who was a great influence on Chick? Bartók! To me it is bullshit. Chick turned his back on the very people that influenced him and gave him oxygen for his artistic life. He accepted that bullshit from Scientology that the more people that love your art makes your art better. So the more applause and acceptance your music gets the better the music is? This is the biggest lie ever that Scientology perpetrates.

Dave: It is hard for me to believe this.

Richie: Look at the results ... just look at the results, *Romantic Warrior*?

Dave: You think they sat down and said now we are getting across to 10,000 people and not just 10?

Richie: They don't tell you that, but it is the implication, the subtext. How else can you explain this, Tom Cruise, John Travolta.

Dave: We don't know this.

Richie: These cats are trained to be successful, not following your vision of what you would like to do. Look at John Coltrane ... his vision happened to be successful, *A Love Supreme*, 500,000 copies. Unbelievable. Keith Jarrett ... five million copies of the *Köln Concert*, solo piano improvisations. But Chick was *not* successful commercially at what he was doing before 1972 and he was at the top of his profession, just like Bartók and Van Gogh, okay? What am I going to say? He was weak? Did Scientology people get him at a weak point? Yes. We all have our weaknesses, me too. As soon as Chick had success with *Return to Forever* and *Light as a Feather* he got bigger and bigger, playing stadiums, and the music got worse and worse in my opinion. He did make his musical contribution between 1966 until 1972. And after that he made his money, and with the exposés and scandals about Scientology he was still committed to it. My final feeling about Chick is that the world of music has been deprived of what he could have done.

Dave: Here is the thing. I was on tour with him in 1978. You and I were in Houston, Texas when the phone rang...

Richie: ... he found you...

Dave: He found me and he asked me to do this three month tour of Japan, Australia, and Europe. I enjoyed the playing immensely ... we did a duo every night, either "Lush Life" or "Crystal Silence." The rest of the music for the tour was from the records *Leprechaun*, *Mad Hatter*, and *My Spanish Heart*. The group included a string quartet, his wife Gayle Moran, Rick Laird on bass, and Tom Brechtlein on drums.

Because Chick and I had a history from the loft I was not just hired as a replacement for Joe Farrell. It was personal ... I knew Chick ... we lived in the same building after all, baking bread together.

Richie: Had he ever hired you before?

Dave: No, I wasn't ready.

Richie: Right.

Dave: This is now 1978, so I play a little better than 10 years before. Chick and I spent a lot of time together on this tour. After the gig we would end up in his or in my room talking about Scientology.

When Chick joined, I also did try Scientology myself for about six months. I detected a definite change in Chick's personality from what I remembered from the old days. What I remembered from 1969–1970 was his generosity of spirit, his unbelievable musicianship, but mainly his general demeanor and personality and him being a giving and loving cat. Plus he was one of the great, is not the greatest musician I ever met.

Richie: Me too.

Dave: So here I am in 1978 with Chick talking about the stuff and I'm asking what happened in 1972? Did they brainwash you? I'm not sure if I used those exact words but we had long talks into the night.

Richie: He loves to talk and he is very articulate.

Dave: But it appears that he did not take it that way because at the end of the tour, landing in Los Angeles, foot down on the ground, he turns to me and says you were against me, you made trouble with the band, and I don't ever want to see you again. He really closed the door, I couldn't believe it. Later that day I talked to Charles Veal, the violinist, and asked him if he could find out more and he says, "I don't know what happened, Dave, but he was really pissed off about some things you said." So our relationship pretty much ended there but of course over the years I saw him again ... he sat in one day with Pete La Roca and you remember, the two of us saw him in Japan and he said, "Oh, you're really lucky because you can record what you want. I can not do this with Polydor." But we never had real contact again.

Richie: There is a photo of the three of us and me handing him a solo piano LP called *Live in Tokyo*.

Dave: Here is my take on Chick. He wants to do well, and sincerely wants to be a force for good. In his mind Scientology was the vehicle for him to become what he really was, a great communicator. This has nothing to do with the music, but of course the music suffered. We both agree on that. But I have to say his intentions have always been positive. It is the way he did it, which you might not agree with, but I felt that he was always honest in his pursuit to be a human being, plus he is one of the greatest musicians.

Richie: I agree about him being one of the greatest musicians, but totally disagree about him being a force for good after he joined Scientology, and I will tell you why. Because unfortunately he has been brainwashed into thinking that being successful is being the force for good! But this is not good for the development of his art. And since he is one of the greatest there is something called artistic responsibility.

Dave: So you say all his bands of the last 50 years are bullshit?

Richie: Yes, in my view every group from *Return to Forever* on. Maybe not all bullshit. There is some well-played stuff, but it was not the true creative Chick ... it was not his best or his vision, which was misplaced. Everything was about communication and self-promotion, just what they teach you in Scientology. The quality of the music went down. Of course he is still a great piano player. But he knows better and he changed his direction only because he wasn't successful. And he didn't have the patience and courage to stay on his original and creative path. In my opinion he should have stayed on his path with compositions like "The Brain," LPs like *Now He Sings, Now He Sobs*, and he should have developed further the piano solo music he recorded for ECM on that level with his full artistic expression. I think he deprived the world of some fantastic music and because of his involvement with Scientology he never developed past a certain point. Think of the fantastic record *Tones for Joan's Bones*. This was his first record ... the most amazing debut.

Dave: Exactly.

Richie: And then he even developed further! Think about these five recordings and his two piano solo records. These are historically brilliant, naturally artistically conceived pieces of art. Like Picasso with his blue period, red period, and Guernica. Also like early Mozart sonatas, the late Beethoven string quartets. The heaviest shit in the world of music. They all have a sense of unimpeded development and to me of course the greatest example of this is John Coltrane and his music.

Dave: So you say that he cut his own development short?

Richie: Yes, he cut it short.

Dave: But you just named several works of Chick.

Richie: Five records in five years! But it was 50 years ago.

Dave: So you say after that he hung up this coat and said I will be commercial from now on?

Richie: Yes, not completely commercial but with the intent of pleasing the most people instead of following his vision. You can't argue with that, it is a fact. And he never wavered ... that's the other thing.

By the way, my fight is not with Scientology. I don't like them but it is not my business. If you want to go join them it's fine. But with Chick it is personal. If Chick's first record would have been *Return to Forever* it would have been fine, a different story. But we know he was one of the greatest of all time. *Return to Forever* is not the greatest. It is arrested development and a shame. I feel bad for this cat ... he knows himself ... he's not high. He is clear and should have known what he gave up!

Dave: So your problem is that the world has been deprived of his genius.

Richie: Yes, I am sorry too.

The point is because his earlier work is pretty much hidden except among young musicians, he does not want it to be widely known. I heard a radio interview with him once, you know he is great in interviews, he makes everyone feel comfortable. And the woman says "Chick, I would like to ask you about your earlier records, *Now He Sings, Now He Sobs* and *Sundance*, what about that music?" And he said, "Oh yeah, thank you for remembering, but I was very misguided then and I was going along the wrong track."

Dave: He probably said that.

Richie, Chick Corea, Dave. 1982 in Japan

John Coltrane

Dave: In my past interviews and books I have said a lot about John Coltrane. But there is one aspect I would like to reiterate that stands out beyond everything outside of the music. And that is the sincerity, conviction, and honesty from which he did what he did. He was like a light to everyone around him. He inspired people, even way back when he recorded for Prestige Records in the late 1950s. This was most obvious it was with his classic quartet featuring McCoy Tyner, Jimmy Garrison, and Elvin Jones.

Richie: How specifically did he communicate this love, light, and humanity ... how?

Dave: He did his job. No extra curricula shit, very few wild stories like there are about Miles Davis, Bill Evans, Chet Baker, and Stan Getz. All those guys have colorful stories. Trane's story is very simple. He had a little drug problem for a minute, got out of it, and went on to produce the greatest jazz music of all time. He was completely dedicated with a group that absolutely read his thoughts and ideas without talking about it. They were comfortable with each other. They were the epitome of what a jazz group should be ... ain't nothin' to say. Just get up there and play. That part of Trane for me stands out above anybody else. Other people have played and conceived great music, but that ability plus his great skills and what he contributed to the music puts him in a category alone. And for me, being 15 years old, seeing that, something clicked with me. That straight ahead, do the job, that's the way I am trying to be.

Richie: You are very pragmatic.

Dave: Your job is to get up there and play your ass off, for an hour and a half. No show...absolutely no show. Tuxedo and tie, no talking, just play. I asked Jimmy Garrison what Trane was like and he said he would've liked you, and you would've liked him. And then he told me a little story. I asked him, what was the relationship between Sonny Rollins and John Coltrane? He said well, they loved each other. I remember a story. After a gig Trane would usually go straight home to Deer Park in Long Island. He would not hang out after the gig. But when Sonny Rollins was playing in town Trane would always go to see him. One night after Trane finished at the Half Note we decided to see Newk at the Five Spot ... the clubs were within walking distance. We walk into the Five Spot, people would be whispering is that John Coltrane? Sonny is playing trio. Trane gets a seat, lights a cigar and maybe has a drink. Sonny sees him, continues to play, walks off the stage while playing, walks over to Trane, this is Jimmy Garrison describing it. Sonny gets on his knees, finishes playing the tune on his knees. I asked Jimmy what did Trane say and Jimmy said he just smiled. That was the relationship between them!

Richie: I never heard that story ... beautiful. The thing about Trane was his humility, in the face of incredible accomplishment. Miles Davis was styling and so could have Trane.

Our Views On

Dave: Could have ... he was a good looking guy.

Richie: Even though Trane did not choose a religious life, his beliefs reflected a broad sense of spirituality. I did go out to his house once, but I never went in. I think I told you the story with Reggie Workman. This is when Trane lived in St. Albans, Queens. I was playing in the Lost And Found, in 1965, as a sub for Cedar Walton. The Lost And Found was a bar on 33rd Street and Park Avenue, with all the whores hanging out there, remember? So it was a duo gig with Reggie Workman, who used to be Trane's bass player. He called me and said Richie, I need you, can you come and play tonight, Cedar can't make it. I said yes, of course, I would go to Alaska to play with him. I was 18 at the time. So I take the subway to the gig, my father warning me not to get into any strange cars. I come to the club, we start playing, and it is okay, Reggie is very kind, and we get through the night. He hires me for the rest of the week and we are becoming friendly. So one day he says hey Richie, I'm going out to see the chief. I said who is the chief and he says John Coltrane, do you want to come? So I said yes, of course I want to come.

It was in the middle of the summer, Reggie had some music that he had to give back to Trane. We are driving there in Reggie's station wagon, the back is full of his kid's toys. I am really scared to meet Trane, I don't want to be an idiot. So we got to Trane's house and Reggie gets out of the car. I can't move, it is like I am cemented to the front seat. Trane comes to the door, a screen door in which he fills up the whole frame. He is tall, about 6' 3" and broad. In his hand he has a tenor sax, an alto sax, and a flute hanging from straps around his neck. I have never seen anything like that, and he smiles when he sees Reggie. So Reggie says come on in, have a lemonade, and I said no. He said what's the matter, are you sick? I said no, I can't come, I don't want to take up his time. So he tried again, why don't you come in, it's hot out here. So I said Reggie, please, you go ahead, I'm totally cool out here. So he goes to the door, Trane is there, opens to door, smiles, gives Reggie a big hug and Trane asks who's the kid who doesn't want to come in and Reggie explains to him. So they go into the house, talking for a while. Then Naima comes out with a big glass of lemonade and says this is for you, are you sure you don't want to come in? And I said no thank you. Not long after, this was only a social/musical call, Reggie gets back into the car. He didn't say anything. He is respecting my decision and then I said to Reggie that I am so far away from Trane in certain ways, I don't want to take up any of his time. Reggie said he understood. I know that I missed the opportunity, but I don't think I could've added anything to his afternoon. Reggie said good man.

Dave: That's the reason. You did not want to take up any of his space.

Richie: I did not want to ask any stupid questions. You know like when people ask us dumb shit, sometimes it is better to shut up. So this was my experience with Trane which was very humbling. The power of his sound was amazing, because a lot of times he played off microphone.

Dave: That's true, when he played live.

Richie: You know when he turned to Elvin and got on his knees, you could hear Elvin's cymbal and Trane screaming, that was the universe coming to visit. The power really hit you, especially if you sat in the front.

Wynton Marsalis

Dave: Wynton Marsalis is important.

Richie: Yes, he is important, but his story is a little bit like Chick Corea's story. Chick showed early genius on his recordings from 1966 to 1971 and then he sold his musical soul to the Scientology cult and in my opinion his music suffered greatly in terms of the creative path that he had established. There is a comparison between Chick's and Wynton's story because after showing great promise when Wynton came to the jazz scene in 1985, and for the next five years he grew and developed. Then he changed when he became artistic director of Jazz at Lincoln Center and became like a present day version of Louis Armstrong.

Dave: Jazz at Lincoln Center is a role model for all concert hall jazz series in the world now.

He came onto the jazz scene at the time like a gift from the gods, clean cut, short hair, with the suit, the tie, and the lineage to New Orleans ... on paper he was perfect.

Richie: And he could play!

Dave: He could play jazz and classical, which put him into a situation that nobody ever had in jazz before. Because of what was going on in the world, media people wanted somebody like that.

Richie: They wanted a spokesman.

Dave: He was the perfect man. If it wouldn't have been him it could've been someone else. Of course he had his jive moments.

Richie: He was too young and inexperienced for that role.

Dave: He made mistakes and said stupid things. But on the other hand he goes out into the community, especially to schools where he is not getting paid. Of course he doesn't need it. He is extremely generous with his time and who could walk better into a public school in Detroit than Wynton Marsalis? I have a lot of respect for what he has done. I never had any interaction with him except for a few words here and there but I have to give it to him for raising the profile of people of his race, particularly, really backing it up and being a form of spokesman.

Richie: Yes, this is all true. Similar to Chick Corea, but not with as much talent. Wynton started out with great promise ... first with Art Blakey's Jazz Messengers, then with his own quintet featuring Branford, Kenny Kirkland, and Jeff Watts. *Black Codes (From The Underground)* was a promising record and it was very influenced by the *Miles Smiles* record from 1966. He did some other recordings with Herbie Hancock which were fantastic. Also Wynton made a brilliant recording of the Haydn D Major Trumpet Concerto which was world class. And then somebody got to him.

Dave: He started to believe his own story.

Richie: He was too young and inexperienced, while some nasty and one-sided music journalists got to him. The first five years of Lincoln Center performances were extremely conservative and mostly about Black music history, which I understand. It was taken away from them, it's payback. But also he is going back to Louis Armstrong which seemingly had him becoming a Louis Armstrong imitator. But he totally neglected contemporary musicians, white and Black, like you in a viral way. It was exclusionary to a breaking point ... it was ridiculous.

Dave: That's true.

Richie: So this is payback, maybe, you punch me, I punch you back. Lincoln Center is a big organization with millions of dollars.

Dave: Thirty-five million dollars raised from what I heard.

Richie: He misused his responsibility as the artistic director, leaning too heavily on the past. I don't know anybody that performed there that was really contemporary.

Dave: Eventually they did, Michael Brecker, Joe Lovano, and others worked at Lincoln Center.

Richie: Wynton continued with his own recordings of the music of the past. The beautiful history of New Orleans and his own music became very much concerned with Louis Armstrong. He hired almost all musicians from his home town, New Orleans. The music was very conservative, ignoring the direction of his first recording, *Black Codes (From The Underground)*. Also he ignored any other musical influences from the 1960s and later. And most importantly he split with his brother Branford and that probably also contributed to Wynton's move to that very conservative direction.

Dave: Wynton's brother Branford went rock and roll for a while, playing with Sting, as did Kenny Kirkland. Their father, Ellis Marsalis, played every Friday night in New Orleans for years.

Richie: Lieb, we have to make a public apology now to Ellis about that incident at a school that happened.

Dave: We did not diss him, we just ignored him.

He asked a technical question ... something on "Stella" if I recall. We didn't ignore him ... we just did not get into depth about it. If we would've known who he was we probably would have.

Richie: We would have done anything for him, sure.

Dave: Because he is a sweetheart.

Richie: I heard that their youngest brother, a drummer, is the best of them.

Dave: Jason ... he is a good kid, an excellent drummer and extremely talented. I played with him for a week at the Blue Note club in New York and we had a great time.

Richie: We can only imagine how Wynton would have developed had he not taken that conservative direction. So far he has not come back to contemporary jazz music.

Jack DeJohnette

Dave: In September 2019, we recorded with Jack DeJohnette, in a trio with you and me. Why did we record with Jack and why in a trio without a bass player?

Richie: I have a long history with Jack which goes back to Stan Getz. For two years I played in the Stan Getz Quartet with Dave Holland on bass and Jack on drums, touring all over the world from 1972 through 1973. When I came into the band I was 25 years old, a bit nervous, but confident, because Stan liked me. We had the Russian Jewish thing, just like my family. I was not arrogant but I was not going to get beaten down. Dave Holland was very English. I knew them both from recording with Chick Corea and hearing them playing with Miles Davis. To me they were the top of the top. When I heard John Coltrane with McCoy and Elvin I was very young and I did not really know what was going on. I just knew that it was great. But this time playing with Jack and Dave with Stan I knew that it was great and why. I was totally inspired by their playing. I had gotten what I wished for. It was an amazing experience because when Jack played behind Stan he was pretty conservative, swinging, but not too loud. However, for the piano solos, because of the way I played and at that time I did play a lot like Chick Corea, Jack opened up and he loved it. But for the first two weeks in this group and on the first gig I was not ready for Jack's totally open approach to playing. This was at the Colonial Tavern in Toronto. You have to remember, at that time Stan Getz was the number one on the music charts with "The Girl From Ipanema," all the charts, not just jazz. This song was in every jukebox in every bar around the country and around the world. He was popular because of this bossa nova stuff he recorded, and less because of his jazz recordings which were limited to the jazz audience.

So the first night on the first gig for me with Stan ... Tuesday night in Toronto. First tune, "Invitation." I'm having a great time comping for Stan who is smiling. We get to the piano solo and I start playing. Jack immediately starts going into his complex and unusual rhythmic phrasings that are very difficult to follow because they seem to go against the flow of the time. After the set I asked Jack what he was doing and he said I don't know and don't ask me because I don't want to know. It is like asking a centipede with 100 legs how do you know which leg it moves first and you have a good comparison.

I think Jack protects himself by not thinking how he plays those unusual rhythmic accompaniments. It is really metabolic and stems from his metabolism. Jack plays organically but he has such perfect, natural time with such an internal sense for 1, 2, 3, 4 that I never heard him fuck up ... never! He does things that sound like a free drummer, say Rashied Ali for example. It just seems that these phrases come out of time and are always correct.

After Stan's saxophone solo the band changes. Now it is the trio. I couldn't follow what Jack was doing. This is horrible to admit but it was just about the four beats in every bar ... basic shit! I couldn't follow rhythmically what Jack was doing with those four beats in every bar. But I missed a lot of the ones and when I tried to change with him, it was even worse. Stan is standing in the corner, looking at girls, but Jack noticed it and also Dave Holland. This happened two or three times in one night, too many times. Why did I try to follow Jack? Because I just wanted to be out there with him. So after the gig we go back to our hotel and I say good night to them. I am in my room and suddenly Jack and Dave knock on my door. "Hey Richie, can we talk?" I let them in. They are very nice, no bad vibe, no weird old school shit like Sonny Stitt. I said sure, they want to hang, great. They come in, sit down and Jack says clearly, "Don't listen to me, *I* can't listen to me." I said, "What do you mean?" Now Dave Holland is trying to help "translate" what Jack said. "In other words, don't listen to Jack for the time or the form. You have good time, you know where it is, trust yourself, trust your instinct. Don't try to catch Jack because you will never get him. You sounded great, you are doing good, it will be fun, everything is cool." Smile. These are great cats. They wanted me to be my best with no bad vibes. That was it.

Dave, Richie, Jack DeJohnette. Woodstock, September 2019

So I go back the next night and I said to myself, okay, I am going to follow my instincts. I do have good time and I do have a good sense of form. I was only 26 but I was doing okay, right? So Jack starts going out during my piano solo, playing some amazingly complex but great shit. We are coming to the end of the chorus, a big one is coming. Jack is roaring like a volcano playing totally asymmetrical and I say to myself no, do not listen to him. He is looking at me and finally he's putting down the one, boom, and we are all on the one together! Jack was so smart, he didn't do that with Stan because he wanted to keep the gig.

The way he plays works because in the end his goal is trying to orchestrate the music. He is not doing it to harm or confuse me. If he would be playing exactly together with me, like Al Foster does, it is fantastic, it feels great, it is like a football team. But Jack is an orchestrator. Jabali Billy Hart is also, by the way. Jack is not playing ding ding ding, he is a percussion section like in the Bartók Concerto For Orchestra and that music has depth and dimension because of the different rhythmic parts. Jack is creating this kind of interest in a small group. So we hit together and I see Jack nodding with the big smile. And from then on I was cool and I could play with him, and of course if I can play with him I can play with anybody. I had achieved my independence from having to listen to the drummer for the time and the form.

Dave: So why not use a bass player on this recording with him?

Richie: The music is different, even with the greatest bass player in the world and great music. When we play duo my left hand is very free to do things, and to re-harmonize on the spot and to create atmosphere in the bottom range of the piano which I can't do with a bass player because I would be blocking his register. The better the bass player the less I can play, out of respect and again as mentioned because of the tessitura. If there is no bass player I am much freer in my role as an accompanist. Even when you are playing free there is always the possibility that there is going to be a clash, or a limitation. Herbie Hancock rarely played in the bottom register of the piano because he always has a bass player and that is his style.

But my left hand is a large part of my sound. I play figures and things with my left hand that help me to create my music and to personalize it. So if we had a bass player I think it would be limiting for my style, not withstanding the goal of the recording situation, whatever that might be. Not having a bass player gives me much more room for expression. Obviously one less instrument can translate to the music being less crowded. I can move the music around in many ways that we could not do with a bass player. The bass has a great sound and adds a lot but it can be a limitation. When you have good time, how much more time do you need? We have the possibility to create some really fresh musical moments. The fact that there will be no tunes will make it even more free.

We already did *Empathy*, our free duo recording with all improvisations, no tunes. These recordings form a complete full circle from when we started at the loft in 1969 and recorded *Night Scapes* with the poet, playing completely free.

Dave: That's why I used Jack, Dave Holland, and Kenny Werner for my *Fire* recording because they are among the few musicians left that know how to play like that, meaning free but not free—figure that out!

Richie: It's great that you did that recording. When you and I started playing in 1968 in the loft, we played free and also some tunes. We weren't very good and could not sustain a mood except the texture of everyone playing together at top volume and no sense of phrasing yet. We were too impatient. We did not know then about motivic development, but we tried. We have both come a long way since then and I feel now that this recording with Jack has the potential for some great music.

Wayne Shorter and the 1987 Tribute Concert to John Coltrane

Dave: What makes Wayne Shorter so special is that his improvised solos are on the same high level as his compositions. We always used to say if a solo passed the compositional review process it would be perfect ... all the ducks in a row!

Richie: He got it from his composing. Remember when he was with Art Blakey? He was writing simple stuff but then something happened when he joined the Miles Davis Quintet with Herbie Hancock, Ron Carter, and Tony Williams. This is a good example for young musicians. Wayne had to be different ... it was mandatory with Miles.

Dave: But this is what separates him from everybody else and I'm not even talking about him as a saxophonist. He is the improviser as composer. Check it out ... "Donna Lee" is Bird's solo, Coltrane's "Naima" is Trane's solo. But Wayne's solos have aspects of composition in them ... rare in jazz but possible.

Maybe because he was a painter ... he went to art school in Newark.

Richie: The bottom line is that his songs are evidence of a deep thinker at work.

Dave: And later the Buddhism in his case. He played with the same group for the last 20 years with Danilo Perez, John Patitucci, and Brian Blade and they mostly improvised. You can hear Wayne still developing when he played with that band.

Wayne has a way of articulating his saxophone style. We all have our own way to articulate because it is personal and in that way it is like the suit that you wear for the day. In other words that's how you say hello, with a certain accent. One of Wayne's ways of showing himself is through his use of tonguing articulation. This is critical because articulation is such an important part of being a horn player. He has a certain way of tonguing notes that is extremely unique. It is almost like double tonguing, it is a hard one.

Richie: How does it differ from Coltrane and you?

Dave: Trane's tonguing was normal, I use a whole lot of shadings.

Wayne's articulation is very special but even more important, he is the major jazz composer of the last 50 years.

Richie: Him and Herbie Hancock.

Dave: Wayne more than Herbie, he composed more and he is still writing. Sonny Rollins did not write much and Joe Henderson is the good example of someone writing almost nothing. But Wayne has contributed a body of music that even if you did not know the saxophone or jazz, would be iconic and important to the world of music.

Wayne's best playing to me was with Miles Davis third great quintet between 1968 and 1969, the concerts at Berkeley, California, or Antibes, France, in 1969. The way they all played at that time was amazing and Wayne is way out there with them, free, but never losing it.

Richie: Every solo was different, the first motive is played and developed. The first time he played with Miles was on the Steve Allen TV show in 1964, and he played an incredibly lyrical and memorable solo on an F blues.

We played with Wayne, you and me, in Japan 1987, Live Under the Sky.

Dave: In over forty years of playing together, we played many concerts, but this concert in Japan really stands out. 1987, Tokyo, Live Under the Sky with Wayne Shorter, Jack DeJohnette, and Eddie Gomez to celebrate the 20th anniversary of John Coltrane's passing.

When we had the so-called rehearsal in the lobby of the hotel, you and me had just arrived at 9 o'clock that night. And then there we are with Jack, Eddie, and Wayne, I am on crutches, I had just broken my leg. So here we are, nobody's talking of course, we are trying to be polite. So I say well, Richie and I could play a duet, that might be a nice change instead of the rhythm section playing on every tune, and everybody said yes, looking for an easy way out. And then we got bolder, you or I said we could also play "India," how is that? Then we also decided to play "Impressions" and "Mr. PC," that was the set. I didn't know Wayne, I only met him once with Miles, so he turns to me and says Dave, I don't really remember those melodies, but I will float around like Eric.

Richie: You never told me that. So he is saying please help me.

Dave: Yes, and he "will float around like Eric." So here I am in jazz history heaven because he is referencing Eric Dolphy with John Coltrane 25 years ago.

How did you feel at the concert?

Richie: I was so nervous, but not scared, and excited. And you know why? We played all standards, Jack DeJohnette was there, Eddie Gomez, and you. It was very cool, Wayne did not say a word, just smiled, like saying, hi Richie, how are you doing. Acknowledgment yes, but I am not going to talk.

Lieb, do you remember when we started playing "Impressions" and Wayne looked at me like asking do you want to play the first solo and I said no. Wayne played a great solo, and so did you. Wayne plays a phrase and then he stops, he stops for the frame of the music to be understood. And for the rhythm section in case anyone wants to contribute. Total interaction, he wants to interact with everyone, like Miles in a way.

So Wayne is playing and I am comping, having a great time, you can see it on the video. And then, you know, it is a G 7 Mixolydian scale from "Impressions," it is all white notes. And then I said fuck it. In between phrases, when he stopped, I played the C sharp in my voicing, I played the A major chord over G, simple. And the amazing thing was that Wayne heard it and included it in his next phrase! And I yelled, yeah! I forgot that I was in front of 20,000 people. He looked at me and smiled. His solo on "Impressions" was incredible. Wayne's solo on "Mr. PC" was also a genius solo and very different for him because he went back and forth between playing totally melodic diatonic phrases, lyrical with sudden jumps to triple time with atonal flurries.

Dave: Flurries, big thing here.

Richie: And this creates a fantastic tension because with the melodies he gives the people a total frame and after more flurries he comes back to the melody. The ability for him to come back to the melody is totally compositional. It is exposition, development, and return.

Dave: First, we played "Mr. PC," then you and I played a duet, two tunes, "After The Rain" and "Naima." I remember lights out, spotlights on you and me, the picture of Trane in the back, you playing an introduction to "After The Rain" and I look out there and I am thinking, here I am, with my main man (Richie), playing my main man's music (Coltrane) for 20,000 fans who love it, this is one of the highlights of my life.

Richie: I remember that concert like it was yesterday. The enormity of what it meant to be playing with your peers and Wayne Shorter. I met Wayne a few times but never played with him. To me he was one of the Mt. Rushmore guys. Jack and Eddie are like my brothers, very familiar, we played together many times.

But to play with Wayne with no real rehearsal in front of 20,000 people, live video and audio recording, this was fail or no fail. It was absolute pressure. It felt like everything I had done in my life was the preparation to get me ready for this. I felt great and was happy about my playing in that period.

The sound was unbelievable. They had these amazing monitors, the sound was clear and warm and I could hear every single note that everyone played. The gigantic Yamaha piano was great, Jack's drums sounded like thunder, I will never forget this. And it also paid the best money I ever made for an hour of playing and live recording for a CD and video with NO TAKE TWO possible! It was the end of the festival on a hot summer night, we were playing at midnight in front of 20,000 silent and respectful Japanese people. When you announced our duet "Naima" people went crazy. It felt like a Stevie Wonder or Paul Simon concert, but this was for John Coltrane and it was amazing.

PERSONAL PERSPECTIVES

Surviving the Music Business

Richie: How did we survive the music business? First of all we wanted it. It was more than the will to survive. We wanted to be the best musicians we could be ... we wanted to be great. We were inspired by the living masters, who were in our faces every night in the 1960s and '70s. We wanted that level of mastery for ourselves, and I think for good reasons too. We wanted that feeling knowing that this was the best we could do. I wanted that for myself, I wanted to be respected, I wanted to be one of those guys.

Dave: I think the word respect is an important one. You wanted to be acknowledged as somebody who could really play ball.

Richie: By the guys who played ball.

Dave: It was like a secret club ... you had to pass the test to get in and you had to live up to it. We all have our testing stories. When masters invited you up to sit in with them or did not invite you, you either played good or not did not play good. Simple enough ... you had to be accepted by the guys that you respected in that crowd, like Stan Getz, Miles Davis, Chet Baker, Elvin Jones, Joe Henderson, Freddie Hubbard, Art Blakey, Sonny Stitt, and many others.

Richie: Absolutely. It was difficult to navigate. Remember, we came out of the 1960s. The political thing affected us ... they were killing Black people, assassinations, Martin Luther King, the Kennedys. There was the civil rights movement and there were racists in congress. The country was very much different than it is now with Benny Goodman and Dave Brubeck who were both on the cover of *Time* magazine before Thelonious Monk and Duke Ellington. Also the music of the '60s was very powerful, revolutionary, not angry, but played with a tremendous energy. That's what happens when you have oppression cause it creates resistance and energy in reverse. So a lot of people said these Black cats are very angry. I don't want to hear that. God damn right they were angry, but there was also a lot of love around. When you hear someone like John Coltrane, your hear energy, but some people mistake energy for anger. They don't understand the difference.

Dave: There is this famous interview where the guy asks Trane about his music being very aggressive and Coltrane says I don't feel any of these things you're talking about ... I'm just trying to play the best I can.

Richie: That was with Don DeMicheal, the senior editor of *DownBeat* magazine who interviewed Coltrane and Eric Dolphy together for *DownBeat*. He asked them if they thought their music was swinging and Coltrane was so modest, it was hard for them to answer this question. I found this interview terribly insulting to these masters and it just showed the level of journalistic ignorance clearly at that time.

Personal Perspectives

But here's the thing—we wanted it, we played or practiced all the time. I gave my life to it after I graduated from Manhattan School of Music in 1972 and that was it... boom! The music business is different than the music and at the time it was not as difficult as it is now ... that was one good thing.

There were record companies centered around jazz, recording artists from Bill Evans to late Coltrane. In general they were run by good people who loved jazz. In some cases the guys in charge were real aficionados. Riverside Records had Orin Keepnews, Columbia Records was run by George Butler and John Hammond, and Blue Note Records had Bruce Lundval. The record business was good ... people were buying records. The atmosphere was good, and again there was a ladder, a pathway. We had the opportunity because of you to record in Japan and the record was called *First Visit*. The economy was booming in Japan, jazz was new to them, and they had a lot of money. We would go there often, 'cause they loved American jazz. They respected our culture so they recorded us and paid us well on those occasions. *First Visit* was our first recording together in Japan after we did *Night Scapes* for Sony.

Dave: *Night Scapes* was amazing. Can you imagine in 1969 a completely free record with a poet for Sony and no "famous" names? They were trying to find what's new in New York, what's exciting and we were on that bus, designated as a happening group. We were 20 ... 25 years old, playing free jazz. We got this opportunity, and even got paid a little bit. So this was *Night Scapes*, Sony, 1969, amazing, our first recording.

Richie: *First Visit* was our first recording together with Jack DeJohnette, Dave Holland, myself, and you. This was an amazing group with the stars in alignment. I was in Japan touring with Stan Getz and Jack and Dave, and you were there with Miles Davis.

Dave: Synchronicity.

Richie: True synchronicity, so of course a guy from King Records said great, let's record. There were no days off on our tours. Too bad, let's record after our concert. Isn't it tiring? No, we are young and strong, 25 to 30 years old, so we met at a studio at midnight and recorded *First Visit*. It has amazing energy.

Dave: We did the whole record in three hours, and then I recorded a duo with Jack, just tenor and drums, at two in the morning, burning. One of the cymbals fell off the stand signaling it was the official end of the recording. I remember when we recorded our duo version of "Round Midnight", Jack was sleeping, laid out on three chairs.

Richie: Well, that was the beginning. Then Manfred Eicher from ECM Records got involved with us and basically started our solo careers.

Dave: In the 1970s and '80s record companies gave tour support. They printed posters and gave us a lot of press. Those were exciting times. The '70s are sometimes dissed for the fusion thing. But then Wynton Marsalis came in the 1980s and cut it all off but the truth is there were some very adventurous groups that played great music for a minute, for a short period of time.

Richie: Getting the actual gigs is something that I am not very good at ... I couldn't do it. When you are calling agents for concerts, or recordings, you have to get on the phone between 9 and 10 in the morning, Monday, Wednesday or Friday. You never call past 10 because that's when their business starts. It's a science, like getting an apartment in Manhattan from an ad in the Village Voice, you call the landlords every day, you're very persistent, you are very kind, you don't pressure them and say why did you not call me back. Because they get 100 calls a week, they don't need you, because you're not a star. But if you are very persistent, sometimes you get something. Sometimes they give it to you just so you leave them alone, in a certain way.

Dave: Or because you played with certain people. If you played with Miles, Elvin, Chet, or Stan it meant something. Therefore you must have your own music ready to go. Whenever we got an offer for a recording we always had a body of music ready that we believed in and loved to record. We did not just have play the blues or standards. In our case we worked together ... it was real. We pushed the success of the group and at some point we had the support of the business with Eicher and John Snyder supporting our projects, up to a point.

Richie: And we even had our own publicist for a while.

How Do We Feel about Our Past Playing Today?

Dave: How do we feel about our playing now?

Richie: My first reaction is—I like my playing, most of it. I like what I am doing *now*. I don't like what I did many years ago. I listened to our recording *First Visit* the other day.

Dave: That was recorded 50 years ago!

Richie: So what? I don't like what I was playing. I am banging, I am rushing, I am not completing ideas, but the energy was great.

Dave: You were 27 years old.

Richie: Herbie was 21 when he played with Miles Davis. Anyway, I am very critical and judgmental. To be critical of oneself inspires the ability to learn ... I am still learning. In general I like my playing from the last 20 years very much, but as a listener I like my playing from the last five years the most. My current living situation allows me the freedom of not having to take every gig to survive. Because of what I have learned about music in all these years my experience finally caught up with me in terms of being able to play what I hear. I am able to concentrate more on the ideas and developments instead of decorations and arpeggios. I don't have to show that I have a lot of technique. That is very hard when you have a lot of technique as I do because I have been classically trained. I used to play these arpeggios because they felt and sounded good, but they had nothing to do with the music I was playing.

Dave: Too many choices. When you are highly skilled this can be a problem.

Richie: The thing is, especially when you are playing free, is to stay within the musical idea and communicate with the guys you are playing with.

Dave: That is very hard.

Richie: You don't want to say oh my God, I have to show that I can play fast tempos!

Dave: But you can do what no one else can do, which is to set up a mood, a little bit like Jabali Billy Hart in that respect. He does it drum-wise of course. In your case it's the ability to frame, like the third movement of Hamlet, you have that Russian Dostoyevsky or Tolstoy stuff in you. It comes from the classical tradition that you know so well. You have the ability to really paint a picture, something I know well because I am a result of that playing, especially in the heavily exposed duo context. Nobody sets the mood like you ... a one of a kind talent. It is your uniqueness and people who know you are aware of it.

Richie: That's the other thing I wanted to talk about. I love accompanying as much as playing a solo. I am basically a collaborator. I never felt I had to be a leader. You take care of that stuff at a high level. When you play free music it's easier in some ways.

Dave: In some ways.

Richie: Because you only have the idea ... there is no comparison. When you are playing a tune, you have 100 comparisons. But if you are in the moment there is no comparison.

Dave: That's why playing free is not just a walk in the park.

Richie: It is not easy and we can't do it all the time. It's okay to play tunes too, or just a phrase, or a brief sketch.

Dave: In our case. But what about Paul Bley who did it on his own terms?

Richie: Paul Bley was incredible and deeply influential ... he was the Ornette Coleman of the piano.

Dave: No left hand, nothing, minus ten, but his right hand ...

Richie: His right hand and concept was so far ahead of his time. Just listen to the way he did not accompany for Ornette Coleman on that famous recording from the Hillcrest Club, Los Angeles in 1959. He didn't comp ... he just played right hand lines for his solos. But his phrasing was so brilliant and original. There would be no Keith Jarrett, no early Chick Corea without Paul Bley and honestly there would be no Richie either. He was an enormous influence on our generation of musicians in the 1960s. He was special because he preferred pure improvising to any kind of tune. In the recording studio he insisted one take of each piece and to leave the tunes in the order he recorded them. I understand that Paul Bley did play with Charlie Parker when he was only 16 years old, so he learned the authentic bebop tradition from the master.

Dave: I have one of Paul Bley's recordings from 1964 recorded at a loft on Sixth Avenue, where they are playing rhythm changes and Paul is be-bopped out. He came to New York in the early '60s.

Richie: Did you hear the trio record he did in the 1950s with Charles Mingus and Art Blakey?

Dave: No.

Richie: I talked to Paul about this. He was very young so the record company hired Charles Mingus and Art Blakey. They did not like him at all ... the white boy! But Bley could play. He could swing and at times he sounded a lot like early Bill Evans. The way Bley played on the George Russell recording *Jazz in the Space Age* was miraculous. That recording features Bill Evans and Paul Bley. That's the one iconic record were you can really hear their linear stuff.

How Do We Feel about Our Past Playing Today?

Dave: They play separately or together?

Richie: Together, both of them, two grand pianos, playing a lot of free stuff. *Jazz in the Space Age*, 1960, is required listening.

Now you Lieb...

Dave: About my playing now I am not as judgmental as you are about your playing. My playing is what it is. Years ago I had problems hearing things from the past, being overly critical. But when we listened to *Forgotten Fantasies* last night I accept that what I played is what it is. For example, I played with too much vibrato. I hear the negative in a minute. A lot of my playing has been with piano players. These last two weeks I played with five or six different pianists and that has honed my skills of course. To play with piano players you have to be careful and I feel good about that.

I am happy about my tenor and soprano playing. I think soon it will be only soprano again, mostly for practical reasons. I am also thinking ahead to the next lifetime and I might end up the way I started ... soprano only. Quest in the '80s was all soprano, and it was fine ... nobody said a word.

Richie: It is not like there was something lacking but I must say your tenor playing has evolved and matured and if it is not equal to your soprano playing, it is very very close. There used to be a big divide.

Our Legacy

Dave: What will our legacy be?

Richie: Our recordings and the books we wrote.

Dave: That's history. And we have our legacy because we have students.

Richie: So what do the students carry from us?

Dave: I would say intensity and commitment.

Richie: The most important thing you can give to a student besides information is inspiration. They must be running out of your house with the intent to go home to practice or to be told the truth which often results in them becoming temporarily depressed. And then they have to build up their confidence again. The teacher must be very honest, brutally honest, but kind and caring. The honesty gets their attention. You know the old story of the Zen master hitting the student over the head with the shoe. And in another other story the student is talking and talking while the master is having tea. So the master is pouring tea into the cup of the student and he keeps pouring until the cup is overflowing. The student says Master, Master, what are you doing? The cup is overflowing. And the master says you are like this cup, you never shut up, your cup is overflowing, be quiet, listen, do one thing at a time, stop talking. Empty your cup.

Dave: So your legacy is what your students remember..

Richie: I agree, and I think we have a good legacy. I love my students, I am devoted to them, I'm proud of them. If I have a student that has not made any progress and I can't help him or her, I feel responsible. Sometimes I feel bad for what I didn't do, or what I couldn't do to help them improve. But most of the students are great.

Dave: The musical legacy outside of the students for me I hope would be the soprano saxophone, making it into something more than a secondary instrument which it has been in the past with the exception of Steve Lacy.

Richie: You absolutely did that.

Dave: In my case the eclecticism that I am devoted to is seen as a positive affirmation of who I am or who I was.

Richie: Yes, because you do all these things well. Usually the problem with eclecticism is that it is difficult to do many many things well, but you did. You picked your spots.

My legacy is also with my students, but there are also certain recordings where I hit the mark. My playing was really inspired and represents the best of me in those moments. I know that these recordings have inspired listeners because I get feedback from all sorts of people that connect certain records with life situations. I want people to love my music and of course more and more, the older you get the more accumulated music you have to offer to the world.

The other thing is that I stood for something, some standard of excellence that I tried my best to achieve. I approached every recording like it would be my last one. I leave everything in the studio, holding nothing back.

Dave: First of all, your life is pretty much framed in your teenage years. It's like Ground Zero when you are 15 to 18 years old.

Richie: The framing of your future life is pretty much over when you turn 18.

Dave: When I was a teenager and used to go to Birdland and other clubs in New York City to see John Coltrane, we would get there early to really check out our hero. For example—what is he whistling, what is he wearing, how does he take his horn out of the case, is he warming up, and if so does he play long tones? All you are doing is thinking about how heavy the cat is, like I want to be that guy. It means really checking out your idol and seeing if you could attain that same level of respect from your peers. You could see the presence of the master coming into the club and looking forward to the great music that would be coming. I always wanted to be that guy and I did get what I wanted to be. In my case I made my bed and it's okay to lie in it.

Richie: You did, you made a nice bed. I always remember one special thing. I went to see Miles Davis many many times, in small clubs, not big concerts. I am talking about the Village Vanguard or the Village Gate. Miles would always come in last. He timed it, he came in smoking cigarettes and with an evil look on his face. Evil?? He doesn't want anyone to bother him. Maybe he says hello to Jerry, the guy at the door, and then slowly walks into the kitchen. He was always peacocked out, always dressed so nice.

Dave: Yes, and he would dress like that even at the Village Vanguard on a Tuesday night, the slowest business of the week.

Richie: And when he walked in, it got quiet, 'specially us young guys. I will never forget that. John Coltrane was different.

Dave: Trane would just appear from the back. You could hear him play a few notes, but never the legendary practicing. That whole thing about Trane practicing between sets, I never heard him do that much.

Richie: I heard him warming up in the kitchen, not practicing.

Dave: But you know, Miles said "I can tell how a guy plays by how he takes his horn out of the case" and you know what ... this is true, even before the guy plays a note. It's deep, at least with the horn player you can tell his alignment and comfort level with his instrument.

Richie: Here is a social question—do you agree that some of the greatest jazz musicians are also some of the hippest and most sophisticated people on earth?

Dave: Oh definitely. The sensitivity, intelligence, awareness, how to handle people ... we are really on top of a lot of games even though we appear to be underneath it. The truth is we are observing with the third eye big time because our profession demands it in order to survive and to be successful. Of course you have to be able to take care of the music which goes without saying.

August 2019, Nideggen, Germany

ROAD TRIP THROUGH OUR PAST

We have been talking about this for a few years—driving to Brooklyn to visit important places from our childhood and to Manhattan where we lived and worked from the 1960s to the '80s. It was a rainy and dark day, perfect to revisit our collective and individual past. It was a wonderful shock to go back to the places we had not been to in 60 years and to experience them together with our friend Kurt Renker. Prepare yourself for a bumpy ride, but also to be entertained.

Brooklyn Born

Richie: Remember Spike Lee? Crooklyn!

Dave: Crooklyn baby, the roots, first time in 55 years for the bro.

Richie: I haven't been back to this neighborhood where I was born for over 50 years.

Dave: And you lived there for how long?

Richie: Until I was 12 and then we moved to Queens to 1623 Sawyer Ave. in Queens Village.

Dave: So you had started with your piano teacher there in Brooklyn, right?

Richie: Absolutely, and then continued when I was in Queens going to Martin Van Buren High School and in my graduating class in 1965 was Mario Savio. Remember him?

Dave: Rebellion Jones?

Richie: Yes, the original student rebellion, he and Tom Hayden.

Dave: What was the name of that movement?

Richie: The SDS, and they were investigated by the FBI. So Thomas Wolfe said you can't go home again. He lied, we are going home!

Dave: We are going home. So you grew up on East Second Street and Avenue P in Brooklyn?

Richie: East Second Street and Avenue P.

Dave: And I lived for the first eight years on 1014 14th Street between Avenue J and K, and that's where I got polio. And then we moved to 1328 East Fifth Street between Avenue L and M and that's where we're going now. So we grew up within three blocks of each other.

Richie: And we did not know each other.

Dave: How many people lived in that square block in Brooklyn?

Richie: But we never crossed paths. Different schoolyards, different candy stores, the Claridge movie theater.

Dave: We went to the Kingsway theatre, and the Avalon.

Richie: And the Elvis Presley film *Beach Blanket Bingo* was playing with Frankie Avalon.

Dave: I saw the Elvis movie *Love Me Tender*, and I went to see *King Creole* on a Saturday afternoon. My mother let me off, I went in, I remember, and everybody was throwing candy and going crazy. I was scared out of my mind.

Richie: What was the song that inspired you to pick up the tenor, was it "Stagger Lee"?

Dave: The song was "Rock Around the Clock" by Bill Haley and the Comets because the tenor sax was the main solo instrument in rock and roll at that time.

Richie: Who played with that big screaming vibrato at that time?

Dave: The rhythm & blues guys, King Curtis, Junior Walker, even Charlie Ventura and those old swing transitional cats. Rhythm & blues is one of the roots of jazz.

Richie: Wasn't Junior Walker a big influence on Michael Brecker?

Dave: Yes.

Richie: And Maceo Parker?

Dave: Maceo, yes, but Junior Walker's solo on the tune "Shotgun" was a big influence on Michael.

Richie: I was reading Bill Milkowski's book on Jaco Pastorius. Did you read it, we're all in there.

Dave: I didn't like it. I don't like a book that dwells on what his problems were. It just made Jaco look like a nutcase. It's not right!

Richie: But he also talks about his incredible genius and his amazing accomplishments on the bass equally. It's a kiss and tell book.

Dave: I didn't dig it and I told him. I was very upset with him. Writing about him taking his pants off at Columbia Records. I just don't think we need that.

Richie: His exploits on the basketball court were the shit that really upset me. When he was thrown out of every place, he had garbage bags on his feet instead of shoes. I remember, he came into Bradley's like that.

Dave: Yeah, but meanwhile, one of his first gigs with Weather Report was opposite us.

Richie: That's right.

Dave: I remember, we played duo in East Lansing, Michigan, opening up for Weather Report. And he was such a nice guy. He was so honored and so thrilled to play with Joe Zawinul and Wayne Shorter.

Richie: He was walking around with his LP, his amazing first recording called *Jaco* with Herbie Hancock on it.

Dave: This was 1976 when he first started, and he was fresh. It is not good to talk about him like that.

Richie: Even if it is the truth?

Dave: We don't need it. The poor guy had a rough time.

Games We Played

Dave: So another thing we should talk about are the games we played in Brooklyn in the 1950s.

Richie: Stickball.

Dave: Okay, let's describe the game of stickball for a second, which is probably not played anymore.

Richie: There are two different ways to play stickball. We played stickball in the street, right in between the parked cars. In stickball, you have one guy pitching, a guy in midfield and a guy in the outfield and it was all determined by the length of the sewers in the middle of the street relative to the distance between them.

Dave: How did the ball stay straight in such a narrow street?

Richie: You had to hit the ball straight, and that was an art. And if the ball went under the car, it was called a clinky and you had time to get it and then you had to run to the sewer covers. And If you hit it past the guy in the outfield, it was an immediate point. If you struck out, you got no points. There were only three guys on each side… that's why it was great … you only needed six guys to play!

Dave: Right, because you didn't run bases.

Richie: No, and every time the cars came you had to stop playing. We preferred playing late at night because there was much less traffic and also because nobody wanted to go home. Right? We played until it was almost dark. Every once in a while a car would come without lights on and that was a drag. We almost got killed a few times.

Dave: Now punchball was a variation of it.

Richie: Yes, just punching the ball.

Dave: Stickball was played with a broomstick

Richie: A broomstick that was taped up at the handle. Punchball is the same as stickball except you punch the ball with the open side of your hand.

Dave: Throw the ball up in the air and punch it.

Richie: That was really great. Then there was a wall game, you told me about this.

Dave: Chinese handball, in between the alleyways, bounces and slices applied to the ball. I don't know why it was called Chinese handball.

Richie: Because Chinese was a derogatory term for putting spin on the ball. Like, you know …

Dave: You cut and slice the ball, right?

Richie: Yes, I was very good at this because I was a piano player and this part of my hand was very strong.

Dave: Like ping pong slicing. You can play in your alley in between the houses. And there was stoopball.

Richie: These are the rules for stoopball. In those days in Brooklyn, most houses had six or seven steps you had to climb to enter the house. The steps were called the stoop. In this game, you had to avoid all the people that walked down the street. And if you hit the crack in between steps, it was worth more.

Dave: Also, when you hit the edge of the steps and the ball came right back at you and you hit it on the fly, that was worth more points.

Richie: It was like baseball. We all played these games.

Dave: It is amazing how ingenious people can be. You are between buildings on a street with cars parked, broken glass, in a residential area, and you still play these games.

Richie: And then the older kids would sometimes come in and bogart, and they would make side bets on us. And if you lost, they would kick your ass because you were losing money for them! We had no money, so we played for bottle caps, Canada Dry Ginger Ale, the thick Coke bottles. And then there were the school gym games of which the most dangerous was dodgeball.

Dave: That was played with a heavy ball.

Richie: Yes, a heavy medicine ball.

Dave: Now what is a medicine ball?

Richie: Think about it, a medicine ball is a leather ball with a lead weight in it.

Dave: Why was it called a medicine ball?

Richie: Because it was good medicine, I suppose. It was used for exercises to build muscles in your stomach. Boys would throw it on your stomach to see how your abs were.

Dave: Six-pack shit.

Richie: Six-pack shit, but I never had a six ... no way. Forget it...I had more like a two-pack. In any case, we had a lot of fun and were exercising at the same time. We played ping-pong with bottle caps on the ping-pong table to make it more interesting. If you hit a bottle cap, it was a dollar, if it turned over, it was five bucks. And if it was knocked into the furthest corner, it was ten bucks, which was a lot of money in 1956. If you knocked it off the table, you got nothing. That's how we amused ourselves.

Dave: And of course, some of the guys had a ping-pong table and/or a pool table. So in the summer people would put the table(s) out in the driveway. You could play pool, which was a hard game that needed a lot of skill which I couldn't do.

Richie: I didn't like pool either and was not good at it but a lot of older kids made money in the pool halls.

Dave: And there was bowling, did you bowl?

Richie: Yeah, but I wasn't too good.

Dave: My older brother Paul was a champion bowler. He used to hit a 298 or 299 score. 300 is a perfect game.

Richie: Did you have a bowling alley with automatic pin replacements?

Dave: No, Paul was a pin boy on the bowling alley right on Second Street, which was his job for which he got paid. That's all he did, setting up the pins and then he ran away so he didn't get hit by a bowling ball. When the spotting machines came, it was a major invention, amazing.

Richie: The worst thing you could do is have a gutter ball in front of a girl, right? This would be a drag, man.

Dave: Bowling was a very, very big sport at that time, right?

Richie: There was very little football, did you notice that?

Dave: But there was touch football on concrete. You couldn't tackle but you could touch the guy with two hands and that was it, right? We played a lot of touch football. When we lived on Fifth Street, it was a dead-end street and there was a field near a Quaker school. This field was really beautiful and you could play ball there. There were no cars, so we played a lot of touch football. Did you have a school yard?

Richie: Yes.

Dave: Did you play stickball in the schoolyard with the box of strikes painted on the schoolyard wall?

Richie: Yes, and we had tennis against the wall along with paddleball, of course, which we played with the older kids.

Dave: Also, there was a spectacular game called handball. It was played with a very hard, small black rubber ball. My father was big on handball…every day in good weather he rode his bike after coming home from teaching, about five miles. The destination was the handball courts where he would meet other teachers finished with school for the day. They would all go to Brighton or Manhattan Beach. What a great scene, teaching all day and then off to the courts!

Richie: Now here is the thing. If you were really macho, you would not use a glove. My father had a pigskin glove but didn't like to use it because it made him (or anyone else who played) seem like a pussy. "Listen kid, if you want to play I can give you my glove." I said, "no thanks Dad" and proceeded to play black ball without a glove. Needless to say, I ended up with my hand bleeding. That black ball was smaller than the more common pink Pennsy Pinkie, but very hard. If you caught it in the palm of your hand, you could get a little more spin or slice which applied to the hand wouldn't hurt so much. Of course, this was a bit rougher than the norm since I was a piano player already getting more serious as the years rolled on.

Dave: But since it was not a defensive game like regular handball, it was about one's serve and how low you could hit it. I remember cats would hit it low, just off the ground.

Richie: Yes, and then you had to catch it. Did you use both hands?

Dave: I did not use both hands. I think I usually used my right.

Richie: I only used my right hand because my piano teacher asked me point blank— do you want to play handball or do you want to play piano? So I had like two fathers, which in some ways was great.

Family

Richie: My father was not able to talk to me about the war until I was 18 years old. He was a combat medic. He landed on D-Day in the second wave, not the first wave, and he made it through. But all his friends were killed in 20 seconds when the LST boat front opened and they jumped into the sea. The LST could not go close enough to the beach because the guys had fifty-pound backpacks not to mention rifles and so forth.

Dave: So they drowned?

Richie: They drowned, and they were shot with the machine guns. My father went to see the movie *Saving Private Ryan* and after the first 20 minutes, he ran out of the cinema. My mother had to go get him and he never wanted to see the film, but my mother brought him back and he saw it and he was crying. He said that was exactly the way it was, and he sent Steven Spielberg a letter, which was heavy. He wouldn't go back to Europe for 30 years. He didn't even want a passport because he associated Europe with Normandy and Germany. But my mother forced him to go.

Dave: Did he go to Normandy?

Richie: Listen to me. Remember the gig we played in 1984 at Fat Tuesdays with Randy Brecker, Al Foster, and Ron McClure? My parents were there. They just came back from Europe and my mother dragged my father to our concert. He was so happy because he had been to Normandy to attend the 40th anniversary ceremony of D-Day and he met guys there that he had not seen since the war. They were sitting right next to the piano, and they were really happy. It was an amazing night for me because my father completely changed ... he exorcised all his demons.

As I said, he wouldn't talk to me about the war for years. I would ask him, So Pop, what happened, what was it like?" "You don't want to know, kid." I mean, he did not talk about it for 20 years. He was a hard worker, leaving the house at 5 a.m. to go to work.

Dave: Where?

Richie: He worked in a shoe factory on the Bowery, near Randy Brecker's original loft. I remember that we used to go to Katz's Delicatessen for lunch ... they had these big pastrami sandwiches. He worked at his father's business, which was making and repairing shoes. When his father died, he became a salesman. He was so good at it that he was eventually hired to teach other salesmen. He had a completely new way of selling shit.

Dave: What did he sell?

Richie: Door-to-door encyclopedias, vacuum cleaners, toasters, everything. He was a door-to-door salesman, but he had his own way of selling things. Most of the other salesmen were hard-ass sellers, pushing, pushing. But my father knew people and he wouldn't sell anything that he didn't use or that he didn't like and he could say that to the customer. So he would go into a house, the wife was usually home, sometimes the husband was home as well and my father would say, "Hello, I'm Mr. Beirach, I would appreciate a little of your time. I have some really good things that might help you and your family and I'll tell you the truth. I use them myself."

Dave: This is when people would still open the door.

Richie: Yes, they opened the door and let him into the house. He went door to door, all over Brooklyn, Queens, Bronx, and Staten Island. He said the best place was Staten Island because of the old Mafia Joneses who had money. So he went in and talked to the housewives since they never worked. It was a great tragedy if your wife worked...it meant you were not a good provider, that you didn't have enough money and you couldn't provide for your family.

Dave: Giant stigma. But on the other hand, my mother worked right away, and she was considered revolutionary because she graduated from Hunter College (New York) already when she was 22.

Richie: Ten or fifteen years later my mother got a job as a legal secretary. Plus, by then the kids were out of the house. My father would do his work dressed in a beautiful suit, tall and handsome, selling things.

So he goes into the house and sits down, and the woman asks if he wants some coffee. His whole thing was the anti-hard sell. He says, "This is a new vacuum cleaner, a Hoover, it collects the dust, it really works, and it's much quieter. Would you like me to show you ma'am or Mrs. Silverman?" So she says yes because she is bored and she's got this nice guy in her house ... he vacuumed and everything worked.

Then if he was selling encyclopedias, he says, "This is very good for your kids. How many kids do you have, Mrs. Benelli?" "I have four kids." "Well, this is the Encyclopedia Britannica." So he opens a sample. "The only thing I could say about this is I have one for my kids," and he shows the lady pictures of his family ... right.

Then he would shut up, be quiet and he just let the woman talk and let her feel like it was hers. He sold the most of any salesmen in the company. After a while he was too valuable as a salesman for the company, so they hired him to teach a hundred salesmen. That was my dad.

School Days

Dave: Now we're going into Brooklyn guys. This is the Brooklyn Battery Tunnel and we are going under the East River. It is hard to believe that Brooklyn is on an island.

Richie: Brooklyn has four million plus people. Brooklyn has more people in a borough than most cities have.

Dave: And the most churches in one place. I read in a statistic about the number of churches.

Richie: In Germany, where I live now, cities are much smaller. When they interviewed me for my job as a professor in Leipzig, I asked how many people live in Leipzig, which is a relatively big town and they said 550,000. So that would be three blocks of Brooklyn, right? (Laughs) They don't even know how big Brooklyn is.

Dave: Okay, we are on the Brooklyn-Queens Expressway. Welcome to Brooklyn. Forget about it … Jackie Gleason in *The Honeymooners* said it all.

Richie: My favorite show, *The Honeymooners*, Bensonhurst! Remember, Jackie Gleason played the Poor Soul among other roles he appropriated.

Dave: My favorite character Jackie played was Reginald Van Gleason the Third.

Richie: Remember the episode of *The Honeymooners* when he went to the animal shelter, and he came home with 20 puppies because he couldn't stand to leave any puppies behind? That was the best show, televised for a half an hour and Ralph always said at the end of the show, "Baby, you're the greatest," and he kissed Audrey Meadows. Did you know that Steve Allen was married to Audrey's sister, Jane Meadows?

Dave: Of course we are going through the Avenues, which are organized by the alphabet A to Z. Streets have numbers, the usual grid system.

Richie: We used to go to Coney Island in the summer, before there were gangs, and ride the Cyclone rollercoaster and the bumper cars ride, my favorite.

Dave: Also my favorite. At Nathan's you got a hot dog, then you go on the bumper car right next to it.

Richie: Yes, cotton candy and also the candied apples.

Dave: And crinkle cut french fries from Nathan's.

Richie: The best in the world! I loved the fried shrimp with a Cherry Coke.

Dave: Did you go to the beach?

Richie: Never, no no no.

School Days

Dave: Okay. I went to the beach on Coney Island and Brighton Beach, which was divided into what they called bays. They had the dividers floating in the water for the divisions. Each bay had a specific clientele. Bay three was for the high school kids, bay five for the bros (Black folk), and bay seven was for the Italian cats. So you stayed within your bay. In the summer, I spent every day in Coney Island. I took the bus from Avenue M down to Coney and spent the whole day at the beach.

Richie: My grandmother lived on Brighton Tenth Court.

Dave: So she was there, right? This is Little Russia now.

Richie: Yes, Little Odessa, Ukraine, the Russian mafia guys were there in Brighton Beach and Brighton Tenth Court. Yeah, it was an amazing.

Dave: Ocean Parkway and Coney Island, right there.

Richie: Oh my God, now I'm starting to get emotional. There was a candy store named Uncle Miltie's near the Claridge Theatre right near my house on East Second Street and Avenue P. Miltie's son was named Babbo, a big fat kid. We didn't know he was epileptic. So one day he was having a fight with one of the bigger kids who hit Babbo. He went down with foam coming out of his mouth, like in a movie, so we knew it was real and happening in front of our eyes. We called his father, Miltie, who was bald, and always wore a white T-shirt with a big cigar permanently in his mouth. There were a lot of guys around taking numbers. A lot of gambling going on there, bookies, but I didn't know what it was, I was too naive.

Dave: We are now on Ocean Parkway. This used to be a bike path, and it was where I learned how to ride a bicycle. And that over there on the left was the horse path. The guys would get the horses from Church Avenue and ride on the dirt path. So this was Ocean Parkway, a cool area, considered very nice, mostly Jewish and Italian.

Richie: This is where you got bar mitzvahed. God, I played so many gigs there. (Pointing out the hall called The Elegant on Ocean Parkway.)

Dave: This is where I had my bar mitzvah.

Richie: When I went to Hebrew school the rabbi tried to kiss me. I smacked him in the hand and ran out, telling my father. My father came after him and the rabbi disappeared.

Dave: Okay, here we go into the lettered Avenues. Mike Garson lived here, my oldest friend, and first piano player I played with.

Richie: Yes, I visited him there. And where did Mitch Kerper live?

Dave: He lived around you, Avenue P and Fifth Street, I think.

Dave: These are all apartment houses. 18th Avenue was Italian and like Little Italy in Manhattan, these were places where they would drink and hang out. John Gotti was the boss when I was in Brooklyn. They called these joints "social clubs."

Now we're getting near our neighborhood with new names. Foster Avenue used to be Avenue F, Ocean Parkway used to be Fifth Street, Coney Island was 10th Street and Ocean Avenue was 20th Street (and still is)

Richie: There's a Hassidim guy with the big hat now crossing the street.

Dave: It is Saturday.

Richie: Right, and Saturday is the holy day around here. They can't do anything, not allowed to turn on the light, not allowed to drive, etc.

Dave: This is Avenue M where my oldest friend Jed lived, on Ocean Parkway.

Richie: That's really good, I don't know anyone anymore from that time.

Dave: My first crush was Lillian, the first kiss and all those rites of passage type things. That was 7th grade...she was from Belgium.

Richie: The first girl I kissed came down to Birdland the first time we played there, Goldie Cantor ... really pretty girl. She was the daughter of the principal of my school in Queens. So I'm kissing the daughter of the principal, risking my life.

Dave: That's for sure.

Richie: Now we are at Avenue I.

Dave: Look how beautiful and big the houses are. This is a very expensive area now. This road is Bay Parkway, going towards the water. Over there was Bromley Studios, where I got my first music lessons. Here was Avenue J, the main area where everyone shopped (except on the Sabbath, when it was like a ghost town). There is the cemetery. I used to ride my bike around here, checking the writing on the tombstones. This is The Elegante I spoke about earlier.

Now we are coming up to my street, Avenue L. There is that field owned by the Quakers where we played a lot of ball because it was a dead-end street, so fewer problems with cars parking and so forth. Jed lived in the second house over there. On Ocean Parkway we hung out all summer, always on the bike, sitting there all night, on our bikes. This was our hang, and the first time I smoked pot. The candy store was here, there was the bakery ... and a nickel for a Coke. Thank you!

Richie: You can tell by the lettering on the signs how long the stores have been here.

Dave: This was the place to get a haircut. Naomi Jacobs lived right here, 1375 East Fifth Street. She is in Boston now, a very nice girl and a real friend. Two apartment houses are there now, that used to be empty lots. Another place to hang and explore ... we would play in this lot until they built the apartment houses.

Dave: We are coming up to 1328 East Fifth Street ... that's my house.

Dave's House –1328 East Fifth Street, Brooklyn, NY

Richie: Did you ever go in to see who is living there now?

Dave: No. This is the driveway where we played Chinese handball.

Richie: Yes, right against the wall.

Dave: Here is the garage, and this is the house, two-stories.

Richie: Amazing.

Dave: Private house, very small. This was like a porch room, and the piano room where I did my first rehearsals. Here was where we played stoopball.

Richie: I never came here.

Dave: No, I didn't know you know then. We lived here from age eight. Before that,

Road Trip Through Our Past

it was 14th Street in the same neighborhood. A little garage, and a little garden in the back, it is still the same.

Richie: I don't remember the number of our house, but I remember exactly where it is.

And it was all Jewish families on that block.

Dave: This is the area we used to hang out in.

Richie: You had it better than me, bro. You actually had your own room! It's amazing.

Dave: All right. Now, let's go to your neighborhood. Look how close it is. Look at that, brother. Okay, so that's Avenue M, all little single houses, small apartment houses, attached houses, that's a concept. Mike Garson grew up right here. Also, Steve Lipman says hello. When I told him we would come here, he said he wishes he could be with us. He lives in Boston ... I'm supposed to see him next week. He retired from Berklee College of Music and runs his own business, advising students on where to go to music school. They hire him to help get an audition.

Richie: We are coming to my neighborhood.

Dave: Only three blocks away, man.

Richie: I am scared now. I am telling you, I have not been here for 55 years. Avenue P, this is it, man!

Dave: McDonald Avenue, the subway/elevator line, Russian bookstore.

Richie: Lieb, do you see that brick building? That's the school.

Dave: That's where you went to elementary school? You just walked?

Just like The French Connection

School Days

Richie: Yes, I walked to the school from my house. This is McDonald Avenue, where I took lessons from Mrs. Schindelheimer, who was my first piano teacher when I was six years old. She was originally from Austria but came to Brooklyn after the war. She was very kind to me, but she was a bit of a fake. She couldn't read music but teaching me using John Thompson's well-known method book called *Teaching Little Fingers To Play*, which everyone learned from at that time. She taught the very beginning students.

Lieb, this is where *The French Connection* was shot!

Dave: The car chase, right?

Richie: Yes, right here. Gene Hackman, right under the Avenue L subway line, remember? One of the greatest car chases of all time.

Dave: See, they are still building new houses and renovating old ones. Look at that house in the middle of nowhere and they renovate it. See how old it looks, so old.

Richie: Of course. Turn right onto Second Street.

Dave: Do you remember the number?

Richie: No, but it is there. Keep going, keep going, keep going. 1649, that's the motherfucker.

Dave: This one? Is it a two or a one-family house?

Richie's House –1649 Second Street, Brooklyn, NY

Richie: A one-family house. My grandmother lived upstairs, and we lived downstairs. This is where I was born ... right here.

Dave: There is a note on the door ... maybe they are looking for you.

Richie: This is fantastic. Right across the street from our house was the Big Apple Supermarket. See were it says groceries now? This building is new but there was the Claridge Theatre ... right there. Wait, wait. Right over here was Uncle Miltie's candy store, and this is the A&P grocery store, right there. And now it is multinational ... all Puerto Rican, Japanese, Chinese, it looks like the UN, fantastic! All these places were in a one block area. And that's my school, right there, Public School 177.

Dave: Look how big it is, it's massive.

Public School 177, Brooklyn, NY

Richie: This is the schoolyard. Did I ever tell you about the time I got my ass kicked by a bully. This is a very important story.

I was in eighth grade, and there was a big Italian kid named Frank Valente. He was three years older because he was left back. You know, a punk, a real bully, black hair, with cigarettes under the right sleeve of his white T-shirt, and stupid ... you remember this look.

Dave: Like John Travolta in *Grease*.

Richie: So I am ten years old and he is thirteen, but you know at that age it's like a hundred year difference. He considered me a "fag" because I am a piano player, right? Any boy, like a piano player or a dancer, would be considered gay. I also played with the school chorus, which was like a setup. Actually, it was a great way to meet girls because who sang in the chorus? Mostly girls, right? So Frank Valente says to me, "Lick my boots!"

Dave: Yes, that's what happened to me. His name was Carmine, right on Ocean Parkway, terrorizing us.

Richie: So Frank said lick my boots, and he said something else after that and I said, no, I don't want to lick your boots. So he smacked me right in the face, hard, and my lip was bleeding and shit. So I started to cry and he called me a little shit. All the other kids hanging around loved it...it was a show, right? So he says, "Hey Vinny, come here." All his asshole friends, bigger than him, came, and he said again, "Lick my boots." So I really didn't want to lick his boots, and I didn't do it. He said, "Okay, you got to carry my books." I said, "Okay, I'll carry your books."

So I am carrying his books and then he turned around and laughed and smacked me again and knocked me down because I was very small. So at this point, I had enough abuse. I broke through the circle and ran home, ran from there to my house. Not a big run ... more like a sprint. It was like 12:30 because this was during our lunch hour in the schoolyard. It was right here, right against that wall under the air conditioner where he trapped me with his boys.

Okay, so I broke through and ran home with blood coming out of my nose, skinned knees and I'm starting to yell, coming into the house, "Daddy, Daddy." My father was at home, so he closed the door and said, "What happened? What are you doing?" And my mother said "Irving, he's bleeding!"

So I was crying, I was bleeding. I'm a little kid, ten years old, you know. He said, "What happened, did you fall down?" I said no. He said, "Sit down and tell me what happened. Everything's gonna be cool, we will fix it." My mother got ice, you know the same shit, right? So I am crying. I'm really crying and said I could never go back to school again. I'm really out of it and he asked again what happened? I said this guy hit me in the face and he wanted me to lick his boots.

My father stood up and said, "What!?" My father was very protective. I said, "He hit me and he wanted me to lick his boots." He said did you and I said, no. "Good boy," he said.

Dave: So you passed the test, the manhood one.

Richie: Not yet. So my father asked but what did you have to do? I said I had to carry his books. He said, "Okay, but how did you get out?" I said I ran away. He said, "Good boy, and now this is what you are going to do. You are going to go back there and you're going to get behind him. You are going to pick up a stick or a brick and you're going to hurt him. And then run right back here to me."

I said, "No, I can't, he will kill me." My father said, "You have to do this ... he is a bully and you have to hurt him." "But he will kill me the next day." My father said, "He will never bother you again." I said, "How do you know?" He said, "I know, I'm your father." And my mother said "Irving, please," and my father said "Beatrice, shut up."

It was the first time I heard him telling her to shut up. It was very dramatic, like some serious reality show, except that it was real. I am standing there bleeding and I don't want to go back there because it's not only him also five of his friends. They will chop me up and eat me. I could not expect help from my friends because I am hanging with all the smart and talented kids ... one of them a dancer who was ten years old and small like me.

So I went back and I swear, Lieb, on the walk back I thought, okay, I had a nice life. I didn't have a chance to get so good on the piano and I'm going to die because it really felt like I was walking into the lion's den. But my father really knew people, right? So I go back and sure enough, he is standing around there with his friends, all laughing, and they didn't see me. He is standing there and there was a fucking stick with a sharp end on it laying right there for me. And I said I'm going to do this, and I was really scared. I was also scared because my father said don't come home unless you hurt him and this is ringing in my ears.

Dave: That's a great story.

Richie: So I picked up the stick and I smacked him with the sharp ends in his calf.

Dave: And he didn't see it coming?

Richie: No, I was behind him and he went down and the stick was stuck in the meaty part of his leg and it was bleeding. And guess what, he started to cry like a little bitch. And I ran. I think I could have done the hundred in like one second. I'm telling you. I was running home as fast as I could.

Dave: So what happened to the cat?

Richie: So the guy is laying on the ground, bleeding and crying, and I felt pretty good. I heard him crying and everybody is shocked. They went to get the principal and the teachers while I ran home to my father. My father is standing at the door looking strong, really good. He said, "Did you hurt him?" I said yes. So he let me into the house and gave me a big hug and a kiss, fantastic. He asked, "What did you do?" I said I hit him with a stick in the calf. He said, "Did he go down?" I said like a brick. So now everything's fine, my father loves me, they fixed me up, everything's cool.

Next morning, 9 o'clock, I have to go to school. I asked my father can I take a day off today Pops? He said no, you are going in. I said please come with me. He said, "No, you gotta face this yourself, kid. You have to learn. He is a bully, you hurt the bully they'll walk away because they'll pick on somebody else. That's why they are bullies, they are insecure. They never travel by themselves, they travel in packs."

My father was so right, man. I don't know how he knew it, maybe he learned it in the army. So I walk back into the schoolyard because you have to go through the schoolyard to get to classrooms. You can't go in through the front. So I go in and I'm really scared, almost throwing up, deep fear. Frankie saw me, and guess what, he turned around and walked the opposite way. He didn't run, but walked away.

Dave: You made your point, baby!

Richie: Amazing, and I never got reprimanded by anyone from the school. I guess that they quietly agreed that the bully had been put in his place. Amazing, I never saw anything like it. And now all the girls liked me, I'm the hero, right? And every time I saw Frank after that, he turned around and walked the other way.

Dave: Nice story, your dad was right.

Coney Island

Dave: This is Kings Highway, the Avalon Theater was here. That's where I saw my first Elvis movies ... amazing. Look, there are Chinese and Indian restaurants. Really, everything is here. And now we are coming to Coney Island.

Richie: For a while when I was a kid Coney Island was really safe...there was no problem.

Dave: But then it got very dangerous because of the gangs, but now they are trying to fix that.

Richie: Over there is the public library where I spent a lot of time looking up composers like Schoenberg, Webern, and Berg. My piano teacher hated them, so I was really curious to find out more about them.

Dave: Chinese restaurants ... we lived on Chinese food.

Richie: We love the Brooklyn Chinese food because when our mothers were tired of cooking we always went out or had Chinese food delivered. This was our first taste of any kind of ethnic food, different from our daily Jewish and Italian diet.

Dave: This obviously is a Russian club because we're getting into the Brighton Beach area.

Richie: Flower shops. ... always a front for the Russian mafia. And look, gypsy cab, whoa!

Dave: Look man ... so crowded, so densely populated ... all kinds of people.

Richie: Look Lieb, the Kiev Bakery.

Dave: Entenmann's Bakery ... remember that crumb cake, greatest crumb cake!

Richie: Best of all, should we get some? Carvel soft ice cream, Lieb!

Dave: Of course ... Carvel custard cake, ice cream cake ... the works!

Richie: Oh man ... in the summer the soft ice cream. Did you see those guys over there? They are Russian mob, for sure. Here we go baby ... bagels. Want me to get some bagels?

You can tell a lot by the signs how long a business has been here. Look at this old lettering ... they didn't change it for 40 or 50 years. Pork chops ... that place must have been around when we lived there as kids.

Where was Leonard's, in Long Island?

Dave: Yes ... in Great Neck, Long Island. I know because my aunt lived near there.

Richie: Yeah, Leonard's was the catering hall where on a given weekend night they had eight or ten different wedding ceremonies going on at the same time. We all played weddings there when we were teenagers, before we were good enough to play jazz gigs. At that time, the live music at the weddings was all the old standard tunes like "All the Things You Are," "Satin Doll," and of course ethnic songs, which is another story all together. Guys like Steve Kuhn played four to five hours continuously for wedding gigs at Leonard's. It was amazing.

Dave: This is Lincoln High School. You think we will move back here one day?

Richie: Never, I would rather move to Pittsburgh. Remember Bob Davis from Pittsburgh?

Dave: He was a great guy who liked us ... African American brother. What was his club called?

Richie: The Encore. We played there with Lookout Farm. Bob organized an afternoon concert for us at the local prison to play for the convicts. While we are setting up the instruments, Frank Tusa asked the stagehand guy, so what are you in prison for? And the guy answered, "I killed my wife." Frank said, "Really?" And he said, "Yeah ... I would do it again." Those cats loved our music.

Richie: We are entering Paradise! Coney Island Avenue ... the F train stopped right here.

Dave: This store on the corner was Madame Stahl's bakery, featuring spectacular potato knishes ... Madame Stahl's homemade knishes.

Richie: My grandmother lived on Brighton and 10th Court. Did we pass that already?

Dave: It is right there.

Richie: This is really Little Odessa. In fact, the big part of the Russian influx was folks from Odessa ... seaside resort like Coney Island. We got to be cool here, bro, this is the center of the Russian mafia in Brooklyn.

Dave: The Atlantic Ocean over there ... we are on an island ... Manhattan Beach.

Road Trip Through Our Past

Richie: Ping pong ... video games right there. The boardwalk was a total summer hang ... billiards upstairs.

Dave: Garden Beach Avenue. Yep!

Richie: There's an amazing night club here where they filmed a scene in a movie called *Little Odessa* in the 1990s.

Dave: I played a gig here with Lenny White and a Russian piano player a few years ago ... Igor (of course) set it up. It was in a beautiful Russian restaurant, like one of these places. It was a daytime gig, a party or something. I wrote an arrangement of the classic Russian "Dark Eyes" which was a big hit. We recorded it with Quest a few years later ... great melody!

Richie: That's great. Unbelievable to go back to this world. There was nothing like this here when I visited my grandma a few decades ago. Brooklyn still looks like the old New York. Manhattan is too slick now ... but this still looks like the old New York.

Dave: There are the beaches in the distance.

Richie: Yeah ... were these big apartment houses around when you lived here?

Dave: Yes ... a couple of big ones. My family eventually moved to Ocean Avenue and Avenue S before moving to Florida, like other snowbirds did. This was a mass migration to the South over ten to twenty years. Again, a whole story in itself. I'm sure there are books about this.

Richie: This looks like Lefrak City, do you remember?

Dave: It's the same period, probably all built at the same time, the projects.

Richie: Neptune Avenue ... yes. And Belt Parkway.

Dave: We are passing Coney Island Hospital, one of the worst in the city. This is

Lincoln High School, and Lafayette High School is in that direction a mile or so from here. If you had gone to high school around here, you would have gone to Lincoln or you might have gone to Lafayette. You might have been with me! That's pretty deep.

Richie: We could have met in the music class.

Dave: That would have been out, man, think about it.

Richie: Maybe it was better that we didn't meet at that time because I could not play that well when I was in high school.

Dave: We met at Queens College. David Roitman was a drummer who organized a jam session there. I just spoke to him. He is in California teaching.

Richie: I saw Billy Mintz the other night. Yeah, he sounded great.

Dave: He looks exactly the same, amazing.

Richie: What about Lanny Fields?

Dave: I think he is still living in the Catskills. My bass player Tony Marino for the past 35 years also lives in the Catskills and he knows all the cats there. Some of them are still around ... some just died there, whatever.

Richie: Lanny Fields was something else ... he was strong.

Dave: He was the first bass player in my loft on 19th Street in the 1960s.

Richie: We are now on Avenue X...these are big beautiful houses. Years ago, they would have cost $35,000. Now ... .forget about it!!

Dave: Brooklyn was off the map for years. Nobody built here for decades and now Brooklyn is hot. The Barclays Center downtown that Jay-Z built, you know, that's a big deal. Some parts of Brooklyn are more expensive than in Manhattan now.

Richie: Yeah, that's crazy ... might as well live in Manhattan. Just miles and miles of residential houses here. I think it's one of the highest concentration of residential apartments in the world, between here and the Upper West Side. Look at those trees ... beautiful ... I love them.

Dave: My grandmother lived on Avenue O and 14th Street. I spend a lot of time there. She watched me when my mother was working. She taught me how to play a card game called canasta. My grandfather did the whole Passover Seder in Hebrew, which took him four to five hours. They had a big TV, *The Kate Smith Show* at three o'clock in the afternoon on the radio, followed by *The Romance of Helen Trent*, and on TV, *My Little Margie*. And of course the Ed Sullivan and Steve Allen entertainment shows on Saturday or Sunday.

Richie: Did you see the Beatles on *Ed Sullivan*?

Dave: Oh, yeah, definitely, are you kidding? And Elvis! When we saw him on *The Ed Sullivan Show*, they would only film him from the waist up ... think about it ... compare that to what is on TV now ... what a world!

Richie: Censorship!

Dave: Censorship ... not showing him below the waist ... too sexual ... unbelievable!

Richie: Such stupidity in the culture of the 1950s into the '60s ... Elvis the pelvis, in his white suit ... actually Elvis had great time.

Dave: He was so talented with a good voice ... I loved him. He was my first musical influence ... not the music so much but the vibe of FREEDOM NOW! ... shaking those hips.

He did a fusion thing combining Black church music with the white Baptist shit, all happening down home in Mississippi ... rockabilly became a thing.

Richie: Rockabilly, Black and white music, but sweet.

Dave: Now this is where I was Bar Mitzvahed at Temple Ahavath Sholom. I went to Hebrew school after regular school twice a week and on Sunday. I was so good at the Hebrew school that the Rabbi took me to his office and asked if I wanted to continue on with my Hebrew studies. No way could I do Hebrew for a few hours every day. The Rabbi's name was Alan Steinbeck ... he was famous and had books published. This was a Reform synagogue, which I already at 13 years old had a hard core view of religion ... another story!

Richie: I really loved the way the Hebrew language looked.

Dave: Oh, yeah, it looks fantastic.

Richie: Did you have those blue books?

Dave: The siddur ... very beautiful ... with all the prayers in one place. It really looks great, like Sanskrit.

Richie: The blue book had very thin-lined papers. I just got into the calligraphy of it, very beautiful stuff. And a lot of the letters look like bass clef ... it was so close to written music.

Dave: I don't know how they read it. It has nothing to do with the western world. At least Russian looks like our stuff somewhat.

Richie: It is like Cyrillic.

Dave: It is worse than Cyrillic because it has nothing to do with our letters.

Richie: It has no connection to any Roman letters ... Latin, French, that's why I like it. The only alphabet thing that came before these guys was the Egyptian hieroglyphics ... the picture language.

Dave: And of course there is Chinese, but they were in another part of the world. How did the Egyptians come up with this picture language?

Richie: They had the symbols like for an archer, a farmer, or snakes but they also had to find symbols for things they could not picture, like anger, fear or love. Egyptology is fantastic. I am interested in so many things, but for a different reason. I just like the way it looks. I care little about what it means because I know I can never figure that out, and it is a dead language. Nobody speaks that now.

Dave: When you go to Israel, they speak to each other in Hebrew, even the news is in Hebrew.

Richie: It's peaceful here ... Saturday ... everybody is inside, no commotion, nobody is shopping. It's just miles and miles of these houses, thousands of people living here, it is amazing ... a total residential neighborhood.

Dave: Look, Dr. Melach Gilbert, dentist. His prices are on the sign, look no further. Extraction $55! I have never seen anything like this before, the listing of all the prices.

Did you see this Japanese book, *The Coltrane Chronicles*, with pictures of Trane? There is a picture of Coltrane from Newport 1966. I was there at the festival. Charles Lloyd played there with his group. I drove Keith Jarrett, Cecil McBee, and Jack DeJohnette from Manhattan to Newport. Jack lived on 82nd Street, Cecil lived somewhere on the Lower East Side and Keith on Central Park West. Coltrane played in the afternoon on a sunny, very hot day. I took a magnifying glass and found myself in the photo of the audience clear as a bell along with my lady friend of that time, Laurel. It was late Trane all the way ... unbelievable.

Richie: I would love to see that picture. Did I tell you about the picture that my mother is in? You know the famous picture at the end of the war, people celebrating in Times Square, where the sailor is kissing the girl? My mother is right there in the back. And one other thing. Ken Burns ... World War II ... the eight-part series? My father is in one of the shots of D-Day. My father was in the second landing in an LST and he is the only one smoking, haha.

Public School 99, Brooklyn, NY

Dave: This is Public School 99, the elementary school I attended for grades kindergarten to second-year high school. This school was very well-endowed. It was an 8th grade school, one of the last in New York City. Isaac Asimov's school with literature, science. This was a special school. Now I will show you where I had my first piano lessons.

I took piano lessons with Luba Galprin, a Russian. I started with her when I was nine or ten years old when I was deep into Elvis. I told her I want to play something from him. She said go get the sheet music. I still have *Love Me Tender* with chords, the guitar grid and left and right hand in C major. She taught me to read music. She could not read the chord changes, but she taught me to read the left and right hand. That's why I am able to read bass clef, because of her. I took lessons once a week.

Richie: Was she nice?

Dave: Yes, you know, big fat Russian woman. And you know famously who went to the school besides my brother? Woody Allen and the baseball pitcher Sandy Koufax. There is a documentary video that I watched on a plane once and Woody Allen walks right in front of that building. He lived right here on Avenue K, so it is said.

There is the box for stickball with the strike box painted on the wall. You get three strikes and if your ball hits the first floor wall, it was a single ... second floor is a double and third floor is a triple. If you hit the ball over the roof it was a home run. No bases, you hit the stickball standing still. Over there are the basketball courts. That was big time, we played a lot of basketball. This was where I spent most of my childhood, when I wasn't in school. And from here I would walk home to Fifth Street. The school is still in good shape. A couple of years ago we had the 50th year reunion. It was on a Saturday. We sat in the school, the principal talked to us—it was unbelievable. Good memories and that school is very well maintained.

Richie: Look at that field, a lot of space here.

Dave: This was Midwood Field, belonging to the city. We played handball and other ballgames there a lot. You had the parks, the beach, restaurants, shopping—you did not have to go to Manhattan.

Richie: No, Brooklyn was self-contained.

Dave: And there was a cultural life. You had temples and the schools so you only went to Manhattan to see a Broadway show.

Richie: But Manhattan was older, more adult, the real shit. And of course it had jazz.

Dave: When I had good grades, my father would say pick a museum you want to visit. The other cultural thing in our family was Broadway. We went at least two or three times every year. We would take the subway to go to see a matinee on a Saturday. I saw *Bye Bye Birdie*, *My Fair Lady*, *How To Succeed In Business* ... and others. My mother really dug them. After the show, we would eat at a restaurant around 42nd and Broadway, which was a tough neighborhood at that time. We would be back home by 7 o'clock at night. So that was a reason to go to Manhattan ... otherwise you stayed here in good old Brooklyn.

Back to Manhattan

Dave: So now we are driving back to Manhattan.

Richie: Remember the first time you went to a jazz club in Manhattan?

Dave: My first visit was with the high school/Lafayette guys. I'm pretty sure Mike Garson was there with me on the way to Birdland. Count Basie's band was playing, and Gerry Mulligan's group. This was during Christmas vacation. The next time was a few months later, in February 1962, to see John Coltrane. And that was it ... that was my epiphany.

Richie: That must have been with Eric Dolphy, after he recorded *Africa Brass*.

Dave: Yes, with Eric. Incredible!

Richie: I also went to the Village Vanguard with an older cat ... Cliff Smith. Remember him ... the alto player? He was a club date musician who loved Miles Davis. He took me the first time to see Miles at the Village Vanguard. It was the most exciting thing I ever saw or heard up to then. Nobody said a word. The guys were wearing black suits with white shirts. They didn't talk to each other ... no joking around for Tony Williams, Herbie Hancock, Wayne Shorter, and Ron Carter. Wayne Shorter was extremely mysterious. They are all on the bandstand, ready to play, and Miles comes down the stairs dressed in a cape with beautiful handmade gloves that had belts on them. He swept in, smiling. He punches Jerry, the guy at the door, in the stomach and whispers "you are getting fat." Miles was smiling ... you could see his white teeth and he was happy. He came into the club with another guy, a big cat, and a beautiful chick. He took off his cape, handed it to the chick, got his trumpet out, walked up on the bandstand and started playing.

Dave: No warmup, nothing, right?

Richie: No warmup, none of that stuff. It was the most exciting thing I ever saw, and everybody in the band seemed to know what to do. They started fast, a tempo like 350, and then all of a sudden Miles played two quarter notes and they switched to a slower tempo. Unbelievable. Then he yelled something at Herbie, who stopped playing and laid out, shoulders down, you know, like Bill Evans did. Tony meanwhile always looks bugged. And he was playing some of the greatest music in the world. In my young, inexperienced mind, I took the looks on their faces for frustration. Ron Carter is up there, real tall, looking at Tony and Herbie, keeping the music together. Wayne is in the corner, holding the tenor, listening to Miles solo and figuring out what to play. And he has that look on his face with his head tilted, like a dog. He is just waiting and then somehow Miles finished his solo and then Wayne came in with his solo. It was an unforgettable experience.

Dave: It was like going into a battle. It's what we do ... no show ... just start playing.

Richie: Really mysterious, no show, no talking, not looking at each other, no smiling, nothing. They just start and Miles is looking at every girl in the audience. Miles would play some of the most amazing phrases. He goes "ahhh" and makes a face like he hated it. Why did he do that?

Dave: I don't know. He did the same when I played with him. Maybe he cleared his throat or his jaw?

Richie: And then, like in "My Funny Valentine" after he tripled the time up, he would leave this gigantic space while Tony continues burning. Miles was completely relaxed, leaving 16 bars out and then he came in right on the dot. I never saw anything like it. I knew the tune, but I couldn't follow the form. The tune is in 4/4. I was counting, but I could not follow. I thought they left the 4/4, but they never did. And right after they ended, Miles started the next tune. I read an interview that Mike Zwerin did with Miles and he asked why do you start the next tune while people are still applauding and Miles answered you have to walk into the applause.

Dave: Walk into it, that is great.

Richie: So Mike asked what do you mean and Miles said don't let them stop, keep it going. Miles wanted to keep things going, so he was already doing the set as one long suite.

Dave: That band played so often that they didn't have to worry about the order of the tunes they played.

Richie: Like us, we don't have to talk. When we have a new tune, yes. But the next time we play it, we don't have to worry about it. The John Coltrane Quartet was totally different from the Miles Quintet in the 1960s. Elvin Jones was sweating already before he started playing. He looked at his drums and started to sweat, even in the winter. Jimmy Garrison was drinking his usual Scotch and milk, while McCoy Tyner, who was straight and a Muslim, was completely cool sitting in the corner. Seeing Trane a few feet away was different than an album cover or a photo. You don't realize how big Trane was 'till you are close. He was very tall and later on he gained weight. They started to play and after a couple of choruses he would be down on the floor, bent over. Sweating and screaming through the tenor, completely engaged. He never acknowledged the audience, never announcing any tunes or the members of the band. I was wondering why they never announced the tunes and my friend said you are supposed to know the tunes by ear. By the way, Miles was the same about not announcing tunes or the band.

Dave: It's like in the classical world, right?

Richie: Horowitz or Rubinstein never announced what they would play, so why should Miles or Trane? But I also saw Cannonball Adderley, and he did talk to the people.

Dave: And he was very articulate.

Richie: He talked to his band, introduced the tune to the audience, and the way he counted the tune off, snapping his fingers, the whole club was grooving. It was amazing. Cannonball was very articulate. He was a high school music teacher. The way he spoke to people and introduced Joe Zawinul, that he came from Austria and that he composed their hit "Mercy Mercy Mercy."

Dave: Joe wrote a couple of hits, "Mercy Mercy Mercy," "Jive Samba," "In A Silent Way."

Richie: Yeah, Joe recorded "In A Silent Way" in his record called *Zawinul* and when Miles recorded "In A Silent Way" he eliminated all the chord changes and put the whole tune over an E pedal. Do you know the original voicings?

Dave: I just re-harmonized it for a recent project.

Richie: But did you hear Joe's original version from the *Zawinul* record?

Dave: I never heard it.

Richie: The original version from *Zawinul* is a beautiful tune. It has a Viennese vibe, a little bit like a folk song. The changes are really beautiful, but they are a little too sweet.

Dave: Rubato?

Richie: Yes, the whole tune is rubato.

Dave: Where does the vamp come from on Miles version, is that Joe's vamp?

Richie: The vamp came from Miles, or probably from Dave Holland, the bass player.

Dave: So he just added in onto the tune.

Richie: Yeah, Joe's original version is rubato from top to bottom. When you get home check it out. It has Herbie Hancock and Joe on the record. He used two keyboards.

Dave: What year was that?

Richie: 1971.

Dave: So this is two years after Miles recorded it.

Richie: Yes, Joe brought the music over to Miles, who decided to record the tune. Miles's version of the tune is so much more modern than Joe's take. Joe was not happy with Miles's version because Miles left out all the changes. But the record sold very well, meaning Joe made good money on royalties. This was right before *Bitches Brew*. Right?

Dave: Right.

Richie: And *Bitches Brew* sold more than 500,000 copies.

Dave: That was a real hit. Joe wrote "Directions," right? So in a way, he (with the help of Miles) put himself on the map.

Richie: Absolutely, Miles really helped Joe by recording several of his tunes. By the way, one of the best records ever recorded from the same period was Miroslav Vitous's *Infinite Search* ... unbelievable.

Dave: A great record.

Richie: Just stunning. Joe Henderson, Herbie Hancock, John McLaughlin, and Jack DeJohnette, I never heard anything like that. There was so much interaction in the band and it still swung really hard. This record influenced all of us very much.

Dave: While we drive back to Manhattan, tell us a story.

Richie: Okay, so we are in an airport. I think it was Ireland after we played the festival in Dublin. We are waiting to go home 'cause the flight was delayed. Steve Swallow was there, and Bill Hardman. He is a really wonderful and total bebop trumpet player who had recorded with Coltrane ... he was one of the cats. Though not as famous as Lee Morgan or Donald Byrd, but just as good, I would say.

Dave: His lines on the flugelhorn, come on.

Richie: Now a month before, Randy Brecker had given me, as a birthday present, a pocket trumpet. Randy came over to my place and showed me how to breathe. I loved it because I felt like I'm Miles. I can't really play, but it feels very hip and I'm bragging about it. This a fatal error I made in front of a legendary bebop trumpet player, who was playing great music with the heaviest cats before I was even born. So in the airport I am going on bragging because I am a little bit out and I'm saying, "Man, I got this pocket trumpet from Randy and I'm playing it and it's really great." So Hardman finally can't stand it anymore and he goes, "Pocket trumpet, that's buuuullllshiiiiiiit." It was like a seven syllable word. And he said it with a vengeance because he hated me, he hated the pocket trumpet, and it was like an affront to his entire gestalt. And all of the sudden I realized what I did ... I really overstepped myself. I made an error, and I insulted a hero. So I said, "Oh man, I am really sorry." He went on about it for some time. He really cut me down in size, don't you think so?

Dave: I would say so.

Richie: I really did apologize to him.

Dave: He is not working anymore.

Richie: I am sorry to hear that. In other professions, doctors, lawyers, at least they have facilities for retirement and caretaking. But Bill is probably in a room by himself with a damn walker now. The Musicians Union, they don't provide for the guys though they try.

Dave: There is the Jazz Foundation taking care of guys. They go to older musicians and they see if they get fed and if they get their medical prescriptions.

Richie: That's cool. But that was an amazing experience with Bill Hardman. I just shot my mouth off and didn't think of the consequences. The way he said "bull shit" was classic and every once in a while I or you will give that saying a place in present time. This reminds me of something my wonderful father told me. He said, "You are still a kid." I said, "What do you mean?" He said, "The difference between a kid and an adult is that the adult thinks of the consequences of his statements and actions and the kid doesn't." And it still is true.

Lower Manhattan

Richie: We are getting closer the place I lived in for the past 44 years on Spring Street. It's good that today is a rainy and gray day because we're going back into the past, into the Jones, you know what I mean.

Dave: This is Warren Street, my second loft. I moved here in 1972.

Richie: The Chateau.

Dave: Chateau Eleana ... that loft on Warren Street was nice. Clean as a whistle ... a beauty. By complete luck, John Abercrombie and Marc Copland moved a few doors down from me. So Warren Street had a lot of music and not much else.

Richie: That was a great hang. I used to visit you down there. You had fun.

Dave: Then we went to Greenwich in Connecticut where Eleana Steinberg, who was my lady during this whole time, had a family "mansion." This was in the early 1970s, I was playing with my close friends Steve Grossman on sax and Gene Perla on bass in Elvin Jones group ... again, another story.

Richie: Your first loft on 19th Street was funky and the next one mentioned above was on Warren Street in Tribeca.

Dave: The last loft at 800 Sixth Avenue wasn't the greatest either. Living in the Apple as an artist was never easy. Firetraps, hanging light bulbs, freezing, shower and toilet in the hall, etc., etc! The lease's first sentence was something to the effect, don't even think about living here ... which of course we all did.

Richie: Wow ... the area has changed so much. Look at that ... Bed Bath & Beyond. It looks so different now. It's a completely different vibe from the old days. In the 1960s and '70s, the city was dirty, dangerous, and funky.

Dave: 83 Warren Street. That was my second loft after 19th Street. Like I said, there wasn't much action in Tribeca ... a lot of warehouses and so on. But these lofts in deserted parts of the city served a purpose for artists to stretch out and work at their art. Lispenard Street ... my grandfather came off the boat at Ellis Island and lived here.

Richie: Bob Berg lived there on Lispenard Street, with his beautiful girlfriend. Terrible that Bob died in such a horrendous car accident.

Dave: He died on Christmas Day ... drove head on into a truck. It was right up from where I lived in the '80s out by the North Fork of Long Island, past Riverhead. So terrible.

Richie: Lispenard Street, oh man, we are right in the middle of it now. I used to know every place around here. Look at this, the UPS trucking terminal is the largest trucking terminal in the world ... it goes for four city blocks from

Houston to Spring Street. All UPS shipments for New York are processed here. Everything is closed today because it is Saturday, but on weekdays this is really humming. Okay, now we are on Spring Street. There is the Ear Inn which has been here for decades. It's still open.

Dave: There is McGovern's Bar.

Richie: Oh my God, man. This is my building, 305 Spring Street, with McGovern's Bar on the ground floor. I lived in that studio apartment for 44 years and it was rent controlled, so the rent stayed very low.

305 Spring Street

Dave: The Half Note club was right there on the corner of Spring and Hudson Street, taken over by a Korean deli now. Coltrane *Live at the Half Note*! You lived on the cusp, bro.

Richie: The Half Note, I went there all the time. They had great veal parmesan sandwiches prepared in the back by the mother of Sonny and Mike Canterino who owned the place. Right across Hudson Street was a small jazz club called

Pookie's Pub. I used to see Elvin Jones there after he left Coltrane's group with Wilbur Little on bass, and Joe Farrell or George Coleman on tenor sax.

Dave: This was 1966, a year before I met you.

Richie: Of course ... and now the Half Note is a Korean deli. Remember this place right on the corner there? It used to be called Rhinoceros ... a private after-hours club, owned by John Belushi. It was a dangerous place to hang. They had some murders there. Now it is a clothing store. We are driving by Joni Mitchell's loft around the corner on 112 Varick Street. She owned a gigantic loft on the top floor and you could always tell when she and Don Alias were home because the lights would be on.

Dave: Great space ... I hung with Don and Joni one New Year's Eve ... she was very nice. Not much has changed here on Hudson Street, but up in Chelsea it is a whole other story.

Richie: A lot of the clubs used to be around here. Sweet Basil on Seventh Ave, Boomer's on Bleecker Street, and the temple of jazz, the Village Vanguard. Boomer's might have been the worst of all hangs. I mean, for drugs and drug violence.

Dave: But that guy Bob, he was a good cat

Richie: He was a great cat, Bob Cooper, very tall, big, ex-football player. The two guys owned Boomer's, Bob, and Gerry the other guy, They were alcoholics and they loved jazz. The club had an upright piano, and this is where Sam Jones, Cedar Walton, and Billy Higgins had probably one of the greatest bebop trios that played there regularly. You could hear them for the price of a beer, there was no cover charge. Do you know what they found when they tore Boomer's down to renovate and to open a new place? $30,000 dollars worth of cocaine and $25,000 in cash stuck in between one wall and the next wall that they had forgotten about because they were so high.

Dave: The stuff that went on in those days, I tell you...wow. One second, that's the Freedom Tower. This is it man, this is the 9/11 site. Tell your story. You watched it all.

Richie: I was in my Spring Street apartment up at 8 in the morning.

Dave: It was Monday, September 11th, 2001. I was coming in to teach at the Manhattan School of Music, my first day there for the new semester.

Richie: I had my TV on, watching it all. First, I thought it was a Japanese horror movie or some shit, right? Then I thought, no way. I ran upstairs to my roof with Howard. Remember Howard, my neighbor? We saw the second plane hit the tower. It was one of the worst things I ever saw in my life and it contributed to my decision to leave New York, moving to Leipzig, Germany, I have to admit. But the worst thing of all of 9/11 for me was the people jumping out of the top floor windows. And I'm thinking, why would they jump out of a 104 story building to a certain death? But of course it was 2,000 degrees in there because of all the flames from the jet fuel. And then I went back down to watch TV. Nobody could believe what was going on. I called LeeAnn Ledgerwood, my former wife and great friend. She lived on 49th Street and 10th Avenue and by then it was like later in the morning. She said you better come up here because they are going to close down the downtown neighborhoods.

So I packed some clothes and started walking from Spring Street up to 49th Street. There were no taxis, no trains running, so I had to walk. And sure enough, on 14th Street and 34th Street and 42nd Street they had soldiers checking IDs and so on ... Marines with M16 rifles out. They had checkpoints and I had to show my passport to get to LeeAnn. I walked all the way up. Nothing worked. I tried calling her from a street phone, but the lines were jammed. It was frightening. It was like, holy shit, we are being attacked. It was completely out, like in a movie. I finally made it up to her house. It was scary, and she was crying and all her cats were crying. It was a whole scene. So the first thing we did was go to the Puerto Rican bodega and bought gallons of water and food and all kinds of supplies. Nobody's phone was working, do you remember?

Dave: I was driving into New York and Caris called me right before I got to the Washington Bridge and she said don't go in, turn around.

Richie: Smart girl.

Richie: This is 23rd Street. I have so many memories of this street. The Chelsea Hotel and the Spanish restaurant in the hotel.

Dave: The restaurant was called El Quijote, and it is coming up on the right. Joe Lovano used to live there in a loft.

Richie: What was the name of that little club on 22nd Street?

Dave: Angry Squire, Seventh Avenue, between 22nd and 23rd.

Richie: I used to play there ... they had an upright piano. Rick Laird played there all the time.

Dave: The piano was at the back of the bar, same setup as the Half Note.

Richie: And don't forget that other club, Zanzibar with Bobby Rodriguez and all the crazy Filipino guys. And the Fort Apache Band with Jerry Gonzalez ... that was all cocaine money. Passing 11th Street and Fifth Avenue ... the real Greenwich Village. I spent so much time here and knew a lot of people, many passed away.

Dave: In the end, this was the best place in the world. This right here, Fifth Avenue, Sixth Avenue, Seventh Avenue, in the teens. It is still neighbourhoody. Everything is here. If I had a lot of money, this is where I would live.

Richie: Now we are coming into Village Vanguard territory. I know every inch of every street here. Elephant Castle had great burgers.

Dave: Seventh Avenue was the 52nd Street for our generation.

Richie: When it was happening it was really smoking.

Dave: The Village Vanguard, I have not been in there since the last Quest gig in 1987.

Richie: We used to play there all the time but after Max Gordon died they didn't hire us again, no idea why. We recorded live at the Vanguard, which in that time was the real deal, walking in the footsteps of the masters, Trane, Newk, Bill Evans, etc.

Dave: And of course you and I ate at the Buffalo Roadhouse all the time.

Richie: Yes, all the time. It used to be right there, and now it is some kind of karaoke sushi place. This used to be John Clancy's, a beautiful fish restaurant.

Dave: The 55 Bar was here and Boomer's down the street.

Richie: Sweet Basil was right here, and that used to be Seventh Avenue South, Mike and Randy Brecker's club. And over there downstairs was St. James Infirmary. This here is the only street in New York with two names, St. Luke's Place and Leroy Street, the most beautiful street in Manhattan. Look at those buildings on the right. They are beautiful townhouses, just stunning.

Dave: Very nice. This is really amazing, I think it was six jazz clubs in a row on Seventh Avenue.

Richie: But then, of course, there were many other places in the village.

Dave: On Bleecker Street...

Richie: The Village Gate, The Surf Maid, Lush Life, and the list goes on. Barrow Street is where E. E. Cummings lived. He wrote some beautiful poems here. And the White Horse Tavern is there, one of the oldest bars in New York. Remember Bleecker Street Records ... that was a great place you could hang for hours checking LPs out.

Dave: And my oldest musical friend, drummer Bob Moses, had a loft at 7 Bleecker Street. His was one of the lofts we used to hang in. Moses on Bleecker, Gates (Gene Perla) on Jefferson Street and me on 19th Street. Randy Brecker had a loft on Grand Street, near the Bowery. Michael Brecker bought my loft and lived there for years.

Richie: I remember Gene's loft. Don Alias was there all the time. So were Jan Hammer and David Earle Johnson. Perla's loft was really out, because nobody lived in that area. You could not buy a cup of coffee down there.

Dave: The Pink Tea Cup over there.

Richie: The Pink Tea Cup. Remember the fried chicken?

It is amazing how the names of certain streets are identified with certain places or events like a movie scene, a music club, or a store. Do you think it will always be like that?

Dave: No, nobody cares anymore.

Richie: We thought everything was going to stay the same and then so many things fucking changed. I mean, it might as well be another country. It's still the city, the Apple, but it's so different.

Dave: A bit like Disneyland.

Richie: It became commercial ... Bohemian commercial. Those stores are only for rich people, but they don't live here. These stores change owners every six months. But this was a great strip here, a great hang. This was the center of our world.

Dave: When we came out of the clubs, it was daylight.

Richie: Then the choice was Wo Hop in Chinatown or Ratner's restaurant on Delancey Street on the Lower East Side. It was a very Jewish vegetarian place, and both were open 24 hours, seven days a week.

Dave: The bread at Ratner's was great. We just ate rolls and butter.

Richie: Remember Lester, the waiter? He used to come over to ask—you want some more butter? We went there once with Joe Lee Wilson, who ordered eggs. Joe Lee, "You got corn? Mix the corn with the eggs." I thought that was a great

idea. The mushroom and barley soup was great. So (at 4 a.m.) the soup, bread, butter, and a coffee was a dollar fifty, and it was enough ... you would be full.

Dave: We definitely had to take a taxi, because Ratner's was on Delancey Street on the Bowery.

Richie: It was open 24/7. I really miss that time. That was the 1970s into the '80s. John's Pizza in the Village, Woody Allen's favorite place, is still there.

Dave: Bleecker Bob is still there, still open. Village Music is there, and the Bagel, a little place in the Village ... featuring scrambled eggs with cheese on top, after the gig.

Richie: The Bitter End and the Back Fence clubs on Bleecker on the left side, still here.

Dave: The Bitter End I played with Ten Wheel Drive. I saw Cream there with Jack Bruce, Eric Clapton, and Ginger Baker playing in front of a wall of Marshall amps ... the loudest stuff ever, until Tony Willams Lifetime and Miles band when I was in the group. Volume became a "musical" tool. The Village Gate is still happening and Lush Life was where the Capital One Bank is now. And the 100 Club with the brothers, featuring a hard bop underground legend, Clarence "C" Sharpe. I came to the Village when I was 15 years old on a Saturday afternoon with my tenor looking for jazz in the streets. NADA! It was all folk music except for the 100 Club ... this place. The first time I saw Pharoah Sanders was here. But jazz in the streets ... I don't think so!

Richie: Yes ... Rashied Ali and Reggie Workman used to work here.

Dave: Yes, yes, yes. All the free cats used to come and play there.

Richie: I saw Donald Ayler and Grachan Moncur III ... it was their hang. Every block in this neighborhood has a reminiscence. You know what I mean, brother?

Dave: The Bottom Line over there on Mercer and Fourth Street.

Richie: What about Strykers?

Dave: That was on the Upper West Side ... I didn't go there often.

Richie: Al Foster was there all the time

Dave: And The Cellar was up there on 95th Street. Miles heard Al there with Walter Bishop Jr. ... another bebop icon. Astor Place had the Public Theatre over there. Now we are getting near the Five Spot. Yep. Remember when we got locked out with Lookout Farm? They booked us. We showed up, and the club was closed. They left us outside in the snow and ice.

Richie: They didn't even bother to call to tell us that they closed the club. Not a very good omen.

Dave: Are you kidding me? They closed the club and we were out there with all our equipment, the Fender Rhodes piano, Altec Lansing speakers, and nobody showed up. This was in February at 7:30. The club was dark ... we couldn't get into our own gig.

This was the original Five Spot, Ornette Coleman, Monk with Coltrane, and Cecil Taylor, the real deal.

Now we are going to drive past The Dom, clarinetist Tony Scott was leading the jam sessions there. The first time I saw Jack DeJohnette was there in 1965. There was a place called the Red Balloon, which was a big hippie hangout, rock and roll and Grateful Dead types. The Fillmore East was one block down on Sixth Street and Gem Spa was right here on the corner serving the best egg creams in the world!

Richie: There it is. They have been here since the 1920s and it is still open.

Dave: They can't still be making egg creams, can they?

Richie: I bet you a thousand. This is New York, baby.

Dave: Okay, get one.

Richie: I will.

Dave: It's unbelievable, he got one.

Richie: We got it!

Dave: Amazing that Gem Spa still makes egg creams? I can't believe it. Unbelievable.

Richie: They make countless egg creams every day. Perfect ... Holy shit! It's not too sweet either. It's like a chocolate soda, and it has no eggs, and no cream.

Dave: Great, good job, man. A little reward.

Richie: I told you, bro, stick with me. Did I take care of you or what? So we copped a real egg cream at Gem Spa. This is historic because we don't know how long the place is going to stay open.

Dave: Cool.

Greenwich Village

Richie: Do you know the original meaning of 86, like when you say he was 86ed? Bradley Cunningham, the owner of Bradley's Saloon told me. There used to be an 86th Street stop on the A train...the express subway that goes West Fourth Street station up to 125th Street. They decided to close the 86th Street stop down because they had so many murders there. So from then on, if somebody told you, "I got 86ed" that means you have been banned from that place. Lovely!

Soon we have to go to Katz's Delicatessen on Houston Street, which is another historic site and of course, like a lot of New York things, connected to food. McSorley's Old Ale House is right here ... the oldest bar in New York City, opened in 1860. They didn't let women in until about 10 years ago.

Dave: They were very famous for that. Oh look ... we just passed the great Carl Fischer music store.

Richie: By the way, New Jersey has the best and the worst of people and best and worst air. Imagine driving through Elizabeth, New Jersey, like there is rust in the air with tremendous pollution. Or Bayonne where all the bodies are buried. And then you go to beautiful places like Teaneck, or Englewood, where Rudy van Gelder has his legendary recording studio used for so many Blue Note and Impulse records. It's an amazing scenario to have these differences within one state, all close to the Apple.

Webster Hall is right here. I played there and in 1967, Bill Evans recorded *Further Conversations With Myself* in Webster Hall with Helen Keane producing. They said that at that particular recording, in order to get the best sound they recorded at 15 1/2 inches per second. Remember when we recorded our sessions at your loft at 19th Street, we used the slowest possible tape speed to get all the long-winded guys a chance to hear what they played. But of course we recorded nine hour jam sessions so the tape had to run as long as possible. Did you transfer any of the tapes?

Dave: I had some of them transferred. Yes, terrible, it sounds like madness.

Richie: But is there any good music?

Dave: There is one good session with three tenors, Michael Brecker, Steve Grossman, and me, plus Randy Brecker, Terumasa Hino, Calvin Hill, and Bob Moses.

Richie: That's fantastic. That's like John Coltrane's *Ascension*, right?

Dave: Yes.

Richie: New York is a great place to live ... the city has so much spirit. But it's more for younger people now.

Dave: That's what it's for.

Richie: We had our time here and we did everything we could do.

Dave: We had a great time. The city was, in spite of its reputation, user-friendly. But if you were born in the 1930s, you really had it great because then you had the 1950s, '60s, and '70s into the '80s, you would have had the best of all times. Untouched by the wars, New York was the best place to be.

Richie: Paris in the 1920s, New York from the 1950s to the '80s. Of course, you would be 80 years old now. Remember One Fifth Avenue, the restaurant? It was beautiful ... pianist LeeAnn Ledgerwood and bassist Steve LaSpina played duo there. And Al Haig played there after he killed his wife, right? He got out of jail on bail ... I don't know how, but he got out and played. There were all these duo places, Knickerbockers, Zinno's, Bradley's, and One Fifth Avenue. You could go from one place to another and hear all these great piano and bass duos.

This used to be Stromboli Pizza, the best pizza in the Village, remember? Okay, man, we're coming up to Bradley's. Oh my God, it's intense. It's coming on the left now.

70 University Place (Bradley's)

Dave: At least it is still a bar.

Richie: Yes, that's true. When Bradley died in November 1987, his wife Wendy took over running the place for a couple of years and then closed.

Dave: A lot of service for the community. So much music in that place.

Richie: God, yes, if the walls had ears. I have a funny story about Bradley and the great pianist Larry Willis. Larry was in this really bad state of being, but he still played great. So Bradley hired him for a week. Larry was taking these unusually long breaks. And what Bradley finally found out was that Larry was also working the Zinno's club at the same time, because Zinno's was a short distance from Bradley's, running from gig to gig. He played with Ron Carter at Zinno's and with George Mraz at Bradley's. George tried to cover Larry as well as he could, coming up with excuses. But then what happened was Larry got stuck in the crowd of a Halloween parade and he came back an hour and a half late. Bradley, who took no jive said, "Hey, you are jerking me off, kid. I admire your moxie, but you're fired." And then two years later Larry tried to do it again!

Dave: Yeah, Larry was something else.

Richie: Larry once stayed at Walter Booker's house. When he departed for an appointment, he left the water running in the bathtub and the front door open. But he could really swing. His biggest claim to fame was that he was best man at Herbie Hancock's wedding.

Dave: I didn't know that. Larry was really crazy.

Richie: And what is that, the famous Roy's Pizza?

Dave: Excuse me, it used to be Ray's Pizza.

Richie: Ah, Ray's Pizza! Correct!

Dave: The famous Ray's Pizza, but a cat bought it. He changed the name but he is trying to keep the same vibe by calling it the famous Roy's Pizza.

Richie: This is a real big con.

Dave: My first date with Caris, we ate pizza there and then went to see you play. Now we go to 19th Street.

Richie: Where you had your first loft, where it all began. We really learned how to play together there.

Dave: Yep.

Richie: Remember our gigantic black book of tunes that we studied to learn standards? In a lot of ways, New York is a bebop town with exceptions.

Dave: Oh yes.

Okay, here it is, 138 West 19th Street. When I moved in, there was nothing here. These buildings were here, but they were all empty. Now look at all the stores, people shopping, look what's going on.

Richie: Man, in this loft we played like every day, 12 to 14 hours a day. Everything looks so different now, it's fantastic. I mean, we had such a great time. Yeah, yeah. This is before everybody was doing cocaine. Nobody knew shit ... we were the underground, and it was cheap. Then, by the end of the 1980s, everyone was coked out. Your dentist was doing it and your lawyer, and it became expensive and stupid. But until then, it was like a secret society, you know?

Dave: Fantastic to see my old loft again. It looks as if they are going to renovate it. Abercrombie had a loft on 18th Street, second floor, just one block down.

Road Trip Through Our Past

Richie: Greg?

Dave: Greg Kogan is still around. I just saw him, he looks exactly the same. He sounded the most like McCoy Tyner of everyone.

Richie: He had the fastest right hand.

Dave: Yeah, he was an amazing piano player.

Richie: I mean no one could play faster. I don't know how he did it. He had long skinny fingers, and he was very furtive when he was playing. He was a very odd guy, but a genius vibe. He ended up, I believe, on 19th Street, buying one of those lofts.

Dave: Very strange, but a nice guy. But he was like so mangy looking.

Richie: He looked un-hirable. But he was a sweet guy who I remember spoke very fast, even for a New York guy. Fast!!

Dave: I first met him up in the Catskills when I was 15 or 16. I have no idea how he got there. But the McCoy stuff ... he really had that down.

Richie: Oh my God. And his double time, I was trying to copy it.

Dave: From 19th Street I moved to the loft on 83 Warren Street near the World Trade Center.

After that my next loft was on 114 Lexington Avenue, I was on the third floor. I lived in this loft from 1975 to 1976, right before I went to California. That's where the picture for our duo recording called *Forgotten Fantasies* cover was taken.

Last stop now, 800 Sixth Avenue. I rented this loft when I came back from California. And that's where we started again. Rashied Ali came up there, and we played with him. Here I rehearsed my new group with John Scofield, Terumasa Hino, Kenny Kirkland, Ron McClure, and Adam Nussbaum.

Richie: That's right. I liked that loft.

Greenwich Village

Dave: The building is gone now, replaced by an apartment house. It was a big loft, and I was on the second floor. I sold the loft to Bill Evans, the saxophone player, when he joined Miles Davis. Eugene Smith's jazz loft was across the street at 821 Sixth Avenue.

Richie: And we didn't even know about it.

Dave: That was in the 1960s into the early '70s. There are some great recordings from Eugene's with Chick Corea, Paul Bley, Thelonious Monk, Zoot Sims ... amazing. So we did it, man, we did it all. Everything up to the year 2000.

Richie: Next time we go back, it will probably be all different and gone.

Richie: Inside the circle above, in Greenwich Village, around Washington Square Park, was "our" version of 52nd Street. Below is a list of some of the jazz clubs and music venues that featured jazz, rock, and blues and operated between the mid-1960s to the mid-1980s in the Village. A few of the clubs we visited when we were young and were studying music. Later we were fortunate enough to play some of these clubs regularly. A few of these places are still there but sadly most of them are now gone. This was an amazing time...

Note: You can find the addresses of all the important place we visited and mentioned at the end of this book in the chapter Addresses in New York.

Jazz Clubs and Music Venues in Greenwich Village

100 Club
Ali's Alley
Bitter End
Blue Note
Boomer's
Bottom Line
Bradley's
Cafe Au Go Go
Cafe Bohemia
East Village Inn
Fat Tuesdays
Five Spot
George Braith's Musart
Half Note
Knickerbockers
Lone Star Cafe
Lush Life
One Fifth Avenue
Pookie's Pub
St. James Infirmary
Seventh Avenue South
Slug's Saloon
S.O.B.
Studio Rivbea
Surf Maid Bar
Sweet Basil
Top of the Gate
Village Gate
Village Vanguard
Visiones
Zinno's

LETTERS TO OUR MASTERS

Richie: Dave and I both had the blessing of being mentored in our early years by jazz masters that picked us to play in their groups. For me it was Stan Getz, Chet Baker, and indirectly by Bill Evans. For Dave it was Pete La Roca, Elvin Jones, and Miles Davis. And we were both heavily influenced and formed by John Coltrane. Sadly all these masters have passed so Dave and I decided to write letters to them as though they are still with us.

Now that we are senior citizens ourselves this gives us a chance to say things to them that we could not say to them at the time because we were either too young, didn't know enough to ask the right questions, or were too shy.

Dave's Letters

Pete La Roca

Well Peter,

You were my first heavy mentor. I had hung with great and influential musicians, but your impact was quite dramatic. I was an unseasoned young man, eager to live up to the job and you were exceedingly patient.

You might remember the "audition" that was about 30 seconds long! It seems that Jim Pepper was supposed to go to Steve Swallow's brownstone to play with Chick Corea on piano, Swallow, and Pete. My oldest musical compatriot, Bob Moses, said I should go there and fill in for Pepper. The rest is a case of being in the right place at the right time. I showed up and everyone was very nice sensing my apprehension. "What tune you want to play?" I started "Softly" and within a few minutes you stopped and said, "Let's rehearse!" That was the beginning of our relationship.

You had a bunch of originals to learn from yourself, Swallow, and Chick, as well as specific standards. I remember Kurt Weill's "This Is New" redefined by Chick. You were a true New Yorker as I was, so speed was of the essence to learn the book. The rhythm section was a dream, leaving me completely alone on the bandstand which was nerve racking to say the least. You wanted to work as much as possible and particularly at the iconic Village Vanguard.

So our relationship began. Things that you uttered became gospel. I soaked in everything I could because I realized the obvious. From jamming with friends to having to really step up to the plate with this rhythm section was a long haul psychologically speaking. I thank you for enabling this to happen. Here was my shot at the jazz life at 22 years old!

Unfortunately, the scene was not so great in New York moneywise. We ended up playing La Boheme, a club on 68th Street and Broadway for FIVE dollars a night for a few months. With such low money only a bassist or piano player who had nothing more profitable for the evening would come in to play. Needless to say, I was truly "there" every night. So I got to play with a lot of heavies during this time as circumstances dictated … Jimmy Garrison, George Cables, Joanne Brackeen, and others. We finally got the Vanguard booking with the A team, Swallow, Chick with Pete. For whatever reason you had enough and seemingly overnight decided on getting a law degree. I didn't understand what happened or why, but the next time I saw you was in the dormitory of NYU with books piled up to the ceiling. And you had offers from Miles and Herbie's new band.

Letters to Our Masters – Dave's Letters

You had tremendous street cred having played with among others Sonny Rollins and Trane. I felt the pressure of being the only horn, responsible for re-entering in the right spot after a drum solo ... keeping the energy level up and of course learning THE book. I wish drummers could see you now because it was so magical. You were way beyond the typical drummer-as-leader syndrome. You were loose but accurate and you visibly loved the music, chanting a lot of oos and ahs when things moved you with a smiling face and loose demeanor. The book was good for me to learn ... blues ... standards ... originals ... all had a distinct flavor to them. And you had Chick at the right time of his musical growth who loved playing with you.

I was teaching school during the day and playing at night. I saw your frustration concerning the playing situation and felt bad for you. But I was learning every day and most of all enjoyed our talks together standing outside the club on 68th Street rapping. You had something that I realized over the time we played together ... ..you were a closet intellectual ... a perfectionist who was well read and tuned into the times we were living through in the late '60s. I remember talks we had about the Sufis, a Persian sect known for their Dervish dancing and the Urantia. You were among the most intelligent artists I have ever known. And you were perfectly tuned in for your future gig as a lawyer because you were a contrarian and extremely intelligent which are good traits for a lawyer. Of course at times you infuriated folks with your steadfast personality. You didn't want to play any 8th note music which you deemed more appropriate for dancing. You might not play for a year but would return to the drums completely fresh. Your skills were naturally developed. You even bought the first Apple computer and printed our lead sheets. No question that you knew your stuff and more. It made a great impression on me that you could sing my parts and the bass lines perfectly in time and pitch.

I can understand some of the aspects of why the law degree, supposing it was a way for you to contribute to society and more. You took care of my family as a lawyer which I thank you for. You famously dropped LSD at times before we played, something I attempted but couldn't bring off when I was blowing. Over the next several decades you would procure a Monday at Birdland or something like that for a few hits with trumpet and tenor added to my soprano. I didn't enjoy that scenario much, especially because I could finally really "deal" with you musically and not be intimidated.

I still use musical tools you taught me. Especially how to avoid the one…the downbeat which has been the most common way to mark off sections in jazz soloing as well as being totally predictable. You not only moved the one around in 4/4 but remarkably in 3/4 featuring your downbeat anywhere in the last part of a phrase.

But most of all it was matters of life, the meaning of the universe and other grandiose subjects that I was just waking up to at that age and you were right there. Thanks my man. You were indispensable to my growth as a person and jazz musician. We had some fun!

Dave

Dave and Pete La Roca

Elvin Jones

Dearest Elvin.

I do hope that you are healthy and feeling good. Getting older is not for the faint of heart.

I haven't been in touch lately. I owe you a lot and want to get that love and respect I have for you on paper.

There were two Elvins on our planet ... the master drummer and the human being. I will start off with the music which is obvious, but necessary to highlight some aspects of your style that I encountered playing with you for a few years. I remember Max Roach referring to you as Emperor Jones. That's a pretty heavy description from one master to another ... a sign of deep respect to be sure.

In the 1960s you were omnipresent with Trane of course but many other artists as well. My desert island collection of must-have albums features Elvin on five out of ten chosen. That's how you influenced me. You are the "keeper of the pass" taking jazz drumming through the lineage to another incredible stage of development. Your triplet approach and general style was a summary of what came before. What you did with Trane was on another level. This is not the place for a musical treatise but suffice to say, the buck stops here when it comes to jazz drumming. You were and are a force to be reckoned with, be it with sticks, brushes, or mallets, and it will be that way into the future.

I was honored to be with you on the bandstand for a few years in the '70s. The first challenge (after getting past the intimidation stage that all young musicians go through) was to be able to take your behind the beat feel on the ride cymbal as a life force. You owned that part of the metronome, (approximate quarter note equals 125-85). I tried to get a hold of that feel but it was impossible to not drag the beat as I did for six months!

The way you played time was both easy and hard. Easy cause you never pushed your way of phrasing on us (Steve Grossman and Gene Perla with me in the *Live At The Lighthouse* band) knowing full well that once we relaxed things would take care of themselves. Hard because of the laid back aspect of your beat placement compared to the more traditional way of playing that range of tempos. Everyone had at least some of Elvin in their playing in the '60s. To play a slow 3/4 with you was unbelievable. Finally, your sound on those signature Gretsch drums (Yamaha came a bit later) was deep. We know that you played pretty loud for John but doing a ballad with you was a trip. Your way of marking off the time with the brushes "caressing" the snare skin at a ppp dynamic exposed the three of us to even greater scrutiny than normal. Believe it, we were under examination nightly ... a separate discussion.

Suffice to say you are the baddest drummer who ever played this music. You always gave your best no matter who was playing with you. I was lucky to be a part of that sound for a few great years.

Now Elvin part two. You are not an egomaniac seeking approval. Being around your personality and observing how you handle the public are all the unmistakable marks of an ego under self-control. I always tell interviewers that besides my father, Elvin was THE MAN in my life exemplifying character, experience, and wisdom. Elvin ... I know you have been around the block more than a few times. You sweat just sitting down at the drum set. ... you can't wait to play ... especially with the *Live At The Lighthouse* quartet. You never abused your status by preaching or being dogmatic. I loved you for that along with your ability to energize and inspire. In fact the whole world loves Elvin. You have a voice that is memorable!

As we play we become ... the music shows the way ... especially in the life of Emperor Jones. Thanks to the Master for being so human.

Dave

Elvin Jones and Dave

Miles Davis

Dear Maestro:

I hope this letter finds you resting comfortably and enjoying the view from up there as well as having time with so many of your old associates and friends. I just imagine you and John Coltrane hanging out together talking about old times. I think about you often and of course since you are now iconic and part of the musical history of the world, there are more than a few times that I relate stories covering the mundane to the dramatic from my time with you, beginning in the early '70s up to your passing. Like when Tony Williams and I were with you in your pad watching fight films with Sugar Ray and Joe Louis, and you got the two of us standing up to throw some punches. "Never look at the hands, only the eyes!" Well Maestro, you are a cottage industry and I talk about you all the time. EVERYONE WANTS TO KNOW ABOUT MILES!

At your funeral I remember looking around at the audience, noting the thirty or so musicians who had somehow been part of your musical life ranging from Max Roach to whomever your last bass player was. (To be honest I couldn't keep track of the Miles Davis sideman association by the late '80s.) I commented to my wife, Caris, who you met when I played with Wayne Shorter for a Coltrane tribute in Japan, 1987, that all of us had two things in common, —we were young and becoming formed as musicians. Most of us played in a manner with you that we never played again, with exceptions of course. Bottom line, you changed our lives musically for sure as well as from the fact that being a sideman to you meant one had arrived at the top of the food chain. After playing with Miles Davis, you were expected to have something on your own to say as a leader.

As I mentioned above, Maestro, you are part of the fabric of musical history like Beethoven, Bach, Ray Charles, etc., etc. What you left the world is beyond belief and description, from my all time favorite *Sketches of Spain* to *Dark Magus* (including me on that one) to *Live at the Plugged Nickel,* the list goes on and on. One thing I always admired in you was the surety and confidence you had when it came to music…no second guessing. And as I tell anyone who asks me what I got most from my time with you (and master drummer Elvin Jones) was the seriousness of the work at hand. Everything before or after those sacred moments on the bandstand could be on another planet at times, but when the downbeat was heard, it was all BUSINESS!

You were never too talkative about music, your own or others, leaving it to a few words rather than a full blown description, much like all the folks from your generation. But one thing you said to me in that off-hand kind of way (meaning a few words, then walking away) was, "Finish before you're done." Like all the tidbits you threw out to me and others, it took years to understand but it seemed that you were saying leave a space for the guys to do something—it might help you to say the least. The lesson being you can and should get a little help from your friends. Also, if you are already thinking about finishing, you're too late to the party.

Dave and Miles Davis, 1973

There's one story I tell that is unrelated to music, but for me reveals a side of you that I saw on occasion and that most people did not witness. I always felt your supposed "hostility" or whatever it might be called was a front to get people to leave you alone so you could do your thing. You were after all naturally a shy person in my estimation.

In '81 (I think that is the right year, but no matter, somewhere in that period) I had a confluence of tough things happen to me—divorce, hepatitis, and a badly broken leg (my weak one with a cast up to my neck). Drummer Al Foster who was with me during the time I was in your band and was also the drummer for my group at the time (Quest with Richie Beirach) came to visit me where I lived, way out about two hours from the city in Long Island, just to say hi and commiserate with me. The next day the phone rings and that voice of yours is the greeting, "Do you need any money?" Now all musicians know that if you are not on the stage you are NOT making any money. We don't have severance or disability pay.

After a few words of small talk you said, "I got a story to tell you. One day when I was 13,14 years old my dad took me outside in the garden and pointed up in the tree. "You see that bird, Miles? That's a mockingbird ... .you don't ever want to be that!" I said to you, "Nice story." You said, "Yeah, I like that. Take care of yourself."

Why you told me that and what it meant is still on my mind. But most of all was you reaching out and checking in with me during those dark days. We did get along well and you WERE a nice guy in the end!

That's it for now Maestro. As I write on Valentine's Day I have not seen the movie that is coming out about you. But I did see the trailer and of course I reserve judgment until I see the film in its entirety, but it looks like another tale of an African-American genius who is violent, a drug addict, beats women, etc. Yeah, you had your shit, but Hollywood takes a wart and makes a plague. And if it is again another Hollywood travesty like Bird, Ray Charles, Marvin Gaye, Billie Holiday, James Brown, etc., I apologize in front.

So long Maestro ... I'll will be looking for you when my time comes.

Peace.

Dave

Wheel of Life
Inspired by John Coltrane

If it wasn't for John Coltrane my life would have been very different. His music and attitude, infused with a strong spirituality, taught me about the values enumerated on my Wheel of Life.

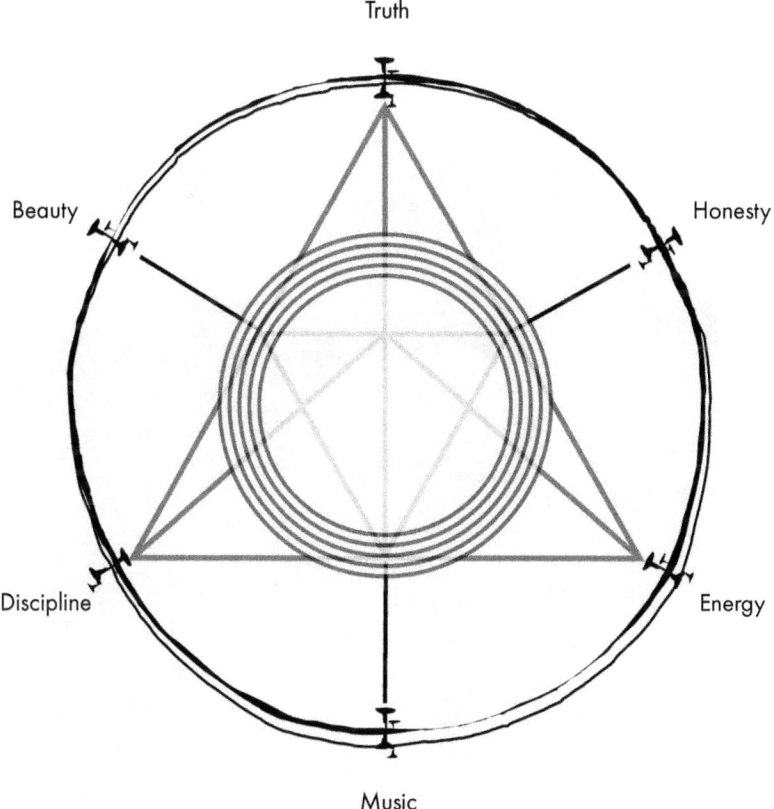

Concept by Dave Liebman, Drawing by Hery Paz. Used with permission.

Richie's Letters

Stan Getz

Stan,

First, where ever you are, I want to thank you for giving me the opportunity to play with you and get a chance to learn so much from you about the music and life. You had an incredible spirit and powerful ability to move everyone within range of hearing you.

I had no idea what I was getting into when you hired me in 1972, and playing for the three years in your quartet gave me the foundation from which I was able to build my musical personality. Having Dave Holland on bass and Jack DeJohnette on drums put it on another level of a learning experience. You taught me so much of what I needed to know about really playing as good as I could every night, six nights a week, two or three sets a night, and sometimes a matinee on Sunday afternoon. I was very young and too inexperienced but it made me realize what playing improvised group music in front of huge audiences really means.

I wish I could have told you how I felt about your amazing sound, your beautiful even tone from the lowest note on your tenor to above the highest note. I felt entranced and moved beyond words, comforted musically, and very warm and loved by your sound alone. But then your choice of notes and conception of pure melody and elegant and totally sophisticated phrasing was always different. And of course where you were always aware of what your rhythm section was playing to support you. You were one of a small group of great bandleaders like Miles Davis, Chet Baker, Bill Evans, or Wayne Shorter of your generation that actively listened and reacted to the rhythm section, and especially to the pianist, which was me during those years.

I only wish you were as sophisticated and confident in your day to day behavior with me and the other musicians in the band as you were In your music. This is the time for truth, not anger, and not over complimentary horseshit. You could be so kind and encouraging to me as a young talented but green piano player on one day and then the next day, or even the next hour, well, you suddenly became a classic Jekyll and Hyde character.

When I started playing with you and we finished that amazing first week In Toronto at the Colonial Show Bar, you told me my intros were beautiful and that my playing was great. I was overjoyed and felt really good. And then after a year of playing for the same money, $600 per week (which In 1972 was okay, remember a budget hotel room was six bucks a night). But I felt I had grown and learned and made you proud. I started thinking about a raise so I talked to Jack and he said go ahead bro and ask him. I was very nervous but I said to myself, fuck it, be a man and ask him for a raise if you think you deserve it. So I went to your room and I said "Stan," and you immediately said no, without even hearing the rest of my sentence! You knew from the tone of my voice that I was going to ask for a raise. And then Stan, why did you say, "Richie, your intros are getting too fucking long, kid?" That hurt me, and by the way, was not true. But okay, you were teaching me about life here, not just music. I felt betrayed and foolish, and I was! More of my inexperience, more of my misplaced hero worship and fairy tale romantic aspirations from me, I am sure.

But the music, and with that rhythm section! Jack and Dave! Fresh from those amazing two years with Miles Davis, Chick Corea, and Wayne Shorter. Every night was school, every night I had the opportunity to learn. Important and unteachable in a classroom. Or the jam session information, that I did learn and still use and try to teach today.

Plus let's remember who you were. In the early '70s, you were on the biggest selling and most widely known albums of all time at that time in history. That iconic tune "The Girl From Ipanema" from the 1964 album *Getz/Gilberto* made you and Jobim world-famous international stars with album sales of over 50 million units globally. It wasn't just the number one jazz record, it was the number one album in the world— like Sinatra, like the Rolling Stones! That song was in every jukebox in every bar in every club around the world.

You were literally catapulted into incredible fame and stardom, and your ego grew exponentially. Now you were not just Stan Getz the great famous jazz tenor sax player, but Stan Getz the king of the new bossa nova wave of music.

Richie

Chet Baker

Chet,

I know you are not here on this planet anymore. There are so many things that I would have loved to talk to you about, and ask you, and tell you. But I write this letter to you now that I am a grown man and I think I finally am beginning to understand you and the incredible importance and emotional depth of your playing. And the even more lasting lessons in how you led your tragic life. The last time I spoke to you was about a week before your so-called accident or suicide death. You would never kill yourself. That was a total bullshit story created by the Amsterdam police to cover up their incompetence. We spoke the week before you died, and you sounded very good, very positive and we talked about recording a whole duo CD together, just piano and trumpet, with all of my tunes that you loved like "Leaving," "Broken Wing," "Zal," and "Elm." I was so honored and humbled and excited. I know you didn't jump, Chet.

If you had made it to be 61 years old with all the crazy shit you put yourself through, you never would take yourself out like that. That garbage story put out in the newspapers had as much credibility as George Bush insisting that there were weapons of mass destruction in Iraq! So I never really had the chance to tell you what I felt and thought about you and your music.

I don't know why I was never able to talk to you like I feel I can now. I guess I was too young and inexperienced and had not much to say to you so I just kept my mouth shut and tried to listen to you and what you said, and of course how you played. It took me many years to realize that you have answered many of my questions in your attitude towards life and within your playing. Your kindness and warmth to people—young musicians like me struggling with trying to learn about the mysterious art of improvisation in a small group. You played one note, literally, and a whole tapestry of sound emerged right in front of me!

Because I actually hadn't figured out in words how exactly you affected me and, of course, the thousands of people in the audiences we played for during those years. Basically, what you were able to do with your music is to STOP THE WORLD. Some musicians, classical, jazz, pop, etc. can, with very few notes, just completely stop the world around them for that first instant of their sound. Two bars of you playing the melody of "Stella By Starlight" or "My Funny Valentine" or "I'm A Fool To Want You" or "Leaving" or "Broken Wing," has the astonishing effect of creating a hushed deep silence that is thick with expression, reflection, and the wordless poetry that is the essence of all great music and especially jazz improvisation.

Your playing is amazingly powerful, even when you play softly. The trumpet, which can be a loud, glaringly insistent, and triumphantly brilliant instrument, becomes a completely different thing in your hands. It sounds like a soft, round but penetrating voice somehow projected directly into the ears of the listener!

To hear your music in person is best, of course, but it is so strong that it comes across even on CDs. It feels like you are playing a private concert to the people, to their hearts. I have seen it and felt it myself many many times. For example, we all come out onto the stage at the New Morning jazz club in Paris or the Village Vanguard in NYC or the Jazz Gallery in Washington. I sit at the piano, the bass player stands behind his bass, the drummer sits behind his drums, then you come out last and sit down on a chair and cross your legs. I don't know any other trumpet player that sits when they play, but you do and it works for you.

You always start the set with a ballad, again breaking all the rules of so-called jazz protocols. Then with the first phrase from the trumpet, maybe "My Foolish Heart," an immediate hush fills the air. Then a space between the first phrase and the second phrase. Electric silence. It unites the whole audience into one mind one heart what we called the collective unconsciousness.

I have seen in the audience big tough-looking men, Black and white, looking DOWN at their shoes. Women look up, smiling gently, both men and women soon weeping silently to themselves. Me too!

Now you are in the Chet zone—magic, pure magic. The same thing of course happens with one phrase from Bill Evans, John Coltrane, Miles Davis, Arthur Rubinstein, Vladimir Horowitz, Ray Charles, Stevie Wonder, etc., etc. The inner man or woman comes right out to meet you from the player's heart directly to the listener's heart. That is an invisible but undeniable connection, as strong and resilient and consistent as titanium wire and indestructible by anyone wanting to interrupt it.

Chet, you were the classic anti-hero. The trumpet is usually a macho bullfighter kind of instrument. Think about Freddie Hubbard, Dizzy Gillespie, Lee Morgan, Clifford Brown, or Miles Davis, who were all fantastic innovators.

The trumpet is a beast of an instrument, hard, high, strong, proud, like a Spanish macho matador. So how did you create a sound that was so soft and pure but could penetrate through walls, through the air, sounding like a private whisper into the ears and hearts of all capable of listening and, more importantly, HEARING.

But let's not ever forget that you weren't just a great ballad player. You could and did all the time totally BURN, with a frightening searing intensity, especially with me, Tony Williams and Ron Carter on my tune "Paradox" on your album *You Can't Go Home Again*, man! All of a sudden it was happening, so strong and powerful that I was dizzy. And playing with Tony and Ron for the first time, I was both terrified and exhilarated, like being on the fastest, safest rollercoaster ride in the world! Tony was smoking. I felt him like a giant hurricane on my back and in my earphones, like being in a wind tunnel, and YOU motherfucker!

All of a sudden, the sweet, deep, soft, lovely elegant ballad Chet turned into this seven foot monster! Your sound was both chilling, with a laser-like sword cutting through the molecules in the air, but still round and pure, not harsh or ugly EVER! It was your ballad sound made much bigger, louder without nails and even more penetrating.

Chet, I so wish we could talk NOW! Because I think I might be able to really understand you better and I might be able to say something that would interest you. I miss you Chet, we all miss you and love you and your music down here.

Richie

Miles Davis

Miles,

Just saying that name gives me the chills. I just would like to tell you my feelings that I was never able to tell you because you were not easy to access. I don't believe in God or any kind of religion but you, John Coltrane, and Bill Evans were my musical heroes and set an incredible example of consistent creativity and the pursuit of the dream of a life of artistic accomplishments.

You had the vision and strength of your convictions to pursue what you wanted to play, with whom you wanted to play. And you took a very heavy interest in your recordings and it shows in over 50 records that changed music history and added so much beauty, fire, and love to the world—my world and that of my close friends Dave Liebman and John Scofield, who had the honor of working with you for some years, Randy Brecker, who loved your playing, and John Abercrombie. Dave and I would go to hear you at the Village Gate or the Village Vanguard in New York City in 1966, 67, etc. It was a mind-blowing experience, literally. And we came out of the concert moved beyond words. Happy, excited, and above all, inspired, always. You gave us so much.

Your honesty on the bandstand—no bullshit show—no announcement—no thank you shit to the audience. We got it. You were working and completely involved with the music. Your band was playing, no talking, it was fucking mysterious! Few other bands were like that! Actually, Coltrane didn't speak much at all, and Bill Evans with his trio didn't either.

But you also came out always dressed to kill, and kill you did! You started the set with the song "Agitation," bang, you were off like a rocket! No easing in, no building it up. "Agitation" was an uptempo burnout tune. With any other band it would have been a climax! But for you it wasn't the climax, was it Miles? No, you had way more to let out of the bag, with your unbelievable quintets. From 1964, *The Steve Allen Show*, the first gig for Wayne Shorter with that iconic rhythm section—Herbie Hancock, Tony Williams, Ron Carter. To the last gig with the last quintet sometime in 1969 with Chick Corea, Jack DeJohnette, Dave Holland, and Wayne Shorter too.

You gave us your heart, your love, and your energy. Sometimes you looked pissed off on stage but I never believed any of that shit. I might have loved your music and felt awed by your presence but I was never the one to believe any of that guru crap. I knew enough about your life off the stage to not be blinded by my great feelings of admiration for your music. And it was even better to know that you were not the saint or high example of all humanity. You were human, a man, a man who had been hurt a lot and also given great respect and love from your peers and fans. That you weren't perfect was a relief for me!

You are so loved and massively appreciated now, probably even more than in 1967 or '69. As I got older I began to understand and love your recordings more and understand your performances better. The music seemed so advanced to me when I heard it in the 1960s. I was in my early twenties in 1967 and knew what you were doing was heavy and beautiful and of great innovative importance but to tell the truth, I and my friends didn't really understand the intricacies of it. Tony Williams especially was a wonderful shock and made an indelible impression on us, but also it was a real band. You had the humility and good grace to leave the bandstand after your solos because you knew that if you stayed up there people's attention would be drawn to you, very gracious.

You sounded sometimes nasty, mean, and shitty during interviews or especially in that jive ass fucking biography by that whore Quincy Troupe who put a lot of his own in your words into your mouth. And there was a big disconnect between your public and private persona. Cool, I get it, we got it.

But to hear you play the melody to "My Funny Valentine," "Stella by Starlight," or "Nefertiti" was to be in the presence of the ultimate musical experience. I can still hear Herbie's stunning intro to "Stella by Starlight" at the Vanguard one night, then you coming in with the fragments of the melody. You opened up that well-worn melody like a flower. It somehow sounded new, fresh, as if I had never heard the tune before. The intimacy, the extreme expressivity without any excess drama or overplaying was extraordinary and remained consistent until 1969.

What happened to your music after 1969 is another story. But for now, Miles, I hope you are cool. You changed the world and gave us so much. Love you.

Richie

Bill Evans

Dear Bill,

It's been over 40 years since you passed in 1980. I still think of you and your great music almost every day. And I can still remember the first time I heard you playing, Bill.

I was 13 years old in 1960, and an older sax player friend of mine named Cliff Smith had just bought Miles Davis's *Kind Of Blue* recording. He brought it over to my house and we put it on the turntable. Wow, the opening part of "So What" with those mysterious chords and rubato bass movements, then the theme in time, with you playing those modal fourth voicings! I was gripped by the sheer power of the SOUND! I had no idea what those chords or melodies were but I was drawn to it like a magnet. We listened, just loving it. I asked Cliff if he knew what the piano was doing, but he said he had no idea either. This was a purely non-intellectual reaction. Then we listened to "Blue In Green," with your intro and interludes and especially to yours and Miles's solos and we got very quiet. The music hit me hard emotionally. I was trying to hold back tears so Cliff would not see me cry, but as I looked up at him his eyes were full of tears! It was too much. Your touch and your incredible depth of expression touched me deeply.

My earlier encounter with jazz was when Cliff brought over the *Milestones* recording and the trio tune "Billy Boy" totally got me, but that was different. "Billy Boy" was a joyous swinging ride like being on an express train with Red Garland, Paul Chambers, and Philly Joe Jones. So *Kind Of Blue* was my introduction to you and since that day in 1960 I have cherished your music. I carry it in my heart forever.

You were so much a part of my musical life that I feel bonded to you in a good way. Of course, your musical influence was enormous in my entire career, but your friendship has been equally important. I remember fondly those times we hung out together in my small apartment on Spring Street in Soho in downtown Manhattan. Those times when it was just you and me talking, laughing and sitting around my big Steinway and playing for each other. Also, those times when I could hear you live, especially at the Village Vanguard in NYC, with your various trios, over many years. I remember one time when your trio was with Eddie Gomez and Marty Morell, on a noisy Saturday night during Christmas time, the first set. The club was filled with ignorant tourists, loud, stupid and just asshole insensitive people from out of town. My girlfriend at the time asked me, "Oh man, how is Bill going to deal with this awful audience?" I said watch and listen! You took the stage, never made announcements or introduced the tunes or guys in the band, just believed in letting the music speak for itself. You didn't want to break the silence and introduce words into the experience of those hearing the music.

So you sit down at the piano and start the set with the softest, most beautiful delicate ballad "My Foolish Heart"! Of course, the first few bars were lost because of the loud conversations. But then, as if by magic, it became quiet. The real devoted listeners shushed the ignorant tourists and then the exquisite power of the depth of your music acted like a big broom, sweeping away the noise and a stunning stillness appeared in its place. You hushed the room in about eight bars! I was smiling because I have seen you do it before. My girlfriend was astonished. Such a wonderful show of your power of transformation, the ability to change the atmosphere. I have used your quiet but powerful method a few times around the world with difficult audiences, and it almost always worked.

I still feel heartbroken that you chose to leave us so early. It was an ongoing tragedy, and I saw it unfold in those last years. You got more and more into drugs and it seemed that, except for the music, you didn't want to live anymore. It shocked me to see you in New York City on the last night of your life. You were so thin and haggard. You wore that striped shirt for days without changing or washing it, but you played some amazing long brilliant solo piano intros on "Nardis" and many other tunes. But we were all terribly worried about your condition.

You choose to leave us so early and only you know why, I miss you very much, musically and emotionally. If you could have only seen and felt the enormous outpouring of love and sadness from the world of music after you left.

Bill, you changed many lives with your wonderful music; I know you changed mine forever.

Love you

Richie

Bill Evans and Richie, July 1977

John Coltrane

Dear John,

Richie here, I wish I could have met you face to face, in the same room with you just for 10 minutes, but when I had a chance to talk to you at your house in 1966 I had very little to say to you of real importance except to mumble my awe and intense love of your music.

When you passed so suddenly and tragically early, you were only 41. I was still trying to understand WHY. I was so moved by your playing and your band. I saw you in Boston in 1965 at the Kresge Auditorium when you had Elvin Jones and Rashied Ali plus McCoy Tyner, Art Davis, and Jimmy Garrison plus Pharoah Sanders, Archie Shepp, and a few guys I didn't know carrying large paper bags full of bells and percussion. To be honest I couldn't understand most of the music, but I knew something was happening on a level beyond my comprehension.

John, the world has become a very difficult place to live in these last 50 years, and the world of music, especially jazz, has unfortunately narrowed greatly. There are still great young players coming up all the time, but who to play for and more importantly, what are they playing? You left a gigantic footprint, and a large beautiful vision, like skywriting on a clear day.

You didn't just play the sax in an extraordinary matter and had a great band. You changed lives with your music, you changed the entire world of music. The entire template of what is possible with the traditional instrumentation of saxophone, piano, bass, and drums was revolutionized. Your innovations enabled the classic jazz quartet instrumentation to became completely expanded and transformed into a much broader foundation for your incredible and incredibly brilliant, and very moving improvisations and compositions. The impact on me and my young friends was enormous, and still felt today, on what would have been your 90th birthday.

After seeing you perform in the 1960s we left Birdland or the Village Vanguard or any place you played mostly speechless, greatly moved, somehow changed forever. More human, less sure of anything, except for the awesome power and true spiritual value of your playing.

You must have felt so good after you finally were able to stop shooting dope and drinking, like shedding an old unnecessary skin to finally feel free of that horrible shit that unfortunately that probably had something to do with your life being so unfairly shortened.

Your influence was beyond the normal instrumental impact on players of your instruments. Your influence was much more significant and cut across *all* instruments like Louis Armstrong, like Bird, and you, similar to the massive and pervasive influence of Bach, Mozart, Beethoven, Händel, and Chopin.

You and your music also had a cross-cultural impact on a great variety of different musicians all across the entire world of music and art. My oldest and

John Coltrane

best friend, Dave Liebman was one of the young sax players who was seriously touched by your playing and your band performances and, of course, recordings. You became, for us a kind of Nelson Mandela figure. Not to worship or make into some perfect bullshit guru, but as a role model for excellence and importantly complete musical honesty of sound and content.

And it wasn't just you, of course. We knew, even being young and inexperienced men, that the band with Pete La Roca, Steve Kuhn, and Steve Davis was cool—but it was clear after your first recording for Impulse Records called *Coltrane* that Elvin Jones, McCoy Tyner, and Jimmy Garrison were your peers and could simply give you what you must have been hearing and wanted for your group all along.

I wish I could have had the words to tell you then about how the power of your sound affected me so deeply! There is no good way to describe in words just what your sound was or did to me and others, but I will try. Your sound, especially on tenor had within it the deep sadness of the horrible shit your people went through in the USA from slavery through the 1940s, '50s, and of course 1960s. It had within it all the incredible joy of discovery, of a group discovery in front of people which is kind of a loose definition of jazz. It had inside of it many, many levels of strength and vulnerability. Of the sweetness of your sound on your iconic *Ballades* CD, to the operatic and almost symphonic projection of your sound on your last recorded CD on that amazing composition of yours, "Expression." It wasn't just one sound, you had hundreds of gradations of power, intimacy, and color. But the quality that I think hit me the most and the element of your sound that touched people outside of the so-called jazz audience was the absolute HUMANITY of the timbre of your sound. To hear you literally soaring over a volcanic and ground shaking Elvin Jones accompaniment with McCoy getting those enormous raging chords with Jimmy Garrison underpinning the whole motherfucker was and still is breathtaking. Like, for instance, on your two solos on "Transition." It must have taken great courage from you and Bob Thiele to release an LP with a 17 minute plus track taking up one whole side of the LP! You increased the possibility of the power and beauty of ALL recorded music by making the tunes longer and longer, filling them with unbelievable creative and growing music, never standing still, not for a minute.

It must have taken even greater courage and fortitude after the incredible musical and commercial success of *A Love Supreme* to release *Meditations, Kulu Se Mama,* and *Ascension*. To say nothing of that great *Interstellar Space* with Rashied Ali and the brilliant *Stellar Regions* and the final awesome *Expression*.

John, you came so far so quickly, from Earl Bostic to Miles Davis to Thelonious Monk and to finally your own groups. How did you do it, John? How? Did you feel you were going to die young and so you pushed and felt time was limited? Or did you just follow your heart and that strong voice inside you that said, "Hey Bob, can we go into the studio with the guys next week to record some new shit that I am writing now?" You could have stayed with tunes like "Giant Steps" and "Naima" for many years, or the "My Favorite Things," "Chim Chim Cheree" concept much longer, or even the "A Love Supreme" suite, a magnificent achievement. But you didn't, why not? You were like a man with a time clock in him.

Whatever motivated you, thank you, John. Thank you for your tireless force for changing your music, always moving ahead, not ever resting on your laurels, and trying to be a force for the good. In my opinion, and the opinions of all of my friends you were a great force for the good, for the good of the jazz world of music and much more.

I wish I could have sat and told you these things but it was not to be, that's okay. Maybe someday when I am up in your neighborhood we can all sit down with you and Elvin, with Jimmy and Lieb and Bird and Miles and Bill and just have our spirits hang.

Happy birthday John! You have given the world so much, and you are still giving.

Richie

PREPARATION & PERFORMANCE

A Jazz Lecture for the Interested Listener

Richie: This is a short lecture that Dave and I gave in Poland to an audience basically of laymen who were very interested in jazz, but not jazz musicians or professionals. The interesting thing for us was that we had never given such a lecture before to people who were not music students or professionals. It forced us, in a good way, to speak in more general terms about our music and to simplify our concepts.

The Challenge of Jazz

Dave: One thing you should understand about jazz even if you don't know much about it technically speaking, is that every time we play something, we try to play it differently. This is a great challenge and needs the assistance of top level artists to have a chance of happening.

Richie: You must!

Dave: You hope you play something differently while keeping the same standard of excellence for the easiest as well the most difficult. Note that this pursuit is quite different from the goals of playing classical music, which are being true to the composer's directions to a large degree. Of course there may be changes of expressive content in the way somebody plays something. But the notes are what they are and they are on the page. In our case, the written notes can sometimes have several compositions fitting on one page. And even what's written on the page can get altered on a night to night basis. Our reference point is the lead sheet and from there we do with it what we like, depending on the moment of inspiration.

One thing you have to understand about this music is that you must listen carefully. We are not giving this to you on a golden plate, if you understand my point. The challenge to listen to jazz is that as a listener you must participate. You don't listen to jazz the same way you listen to pop music, with all due respect to the wonderful pop music that exists. Pop music is music for the body, mostly, and for feeling good and partying.

But jazz is challenging and meant to make the audience become involved in the conversation. Now that doesn't mean that you should start speaking in the middle of our performance. But when we play jazz, or in any typical jazz performance, a lot of our spontaneity depends on our feeling of how the audience reacts. When we play we can't tell what you think because the audience is sitting there and nobody is talking. But we do feel vibrations from the public. And vibrations mean everything to us and our performances. The vibes emanating from this music which may begin with the written page or not (depending on the specific genre) to something that is in the air, basically unseen, is what we are talking about. So when we play this kind of music, Richie and myself, and the people that we play with, we usually try to get the audience to be completely involved in what we're doing. With a good audience this experience is usually very very gratifying.

Richie: Let's think about improvisation in general. Everybody improvises all the time in their daily life. You don't get up in the morning and write a script for what you are going to say or do that day because you don't know what is going to happen ... much of our life is an improvisation.

Our life is also a conversation. It's not just a solo improvisation. It has to do with interaction between me and Dave, between us and you. That's very important.

That's another one of the differences between jazz and classical music. In classical, string quartets, ensembles and orchestras are of course interacting, but it's written into the script ... it's all scripted. Our music is not scripted in the least.

Imagine a symphony orchestra with a hundred musicians sitting there, waiting for the maestro. Leonard Bernstein walks up to the podium and the conductor asks what should we play? So Bernstein plays a short phrase on the piano and there are a hundred musicians who are supposed to know what to play. No ... it would never work, but that's what WE do.

We make something from almost nothing. And I will tell you right now, it's really fun and a reason to get up in the morning and travel, to get on a plane, check into a hotel, get to the concert hall or club, and play in front of you, differently every time!

There are all kinds of jazz from Louis Armstrong to Cecil Taylor—soft jazz, bebop, fusion, all different styles. The only thing that I would say that is a requirement of this music called jazz is that it has an improvisational element.

Dave: This is the common thread we expect.

Richie: Style is something else ... electric instruments, jazz-rock, traditional. Even boogie-woogie, that I don't like at all. But I recognize boogie-woogie as being a legitimate style of jazz. Jazz is not a WHAT, it is a HOW.

What is classical music? Classical music has these amazingly beautiful melodies, right? We can't hope to improvise as great a lyrical melody as a Beethoven or Chopin composition. And by the way, they don't compose in real time, sometimes it takes them years. It took Brahms 22 years after he published his first piano concerto to publish a second. Imagine what we could do in 22 years? When we play we have a nanosecond to decide what to play.

There are thousands of excellent classical pianists in the world, just check all the piano competitions—16-year-olds, 17, 18, 19-year-olds—amazing geniuses from all over the world playing fantastically.

And how many great young jazz pianists or saxophonists are there in the world?

Why are there so many great classical pianists and so few great young jazz pianists? This is a very important philosophical question, jazz improvisation versus classically composed music. We are not comparing them in terms of work since they are both fantastic. The answer is that jazz musicians must improvise the CONTENT of their solo in front of a live audience or in a recording studio.

Dave: Why is it so difficult and such a challenge to improvise in music? You have to be creative, and have great technique. You can't be looking for which scale it is or what note is in the chord in the middle of an improvisation.

If I have a conversation with someone and I have to keep searching for my next word I lose my audience. So technique is definitely a big part of improvising as it is for anybody who plays any style of music. Besides technique, creativity is essential. You have to be able to think on the spot and not be self-conscious about it. You just have to do it and not worry about the consequences while having a conversation with the other musicians.

When Richie and I play duo it is not the typical jazz quartet situation with bass and drums. If we go to a jazz club tonight, I'm sure we would see drums and bass, and some kind of horn, saxophone or trumpet ... maybe a singer or guitar also. Therefore in the case of our duo it is, of course, a very, very exaggerated situation because we don't have bass and drums.

But we certainly still have rhythm. We don't have the bass but we still have the function of what a bass does. And that is all taken care of by Richie, whereby the piano has to be the bass, the drums, and the piano. He has quite a big job in a duo situation. When we play with drums and bass, which we do a lot of course, then the situation is spread out and so is the energy. Drums, you take care of the rhythm; bass, you have the rhythm and harmony; piano, you have rhythm and harmony. So we all have a conversation and function.

But to repeat this is an exaggerated situation. We love the drums! But the technical challenges are very critical when playing in a duet or solo format.

So this is one of the reasons why you go to school to learn the history of this music. It's very important to know the tradition. Jazz has a 120 year history. Obviously this is a lot less than classical music, so it is a little easier to catch up. On the other hand, a lot has happened in these 120 years of jazz music, as much as in 400 years of classical music history in some ways. Therefore we have to understand the past.

So here are some very important names. Louis Armstrong was the founder of jazz. Duke Ellington had a big band for more than 50 years and wrote thousands of tunes. John Coltrane was a great influence on my playing. There was Miles Davis with whom I worked. Bill Evans who was a big influence on Richie. There was Charlie Parker, Sonny Rollins, Art Tatum ... there are so many and it is very important to know these people because they represent the evolution of the music. Jazz did not stand still in these 120 years. If you listen to Louis Armstrong and then you listen to our music, it is quite different yet quite similar in approach and that is very important. When you're learning something about an art form, it is to one's benefit to know the history and to a certain degree to be able to repeat and imitate it ... for sure in the learning stages.

So those are some of the requirements that make jazz so challenging. Is it that more difficult? Everything is difficult if you want to be good. But the specific challenge of jazz is like no other music in the western world. We have improvisation in the traditional music of other countries and cultures. You go to Bulgaria, there is fantastic improvised music ... certainly when you go to India there is amazing improvised music.

Richie: India's music is one of the great sources of world music.

Dave: Latin America has great improvised music. The first Aboriginal people in Australia played the didgeridoo using sticks on the ground for percussion. The didgeridoo came from a tree ... the sticks came from the tree ... while they played on the stones. There has always been improvised music because people want to talk to each other, whether it's musical or non-musical. One way of communicating between people is through an instrument and/or a voice.

But the thing that makes jazz very challenging is that we are encompassing western harmony, which Indian music does not do, for example. In Latin American music outside of Brazil there isn't much harmony, which for this conversation means the tradition of western music from Bach to Beethoven, and Mozart, Chopin, Schoenberg, Ligeti, and Stockhausen.

This music is a lifelong challenge to maintain a level of excellence. More important to you, the question is not whether you become a jazz musician or not. The important point is to enjoy the music. This music you will have forever. The guy who lives next door to me didn't know anything about jazz. But because of me he started listening to it and now he loves it. He comes every time I play. Ninety-nine percent of the time listeners don't stop listening to jazz music for the rest of their lives.

In other words, when something is deep and has a lot of passion, motion, technique, philosophy, and sophisticated thinking, which this music does, it is not some music that you turn easily away from. You can't help but love it.

We're not trying to tell you that you have to play music to enjoy jazz. Jazz is something for life. When people get into jazz, their world opens up sophistication-wise with very personal responses different from western classical music. When you love it you will probably listen to other styles of music with a different ear ... something for you to think about.

Richie: But why are there so few jazz musicians that are excellent? It's because classical musicians have the composer offering the content and knowing what's coming. They know it's going to be Beethoven or Bach or Chopin or Mozart... composers who all wrote great music. But classical music is about exalting the *composer*. Interpretation is important, but the possibilities are limited, even among the greatest classical performers.

Jazz is instant composition. The requirements of a jazz pianist on a night to night basis are demanding. People really don't realize what you need to know to create solos every night in the jazz language. You have to come up with a great and fresh solo on the same tunes, even if you play five nights in a row. It has to be different every night and excellent. Classical musicians spend their life perfecting a piece and for the most part they try to play it the same way every time. That's also difficult because even though you repeat it, you have to play it with a sense of intensity and freshness, as though it was just written.

It is the exact opposite for us. We have to play our tunes as though we had rehearsed them for five years. And then when we do the improvisation it has to have the compositional unity of a great written piece of music.

In the end, people, normal people, not musicians, just want to hear great music. They don't care whether it was written two hundred years ago or in the last one hundredth of a second. Now here's the other thing. In the end if our music is recorded and you listen to it ten times, it turns into something like classical music. The recording becomes the new manuscripts.

Dave: When we improvise in the free style it's different. Before we play we might talk about the weather, but little or no talk concerning the music we will play. Actually it means we are just playing from the top of our head without any preconceived agenda. This is like walking out in the woods on a beautiful day or walking in a city and not knowing which way you're going to go, hoping that it will be safe and that you will encounter something of value ... true improvisation. You try to come up with something interesting and if you don't, you say, hmm, okay, maybe the next time. We just go with the present tense as best we can.

2009

Preparing for Performances

Dave: I was asked to talk a little bit about solo performances. In my case playing solo saxophone. How do you prepare yourself? A solo saxophone performance is quite a rare thing. You don't see it too often and there are some reasons for that. One well-known musician who played a lot of solo gigs, but only on the soprano saxophone, was a gentleman named Steve Lacy who was an American living in Europe for many years. He was famous for the body of music he created under such restricted settings. Tenor saxophone is one thing, but soprano? That's really concentrated to say the least.

I haven't done that many solo performances but I did make a few solo records. Of course working in a recording studio is different than a concert. From my limited experience of playing solo, even if it is only for a few minutes, I must say that it is among the most challenging settings I could imagine. The most obvious aspect is that you have nobody else to look at and to help you through.

I have an interesting story pertaining to this style. It has to do with another great musician who played an odd instrument for solo concerts. His name was Albert Mangelsdorf, a German trombone player. Playing solo soprano sax is tough enough, but trombone? You could have a problem. Albert was a great guy, an excellent musician and famous. He played solo trombone concerts for large audiences in Germany. One night I asked him what is it like to go out and play a 90 minute solo trombone concert in front of 3,000 people? And he said it was lonely ... I would never put it into those few words ... thanks Albert! He wasn't talking about the music. When you get off stage, there's nobody there to hang out with ... nobody to eat with ... nobody to travel with. He was talking about the social aspects of it.

But let me say that musically it is exactly the same for anyone. You don't have anybody there to support you and truthfully to help you musically when you have nothing to say. You can only leave silence for a certain amount of time before somebody starts throwing tomatoes at you. This is a particular problem.

But let me take this subject to a more generalized question. How does one prepare for a performance of this sort? Let's say it's a typical jazz gig, whether it's duet, trio, or a bigger group. Big bands are different because you have 18 people playing behind you. Every musician has his own way of preparing to perform. There are legendary stories of musician's pre-gig routines, anecdotes that are circulating out there. We don't know for sure but we think they are true. We certainly know people privately and personally, who have ways of preparing for a performance, ranging from dietary restrictions to prayer to demanding a certain brand of bottled water, on and on. If it includes the spirits, then even better!

Some people are really serious and maybe meditate or something of significance to themselves. Michael Jackson was very famous for him and his musicians holding hands before the concert creating some kind of wishing well, and so forth. Everybody has their own way, but the important thing is that in the end it is up to you to find a way that makes you comfortable.

A Jazz Lecture for the Interested Listener

Richie: I went to see Sonny Rollins at the Village Vanguard and before the set I went behind the stage to say hello to him. I pulled the curtain away and he was standing on his head, meditating. So I was shocked and said sorry Sonny to interrupt you ... he immediately said it's okay Richie, see you later.

Dave: I'll tell you a story. I played with Elvin Jones, who was the drummer for John Coltrane for several years. My time with him was my first real initiation into the jazz business. My routine before the concert was to warm up, practice licks, and have a million saxophone reeds spread out, trying to find the perfect one for the concert. I mean I was a nervous wreck, but in a relaxed way. Elvin Jones, of course was drinking beer while I was in the dressing room trying to get ready for the concert. Then I got my most notable job, playing with Miles Davis for one and a half years. Not only did Miles not warm up, but apparently he didn't even touch the trumpet for weeks between gigs. With the Miles group we would work three or four weeks and then take a break for two weeks. I couldn't believe it...this was Miles Davis for God's sake! I had to think about this. Miles is like the king of the trumpet and he doesn't prepare, so it seemed. He doesn't warm up, at least when I was backstage I didn't hear him play too many notes...only blow some air through the trumpet. But not only that. He would show up two minutes before we went on stage.

And you know what that did for me, observing Miles in this pre-concert situation? It relaxed me. It made me have a very different attitude towards preparing for the performance and in a sense just trying to make it whatever life is about that day. Here is the point—try to make the playing an extension of the present time you're in, rather than treating it as something so different from your real life.

And then what happened to me was instead of making such a big deal out of it, I tried to get on the stage the way I was feeling that day and have the music reflect that in my playing. I am not saying I was sitting backstage, philosophically thinking okay, today I am in the third altered state, you know? It wasn't like that. It was just whatever was happening, being in present time and it made me be much more aware of what I was doing in the moment, which, of course was conversing musically with the other musicians. It is very important to learn how to be in present tense. So that became more important to me.

I am not telling anybody their way of doing it should be like anybody else's. Some people may practice before the concert, I'll tell you who was very, very notable this way. I worked with Michael Brecker in a group called Saxophone Summit. Michael, who died in 2007 of course was one of the major saxophone players of our time and technically completely brilliant. We had three sax players in the group ... Joe Lovano, Michael, and me. Backstage before our concerts Joe and I would be sitting together, sipping some wine, enjoying the atmosphere and each other and the other guys in the group just hanging out. Michael would be in another room, practicing and playing some ridiculous technical stuff. Sometimes Joe and I would say, "Hey man, come on now, get over here." And then he'd say, "Oh yeah, great," and he would come out of his room and be so glad to be relieved of what he was doing. With me and Joe there, we had to turn off the switch for him and say, come on and relax. To practice was his way to warm-up so he had a very different procedure. And, of course, he certainly had great results with it. So you've got to find your own personal way.

2008

The Five Elements of Learning Jazz

Richie: Practicing is important. I am going to give you a list of things to do because I think this might be the most practical information other than actually playing. The main thing a teacher can give you is inspiration to practice, inspiration to be your best self, and practical fundamental topics of technique.

You can separate the entire study of music, any music, or any art into elements. The first element is technique. That means exercises ... you play smoothly and then as fast as you can ... hands separately. Piano players ... you train your hands separately first ... never together at the beginning, because each of your hands are completely different. Sometimes people come to me and say Richie, show me your method. If we were all given by God the same hand I could show you a method. But everybody has different hands ... everybody. So there can't be one piano method. Everyone has to teach themselves. If you are serious you have to practice technique at least one hour a day.

The piano sound is neutral ... it is without nuance, so you have to create the illusion of a smooth, very smooth singing, warm sound on the piano. So true personal expression is very important.

The next task is learning jazz. The key words are phrasing, dynamics, and articulation. How are you supposed to learn what the content of jazz is? The vocabulary of jazz is studied through the act of transcription. You must write out certain solos ... not from your favorite records, but from musicians that have been especially given to us to play certain kinds of solos that make sense when you add them up...given the history of the instrument. Just like every other art form. If you are an art student, you don't start with Jackson Pollock or your own stuff. You start with Michelangelo and Leonardo, Canaletto and Raphael, you duplicate and imitate them. A teacher says to you, man, you have to learn this solo by Wynton Kelly or John Coltrane and you say yeah ... I like that solo. If it's your hobby, fine. But if you want to become a professional you want to make music your life, you die for it, take a bullet! You must really learn the solo by getting inside of the phrasing, articulation, etc. Not just the obvious things but more the DNA of the solo in question. You come out on the other end of the solo. After four or five years you've transcribed maybe 12 solos, and that's all you need.

So the first part is technique, the second part is phrasing and dynamics, and the third part is transcription. The fourth part is repertoire. You have to learn tunes ... you should know 300 tunes. Hank Jones knew 3,000 tunes. Of course he plays for singers all the time. Tommy Flanagan also, and Jimmy Rowles—these cats know thousands of tunes. I know about 500 tunes ... I should know more but for me it's enough. "Autumn Leaves," "Night In Tunisia," "Round Midnight," "Stella By Starlight" ... these are some of the basic tunes you must know from memory. One of the worst things that you can see is if I call a tune in my class ensemble and I say, let's play "Green Dolphin Street" and I see the kids reaching for the Real Book trying to read "Green Dolphin Street." If you have to read "Green Dolphin Street" you have to get out of my class, I'm sorry. So you must have a certain amount of repertoire down!

And number five is composition. Everyone should write music on his or her instrument. It doesn't have to be great. It doesn't even have to be good, but it just has to be the act of composition. This gives you a chance to understand what it's like to construct quality music. It slows down the process of improvisation. That's the thing which makes it so hard to learn. Improvisation goes by so fast ... do you know what that was? Wait, wait, what was it?

If you are writing a tune with chord changes it forces you to check out what other possibilities there are for reharmonization. Sidebar—for me composition is best done at night with technique done in the morning. This is what I was taught to do. Let's say you want to practice 10 hours every day. It takes about 16 hours of time to practice 10 hours because obviously, you can't sit there all day. You get your own practice routine. Get up at nine in the morning ... you have breakfast ... say hello to your girlfriend ... walk your dog ... whatever. Then you sit down and practice technique ... then transcription and phrasing ... dynamics ... another hour or maybe two depending upon how serious you are. You tell me how much time you want to spend and I will tell you how good you're going to be. If you spend too much time, then you lose your mind and you will be in a mental institution and you can't play. So you have to have a personal life ... a little!

Preparation & Performance

Part of your jazz education is playing with others. Jazz is social music. It's not like a painter or a poet. They can stay in the house in the same clothes for 10 years and they don't even have to take a shower. They have to just sell their art to their publisher or dealer. The dealer hopefully sells it and their art goes out into the world and they get money. They can be very introverted and cloistered people who are very sensitive ... it's fine. Proust never went out of his house. He had a wall built of cork so he wouldn't hear anything from the outside.

But jazz is social music and you need other people to interact in a group. It's one of the great things about jazz and it's also a tremendous pain in the ass because every time you play it means phone calls and emails to organize a rehearsal, a recording, or a concert. So if you don't like people, if you are introverted, go somewhere else ... don't play jazz!

The next thing is saturated listening which is different from listening to your favorite music while you're washing the dishes or reading your emails. Saturated listening means that by the end of the day, you should be sitting in a comfortable chair, or lie flat on your back, with really good headphones or speakers. Listen to a bunch of music that you may not understand, but that you know is great and that has been assigned to you by your teachers and professors to listen to. Maybe some heavy classical chamber music ... an amazing jazz solo you would like to learn ... music like that. Maybe add on some Pygmy music from Africa. You listen to it over and over again until it becomes part of your unconscious and permeates your brain. This sounds easy but it is actually hard work.

I did this when I wanted to develop my music in the late 1970s. I was not satisfied with the language I had been using so I wanted to increase it and make it richer, more beautiful, and more personal. So I listened to great contemporary music from Takemitsu, Alban Berg, and Ligeti that had nothing to do with jazz ... right? I did this for years and it really affected my music. When you improvise, you play what you hear in your head. So how can you control what you hear during the moment of creative improvisation? A lot of music you hear every day is not worth listening to because it is muzak and not intended for serious listening. But with selective saturated listening, especially before you go to sleep, it gets into your brain, into the frontal lobe that controls judgment, love, and beauty. The medulla is the back brain, the reptile brain. It's used for fighting, looking for food, hunting, gathering, and survival.

The front part of the brain can be trained as it does have self-awareness. The back brain has no such thing. So you want to train and saturate the front brain over a period of time with the music that you want to learn and absorb. When you go to play, you will find that you are drawing from this reservoir, from the music that you have listened to so intensely. That's how you increase your musical palate and capabilities.

Finally, the last thing you need to work on is what we all know as the business—networking, getting concerts ... the real world—because you can't just sit at home playing in your room. You have to get on the phone and your computer to connect with other musicians. You have to try and climb up the ladder. It is especially tough to be a jazz musician, but it is a noble profession. If you're a doctor, a lawyer, or an architect, there's a ladder. You go to school ... you meet people in school ... you graduate ... you get jobs ... you help your friends. It's called the old boy network in any profession. Of course it includes women as well and you can profit from these lessons learned for your whole life.

The point is that there is a track, a pathway. Is there a way for jazz musicians? For a long time there used to be. You started by getting gigs as a sideman. Maybe you started playing with Art Farmer, then with Art Blakey, then maybe with Stan Getz, Chet Baker, with Joe Henderson, then Miles Davis or Elvin Jones. But now those guys are all dead, okay?

The guys that have replaced the old masters can not do things the same way anymore. The business changed with very few clubs hiring groups for a week. So life as a working jazz musician today is very different from the times we learned when we came up 60 years ago. Today musicians learn in schools, not on the road like we did. But of course, the best musicians always survive and there is always room for one more badass piano player on the scene, but it is not like it was before.

So those are the things you need to learn. You should also play with other musicians three times a week, three hours each time. You should work on your compositions at night when you feel good, not every day. What do you do every day? Technique, transcription, repertoire ... that's the basic bones of how to become a jazz musician. You do that for three to five years, finally getting out of school. You work on your music until you feel that you are ready make a personal statement and document it on record.

Dave: Learning music has something in common with learning a language. If you learned French in high school or wherever you learned it, you get a lot of the material from books. Maybe your teacher speaks a bit to you. But if you go to France there is going to be something missing from your rendition and that is the sound and flow of the language, but of course you can learn it the best way by being in the country. You watch television or films and eventually you get the sound of what it is to speak the language and then suddenly somebody says you're starting to do very well with this French stuff, etc.

Now in jazz the problem is not the notes that are on paper ... we have plenty of books to describe the harmony. What is not on paper? It is this thing called rhythm. Technically it's called the eighth note feel. It's the way of connecting eighth notes (some people say triplets). It means the flow of the conversation, and it means a dotted eighth note. Sometimes it means a triplet with the second part of the triplet left out. Now on paper I can do that. And I can hear when somebody is doing it correctly. But what is the major challenge and a problem for many people? It is connecting the mind and body. In this case hearing it and having the fingers execute it. I can hear it ... I can recognize it. Oh, that guy swings. The slang word we use is *swinging*.

I can hear somebody playing it ... I know what it is, but as soon as I try to play it I can not do it. It is unbelievable because I had just heard it and I know what it is. Even if I have the written music with a transcription of a beautiful solo, it's incredibly difficult. You can read it as normal written music but you can't get the authentic rhythmic feel. The reason is this is not something you learn intellectually ... or by turning a switch on. I have not met anyone who has been able to show me a better way to learn the basic jazz feel. I wish somebody would, especially if you come from a culture where you don't hear that kind of rhythm, which makes it even more difficult. The problem in my opinion is that just getting that feel and flow can only be learned by intense listening and imitation. It means somebody plays it for you and you copy it like them, just like learning French. All right?

When we talk about transcribing we mean that you are going to take a solo and copy it from soup to nuts, with mistakes included! It's like if I were speaking to you and made you memorize what I say. I would say it over and over again and make you repeat what I said.

In a country like India, that's the way they teach. Nothing is written down because it is all an oral tradition. You sit with the master. In fact a young student will probably live with the master and his family like one of my students did. You just play what the master plays until you get it and then you move on to the next phrase, and the next one, and the next one. And in India, it's about 13 years before you are allowed to play in public, or give a concert. Thirteen years, right? It is probably shorter now. But the oral tradition is still there, and that is the way traditional music is still taught in India, Africa, and other countries.

We can and should use this method to learn jazz. Instead of an Indian teacher we are going to use Miles Davis as our model, and a particular solo from his very famous 1959 record *Kind Of Blue*. The tune is called "Freddy Freeloader." By the way a freeloader is somebody who comes up to you, begging for money. But Freddy was not like that ... he was a friend of the Miles Davis group, doing errands and generally helping out. He was a bartender at the Showboat, a club in Philadelphia and loved to hang out. He was an interesting gentleman whom Richie and I actually met at the Village Vanguard.

"Freddy Freeloader" is a 12-bar blues written by Miles Davis with an unusual turnaround phrase. Now you have to do deep listening since your first goal is to be able to sing along with Miles' trumpet solo, using scat syllables. First singing along with Miles, then evolving to a cappella. (This does not apply to fast double-time passages or uptempo.) What do you think would be the reason that I insist upon you singing the solo before you touch your instrument, even before you put your pen to paper to transcribe it? What does the singing do for you? By singing it you internalize the music physically. It becomes part of your language, part of your physical body. You don't know why ... you are not pressing buttons ... you are not pressing keys ... you are not pushing the notes on an instrument. You are just doing what we do every day which is sing along with some music you love.

By the way, for anyone who purports to be a musician in this world, singing is a necessity, like playing piano. You don't have to be Ella Fitzgerald. But you should be able to vocalize to a certain degree. We have to get past the point of shyness and a certain degree of incompetence and embarrassment from singing. Anytime I tell my saxophone students you have to sing, they go, oh, I don't sing, I play, I push

A Jazz Lecture for the Interested Listener

buttons. So I tell them you are a singer, my friend. The saxophone is an extension of the voice—the piano is an extension of your fingers, which is an extension of your body, which is the extension of your voice. So please, we all sing! So let's get that over with right now ... okay? You may not sing like a professional singer, but close enough is good enough. All right, so now you sing along with the solo. Everybody can do it, you do not have to be super talented. You just have to want to do it.

As I discussed we learn music by osmosis. You learn by listening over and over and over again. And after a while, you're singing it. I bet anyone who is interested in music, if you are a jazz player, or if you are just interested in jazz, I bet right now you can sing along with some solos. This is not difficult ... just don't start with a very difficult solo.

When you sing along you try to imitate everything that Miles played, the notes, of course, an A or a G or whatever, the sound, the dynamics, the articulation, the rhythmic phrasing which is made up of all the things I just said. And hopefully something of the emotion, whatever you feel it is.

Now again you don't have to be a genius to do this. You just have to put the tape on ... listen in the headphones ... walk around with it while you sing along for a couple weeks. Start humming if you feel it. You can use any syllables or consonants ... it doesn't matter. We don't care. There are no rules. There's no "correct way."

The second step for serious jazz students is you write the solo out and that means that by the time you are finished, you figured out all the rhythms and pitches because you have notated it on paper. And when you are finished you feel good ... you have transcribed what Miles Davis played on that famous tune ... you have accomplished something truly worthwhile. Now I know there are many books available with transcriptions of jazz solos with the work already done for you. But it is up to you if you want to get something out of it. You learn the most if you do it on your own. Of course it can be difficult, especially notating the rhythms can be tough. So just slow the tape down and learn how to conduct one, two, three, four, and after a while, you can physically see the architecture. By the way, reading and writing rhythms is just like reading anything ... you get better as you do it. You weren't so good in the second grade, but by the time you were in the fourth grade, you knew more words ... .it's exactly the same with music.

Why do we want you to write out the solo? Because we need it on paper in order to analyze it efficiently, the way classical musicians do. We look at themes and variations and ideas. We figure out what the guy was musically thinking about as best as we can. I'll get a little technical for one moment here. You might say, oh, the chord is an F7 and Miles played a B natural, what was he thinking about? Well, I don't know, maybe the blues scale? We try to get inside the man's brain. This is pretty difficult and really detailed work. The guy has been dead for decades and even if he was alive he couldn't remember what and why he played a particular note. But most of the time we can come up with a hypothesis that is fairly accurate because you know, there are only 12 notes in the end. There are only so many choices. And you know what happens after awhile? You see the same solution,

Preparation & Performance

the same note(s) here again and you think oh, I've heard him play that. He did that three years ago or three solos ago or three measures ago ... so you get familiar with it.

You know what this does for you? It makes it possible for you to intellectually understand more of what's going on. After awhile we take some of the lines ... maybe three or four from the solo and put them on a separate page, leading to writing variations. You now have what you played in the beginning. You choose the "best" lines and memorize them ... transpose them into the 12 keys ... and at different tempos. You then play them on another song, noticing that lines repeat themselves though they may appear to be fresh. These chord progressions come up all the time. Suddenly you have taken Miles Davis and you've made his music your own. This is the process and the goal ... that's why we write it down.

But the most important thing is coming now. To speak the language and to get the inflections and the accents we have to play along with the recording. First you play the solo very slowly like an exercise ... in fact a classical exercise. We will get to the point where you play along with Miles and hopefully you can't tell the difference between you and him. Then you improvise on the piece using it as a reference. This is not a guarantee that tomorrow you will sound like Charlie Parker or Sonny Rollins. One thing is for sure ... you will know a lot better what it sounds like and feels like on your instrument. This isn't talking about the music ... it's about doing it!

Of course, after a while you build up a repertoire of transcribed solos. You work with them to the bone, but the end is within sight. I usually say transcribing and learning five to six major solos are enough. The student has learned five or six solos in detail meaning having written them out ... sung along with them ... leading to analyzation and memorization. When they finish the five transcriptions it could be 20 to 40 hours of work per solo. The process gets faster as they become better at it. By then the musician should incorporate and use a combination of the solos and "quotes" on the bandstand. When they borrow something played by a master you can feel the beauty of the process. We are all "borrowing" from everybody since Louis Armstrong. It's a big reservoir meant to dip in and out of. For experienced musicians like us, we can probably say the student just quoted something from Rollins in 1958, take two with Max Roach on drums, etc. Of course, what we are saying is that the process is valuable and represents positive work, predicated on wanting to REALLY know what is behind the curtain. You couldn't be more complimented at that point of your evolution. You are part of the transcription club meaning you gain respect from the elders. For someone of our experience, to say, you sound like Coltrane in 1958, man, that's great. We know you worked hard because nobody gets there by swallowing a pill or by taking a walk in the morning. It involves many hours of work.

I don't know anything more important for a musician than doing the transcription routine. You don't need school for this. I'm not saying don't go to school, I'm saying you don't need school in these times. You don't need a teacher for this but of course a teacher can guide you. You don't need anything except a battery-powered tape recorder, computer, your instrument, pencil, paper, bread, and water. You also need time, and most of all desire. You must want to do it.

Did we all do it like this? No. Did Charlie Parker do it like this? I don't think so, he didn't have batteries. You know what I'm saying? But did Miles Davis listen to his teacher? Did Charlie Parker talk about his teacher in Kansas City? Yes. Every great musician, if they are telling the truth, will tell you it was him, not me. In my case I go to John Coltrane and Sonny Rollins, because we always give it to the fathers since we are their sons. If we study them we know exactly how great they are, because we now have them inside ourselves.

Ten Thousand Ways

Richie: Now that you have theoretically mastered transcription and application of the transcription, another useful thing to work on is the reharmonization of standards. Transcription of the jazz solo is predominantly a linear and melodic exercise. Reharmonization deals with the harmony of the standard tune retaining the melody exactly. Reharmonization will give you he ability to personalize the approach to a standard tune and have it show your individual creative take on the standard.

Dave: Let's talk about how we approach standards like "All The Things You Are," written in 1943 by Jerome Kern. It is a classic jazz tune ... the melody is simple but it is a difficult tune, and that makes it challenging to improvise on it. It shows your ability to be able to negotiate harmonies that move around rather quickly and that's why we like it. We also like the melody but what Richie has done is put new harmony to it.

Richie: A little preamble about why this tune. There are certain tunes in the jazz repertoire—I would say about 40 or 50—that we call chestnuts. It means everybody knows them. Most of them are great tunes. Sometimes you don't want to play them, not because they're not great, but because they've been recorded too many times, etc.

But they are great for a reason. These are the tunes you have to learn if you want to know the jazz repertoire. This is because any original composition that you or Wayne Shorter or anybody else will write is based one way or the other on these standards. They are the foundational vehicles of jazz music. In classical music it is Bach, Mozart, Beethoven, Chopin, Schumann, etc. They are the foundation ... the historical record. In the jazz standard world you've got Jerome Kern, Cole Porter, Johnny Mandel, Bronisław Kaper, and more composers like that. Considering what a microsurgeon has to learn about the names of the nerves and other parts in the hands, the parts we have to learn don't seem too numerous. They have to absorb a hundred thousand different things. Of course, they go to medical school for ten years and in jazz sometimes the schools are just a section in the basement, passed along from one guy to the next.

In the repertoire, "All The Things You Are" is one of the tunes you have to learn. Now I don't like this tune the way it was written in its original form. I never liked it because it is very symmetrical. You know, in 1943, it was an amazing, brilliant, scandalous, genius kind of a tune. They said nobody will ever be able to sing that tune, it was from a Broadway show, as most of these tunes were ... *Oklahoma, West Side Story, My Fair Lady* ... shows like that. Of course these tunes also had lyrics. Sometimes horrible lyrics, sometimes deep, depending on who wrote them. All right, Richard Rogers wrote the most amazing melodies with the worst harmonies.

So what we do is take a tune and do what Bill Evans once told me. He said Richie, you better learn these tunes whether you like them or not—no one cares, learn them and love them. He said of course the best way to love them is to make them your own. In order to make them your own, it involves reharmonization, personalization, re-orchestration, and recomposition.

Now this is still a great tune and with every great tune there are at least a thousand different ways to do it. The fundamental structure, the infrastructure of the tune can be manipulated because it is so well-written. A great piece of meat and an amazing fresh fish can be prepared in 10,000 ways. A meatball is a meatball ... you know what I am saying.

So now I feel that "All The Things You Are" is a fantastic tune that I didn't like so much but now I like it because I did it over with a radical reharmonization and made it my own.

When you listen to a standard, try to listen with more open ears and find the quality in each tune. Not like, oh, I like it or I don't like it. No one cares if you like it or not. The question is why is it good, why do you like it? Listen with these questions in mind. Of course you are going to listen with emotion, but focus on the treatment of the tune for awhile. The melody is given, but what you put around it and what you put inside of it is critically important. It means very smooth, arpeggiated, pianistic passages, come from Ravel and Debussy, not from Jerome Kern, not from 1943. My reharmonization brings more color to the original chord progression and the rhythmic placement of the chords is different. The original tune is very symmetrical, but we don't want that. We want to take the squareness out of it, to make it more round, more luxurious, more engaging, more inviting. I really love our recorded duo version of "All The Things You Are" on our CD *Outspoken*. (See the "Richie's Tour" chapter for highlights of our recordings.)

Dave: If you are not a musician here's one thing you will get from even doing a little bit of this. You will get an appreciation of what quality means and why something is universally acknowledged as great. It is very easy to say something is good because somebody tells you that something is good, or a magazine tells you it's good or your father tells you it's good. And that's okay when you are young. But when you get more mature, when you are somewhere in your twenties, you start to really want to know what good means to you. What is really good and what's not so good. What's really great? Why is a $400 bottle of wine better than one for four dollars? Why do you have to pay $300,000 for a Lamborghini or a Maserati but only $20,000 for a Chevrolet? They both drive you to where you want to go, but what is the difference? Well, there is a difference and some people know it and incorporate it into their daily lives.

I care about music and I want to know why they say Sonny Rollins was as great as he was. I want to know why Miles Davis was so great. I don't want to just believe somebody telling me that.

I don't want to believe it because a history book told me. When you get into this level of analysis and of listening, you get into the DNA, you get into the molecules, you get into why it is great because you're going to really understand it. So there is something here that can be gained by everyone who reads this, regardless of whether you ever want to play music or not. And that is focus and understanding quality. This assumes, with the assistance of your teacher who should be able to tell you who and why to transcribe a chosen artist, you pick a solo of quality. (By the way I should transcribe on my instrument to get started.) The teacher should say to you here are three possible solos that will help you with your specific weaknesses ... you choose one. If the teacher doesn't help you, go to another person, somebody else who knows—who you have respect for, who you know, who knows the music—probably some older person.

We really hope that this information gives you a better and deeper understanding about the music that we love so much and that we have been playing for the last 60 years. Even if you are not a musician we hope that you can gain some inspiration and insight out of this and that it helps you to get more enjoyment and a deeper understanding.

Our Approach to Preparing for Concerts and Recordings

Richie: This is a free ranging discussion in which Dave and I discuss how we approach playing concerts and recording situations, how we choose instruments, sidemen, repertoire etc. This is more for the professional jazz musician but anyone who is a seriously interested jazz listener can find a lot of information that will help to understand our music, and jazz in general.

Choosing Players and Instruments

Richie: Today Dave and I will be discussing the specific relationships as related to chromaticism in terms of my chordal accompaniments. We will examine solos between the piano and sax or any harmonic instrument and soloist. We also examine the various functions of the piano in the context of a full rhythm section—piano, bass and drums—in support of and interacting with the soloist. We will also be talking about some of our specific likes and dislikes, things that we avoid and pursue in terms of what kinds of musical support we want in the context of small group improvisation in a chromatic and contemporary jazz setting.

Dave, can you tell me what your thoughts are about choosing either the soprano or the tenor sax for a tune during the course of an evening?

Dave: Because the soprano is in the same register as the piano for the duo and chamber music, I enjoy playing that horn in those types of musical settings—it doesn't stick out as much. It is hard to control the upper register, as we know. Our mutual friend, bass player Ron McClure used to say, it sounds like a pet store on fire. This was in the 1980s and it was obviously true and it took me a minute to get that together ... and I'm still working on it. But the soprano really is good when playing unison melodies. And it really works for intimate kinds of music, right?

The tenor is the big one, the daddy. When you bring out the tenor with a quiet sound often you need the drums and bass to offset the range. You do need the bottom because otherwise the tenor gets a little lost in the low register.

Richie: So are the tenor and the piano practical in terms of blend?

Dave: On paper it is and you can make it work.

Richie: We do make it work.

Dave: It depends on the range of the tune. The thing with the piano is that from middle C down that's where the tenor saxophone is home. And that is not the most brilliant part of the piano. So there is a tendency to go to the bottom and then the tenor is low and it can easily get a little foggy. Which means that the tenor has to go up and play higher, which John Coltrane obviously figured out.

Richie: So Dave, do you play differently with a pianist like me on a tune like "Softly, As In A Morning Sunrise"? Let's say as opposed to another good pianist that you've never played with before. What specifically determines your choices and are they based on the limitations or gifts of the pianist?

Dave: It depends on whom I'm going to play with and if I have any previous experience with him or her. You can't substitute for experience. "Softly, As In A Morning Sunrise," to use that tune as an example, is a standard played a lot, dozens of times. So you have to know the direction that the accompanists want to go, especially the drummer and bassist in that situation. A great deal of what is happening has to do with experience and common knowledge of being aware of each other and then building upon it.

With you, we've had a long musical relationship with a desire to communicate verbally as well. You and I seem to have been on the same page right from our beginnings in the late 1960s into the '70s. Everybody is different and when I play with another piano player, bassist, and drummer, obviously it is a different result. But I know with you, because of our common experience, I can pretty much go anywhere. This is especially true when we play with Quest. When I try to describe that feeling I always say that this is the one band where I don't have to think about anything other than myself. I just listen to myself and to what is going on around me, meaning we are able to pull the music off without me having to be overly concerned.

Richie: Let me put you on the spot and ask you a very specific question from your long history of touring around the world. You are known as one of the guys who goes and finds a really good local rhythm section. So now let's say you're going to Belgium and you don't have your normal cats there, but you have a really good piano player. You don't know him ... .you never played with him but he's good and around the age of 40 meaning he is probably experienced. You're going to play "Softly, As In A Morning Sunrise." What are you going to do?

Dave: I can't assume that he will be able to jump on the same musical bandwagon that you or I am on.

Richie: Why can't you assume it? Because it is not common knowledge or because chromaticism is not common practice?

Dave: It is not common practice and to exaggerate a little, I would know after eight bars ...

I mean pretty quickly. I would probably play harmonically safer than normal. I probably wouldn't just throw it right out there. I thought about this a lot when I wrote my chromatic book and started teaching that material. You don't try to force a square into a circle, something that took me awhile to admit. I used to force myself onto a poor rhythm section to make a point. Not a psychological point, not to gain anything, but to make a point of like well, this is the way I play and you have to accompany me. In some cases I might be prejudging a little too quickly because who knows what the musician's capabilities are. Given that the piano player is playing with me, maybe that's a side of him that hasn't emerged before.

Richie: Maybe he wants to learn.

Dave: That's the thing you can't generalize.

Richie: Would you talk to him before the concert in the dressing room?

Dave: No, not about the music except maybe talk about the form or whatever is easy to describe.

Richie: Why not?

Dave: I wouldn't want to make things more nervous and intimidating for him. They know how I play. Our history is long and well documented. I always think of Joe Henderson who for so many years picked up rhythm sections. Everybody knew the six or seven tunes he was going to play and he expected them to know these tunes and he was right. We come in with a dossier already that's been documented for 50-plus years. And in that sense they kind of have an idea of what will happen. In this case, they probably know a version of you and me playing the music. So it's even more specific than with just another piano player.

Richie: Can you tell me what you like and need in a pianist accompanying you ... what to avoid and what you don't like?

Dave: First of all I don't want to be crowded.

Richie: What does crowded mean musically?

Dave: It means overplaying rhythmically ... comping too much, staying in the same register too long, same touch, no dynamics.

Richie: Can you be crowded harmonically too?

Dave: Maybe the piano player tried to do more than even you would, bro, therefore complicating things. Maybe they think the answer is this particular voicing and then they get hung up on it. You know, it's jazz, and we try to be open. And even in this pretty refined area of knowledge we are talking about we still try to be loose, as jazz music is.

Richie: I would say in general an accepting attitude to begin with when you go up on the bandstand whether you know the person or not is very important, especially with a pianist who is sensitive. Playing with him for first time, he will appreciate this accepting attitude and use that to build his confidence, because it is going to be compared to whomever.

Dave: Now we are talking about the psychological aspects of what we do which is meeting new people for the first time, trying to make music with them, and that is an extremely challenging task. So you want to make it as comfortable as possible for them. You want to get through the night, get paid, get to your hotel room, and not make a big deal out of set two for example. You're not trying to make a point and that's the difference to 30 years ago and now. Then I was trying to make a point ... this is what I do, come on with me or whatever. But now if I have to play more inside to make the gig more comfortable, I will.

Richie: Because you can.

Preparation & Performance

Concert vs. Recording

Richie: How different is a concert to a recording?

Dave: A recording is memorialized forever and therefore you probably don't walk in with a pickup rhythm section unless you just play standards.

Richie: And usually there is a rehearsal for a recording so at least, you know the other musicians a little. This is a very important thing to do because this is a process that goes on mostly behind the scenes. Let's say a piano player calls you and says Dave, I want you to play on my record. He sends you his music, he can play good but he is not number one. He wants to learn from you and he wants your name on his record. So you would have more preparation and more demands, even if you are a sideman.

Dave: Possibly, but also you don't want to poison the atmosphere.

Richie: So how do you get to that point without destroying the scene? I mean you have to protect yourself.

Dave: It usually ends up that I am running the record date, and so would you. It's because we are senior, and if it is only out of respect and because of our knowledge, that would be enough. The other musicians in general want that as long as you are cool and don't sit there nitpicking and so on because that would not do any good. For example a bit of rearranging could make the tune work much better. Or the tempo feels too slow, etc., etc. This suggestive atmosphere can be a sensitive matter and you can always retreat immediately if there is any push back. We are just trying to make the tune more of a success.

Richie: Very good. When you play in a traditional piano, bass, and drums rhythm section, do you find yourself focusing on a certain instrument at different times? What determines your choices? Are they automatic, reflexive, or instinctive? Are they conscious or unconscious? And is it important for a saxophone or trumpet player to know the musician's preferences and speak about them to the pianist?

Dave: It depends how much time we have to work together.

Richie: Let's say you play for five nights in a row in Paris.

Dave: If we have that much time together we can probably sit down before the gig and talk about the music. For example I might say to a piano player, "Here are a couple of voicings that I like to use on this tune. When you hear Richie play it he did this kind of thing and it would be nice if you could include that into the scenario for the next few nights," and so on.

Richie: And if you only have one night?

Dave: As I said, there's not much you can do except keep the vibe cool because you are not going to win any points by trying to get heavy and say it has to be this way or it has to be like that. This is jazz, it is the way it is and that's the way it goes. A guy can't change the way he plays in 10 minutes. You are pretty much stuck with what you got. Hopefully you did some research ... you talked to somebody who played with this guy before. Hopefully you hear that he is known to be really good

Our Approach to Preparing for Concerts and Recordings

and modern, that he plays like Keith Jarrett, Chick Corea, or Herbie Hancock ... we know what that means! But let me say this—jazz is drums and my first job is to get the drummer on my side. First drums, definitely and personality-wise because without them on your side you are dead in the water.

Richie: Let's talk about what we mean by the drums. This is how I feel and I think you feel the same way. If you have a great drummer and you have an okay piano player and an okay bass player and a lousy saxophone player you still can have a good band. If you have a shitty drummer, even if you have a great piano player and a great bass player and a great saxophone player, you still have a terrible band. The heart of any jazz band is the drums because historically and emotionally that's what distinguishes it from classical music. Without the drums you have beautiful chamber music. I had a trio with violinist Gregor Huebner and bassist George Mraz. We made three recordings for ACT Records ... played many concerts ... people loved it, but it was not really a jazz band. Improvisational/contemporary music, yeah, but jazz, no. Maybe this is a little too extreme for the younger generation, but I really think it's true. Why the drums, what is so great about the drums? Energy squared and percussion projected.

Take Miles's 1960s band member Tony Williams. Tony stops playing and then you have Wayne Shorter, Herbie, and Ron Carter playing a beautiful ballad or fast time. Then when you hear the music with Tony it sounds complete and orchestrated. It is the function of the rhythm section ... the heart of a jazz band.

So that's why you say, and I totally agree, that the first thing you listen to is the drums. Then second?

Dave: The chord player, if there is one. But also the bass, that is not in the forgotten category. The truth is that the bass makes it possible for the drums to be free in creatively supporting the music in the band. Most bass players are very good and remember, they can only play one note at the time. The bass player is very important but my first duty will be of course to the drums and then to the piano or guitar.

Richie: I agree, but I have to say one thing in defense of the bass. For example in the Miles Davis Quintet with Herbie Hancock, Ron Carter, and Tony Williams there would be no great music without a great bass player. Because Ron Carter was the kind of invisible anchor and solid stabilizing element that gave Tony Williams his great freedom. Because Tony and Herbie were active rhythmically and interactive and Ron was the perfect accompaniment, right? Ron Carter made a lot of things possible because he held down the fort and he liked doing it. It's not like he was a gazelle on the bass like Eddie Gomez or George Mraz in the upper register. No ... that would have not made the Miles Davis band work ... all those subtle grooves, those quick changes of tempos, of dynamics. So the bass was kind of the invisible hero.

Dave: It's when they lay the foundation to a house in concrete, that's the bass. And then the walls come up, right?

Richie: Yeah bro!

2019

Piano and Guitar Accompanists

Richie: Okay, Dave. Who are your favorite accompanists on the piano and guitar and why?

Dave: Well, you are my favorite on piano because of your rhythmic and harmonic thing. So you have a combination of both and also, you know what I need. I enjoy all the guys I play with, and I feel privileged because just in the last three weeks I played with Kenny Werner, Phil Markowitz, Bobby Avey, and in Chicago with John Campbell. I mean, most of the time they are not as active as you because they probably don't have a chance to play as much, even the great ones I mentioned. It is the common language that you and I use. Maybe because they're not playing with somebody like me who leaves them a chance to do it? It isn't an ego thing. We are who we are and we have a special way which has an effect. That might make another guy say, "I always wanted to play this way so I would like to play with Dave because he calls for that kind of stuff." Marc Copland for instance plays very soft and he is quite laid back. He leaves a lot of space and for the most part he plays in a certain register of the piano, in the middle.

Richie: He is not active rhythmically?

Our Approach to Preparing for Concerts and Recordings

Dave: No, he is not that rhythmically creative, but his voicing are to die for.

Richie: Do you like it?

Dave: I enjoy it very much. I can play very lyrically with him.

Richie: What about burn?

Dave: He can burn but he is not doing it that often. We just did a record where he burned.

Richie: When we play I am physically active because I think I know what you need. You want to keep the music going, but you also want space. What is the point where it becomes too active?

Dave: Crowding the notes, playing too much rhythm, overshadowing the drums even. I mean we've had this discussion for years. We want you and the drums to be together. You played with Al Foster who has a certain type of interactive style.

Richie: Absolutely.

Dave: Al was very complimentary and then we started playing with Billy Hart who is rhythmically at lot more independent and it changed our playing, which is what we wanted. You determine the drummer's style and you try to fit your style within it if you can. Sometimes it works and sometimes it doesn't. If you have dozens of years of experience like we do you know what is going to work because we have been there ... we have a communication.

2016

Preparation & Performance

Richie: Do you consider the guitar as an equal in value to a piano in terms of comping, and If not, why?

Dave: Well, the guitar can really play rhythm. But when the piano starts playing rhythmically it can be overpowering for the soloist depending on who is playing. What idiom needs that kind of rhythm? Rock, funk, whatever you call it. John Abercrombie and Vic Juris were my favorite accompanists. They played smoothly but percussively at times. A guitar can play a fifth or a fourth interval rhythmically and it makes sense. If you do that on the piano it is not in the best taste.

Richie: The guitar has amplification and two notes together are a lot stronger than on a piano because they come popping out.

Dave: And if the guitarist is using his rhythmic aspect of comping sparingly, then I am happy. Of course with voicings guitarists are handicapped since they only have four fingers and an open string. They can't play a six, seven, or eight note chord voicing which a pianist can do in a minute. So you can't expect that as you can't get water from a stone. I would much rather have a guitar play colors. That's the other thing. The electric guitar can get great colors with all those pedals. I want them to do color and rhythm and leave the harmonic thing out for the most part. If I have both piano and guitar it's another story—the guitar becomes like a second horn.

Richie: Let me ask you specifically. You played with great guitar players—John Scofield when he was young, you played with Pat Metheny, Mick Goodrick, Vic Juris, you played with John McLaughlin in the early '70s, and with John Abercrombie over the years. You played with the major guitar players of the world. So who do you like and why, and what was it like starting your career by playing on John McLaughlin's recording *My Goals Beyond*?

Dave: On *My Goals Beyond* I played on the more ethnic ensemble tunes and I was like a flavor. I did like John Abercrombie, may he rest in peace, because he was very discreet and he didn't overplay. When a guitar is overplaying it can really get in your way, almost more than a piano. Because the electric guitar is out front physically and that speaker is out front while the piano is in the back. Let's face it. The guitar has a lot of presence because it has volume. Of course in the rock and pop tradition the guitar is number one. Our generation was affected by rock. We grew up with Jimi Hendrix and the Cream, etc. So we have been influenced by that ... we grew up in that era. Jazz or not, we definitely heard Jimi Hendrix.

Richie: What about John Scofield?

Dave: John is a single-line monster. I asked him to stay away from harmony when he played with me. When he was with me in the late 1970s, he said he wanted to play that stuff that Steve Grossman and I played with Elvin Jones. We did not have a chord instrument in Elvin's band so it was very open. One night we were playing Seventh Avenue South in the Village in New York City ... my group with John Scofield, Terumasa Hino, Ron McClure, and Adam Nussbaum, and on occasion Kenny Kirkland. Miles Davis came down with Bill Evans, the sax player, to hear my group. After the set I hung with Miles and asked him what do you think about

Our Approach to Preparing for Concerts and Recordings

my guitar player? Because I knew that Miles was putting a new band together. Miles said I don't like him and I said he *will* be your guitarist but tell him to stay away from voicings ... just play those great blues-tinged lines! In the 1980s Scofield was really a good fit with Miles. He played single notes ... he had the rock influence. You don't hear that in the other guys so much.

Richie: Scofield played great on *Decoy* and was perfect for Miles. With Mike Stern you have a total rock influence, like Hendrix. In John's case he didn't forget he was a jazz player primarily.

Dave: Stern is not my favorite guitar accompanist.

Richie: What about John McLaughlin?

Dave: John is always the lead guy and didn't play much with keyboards.

Richie: If you remember, with the Mahavishnu Orchestra he had Jan Hammer but there was never a real interaction between the two, it was just chords.

Dave: Mahavishnu Orchestra was more of a rock and roll band than a jazz band.

All Piano Players are Geniuses

Richie: You played with many great guitar players, but you played with even more great piano players like Chick Corea and McCoy Tyner. Did you ever play with Bill Evans?

Dave: I sat in with him for one tune with Philly Joe Jones playing drums.

Richie: You also played with Phil Markowitz, Kenny Werner, Marc Copland, Bobby Avey, and Bobo Stenson.

Dave: Number one, all piano players are geniuses!

Richie: It's called eight octaves, two pedals, harmony, melody, and rhythm. In other words, there are so many things to know.

Dave: Piano players write the best tunes, they are the most educated, they know everything from left to right and the reverse. Most piano players fulfill that duty. Bebop guys are maybe a little bit more specialized because they are more blues oriented. Now with this said, we are talking about mostly white guys who are very classically trained.

Richie: McCoy Tyner was not a white guy and he was classically trained at the Philadelphia Academy.

Dave: Talking generalities. Each of these piano players has their own personality. But when you play with someone like McCoy, the same I would imagine with Herbie Hancock, who I have not played with, or Chick Corea, you are walking into their territory because they are senior. Obviously they are more recognized by the world and they have a palette that they've been using to be as successful as they are. We know their names ... they do not need a second name because they have a life-long history of performing.

So I walk in and I'm not senior. That's the opposite as if I play with a pickup group, so now I am the guy coming into that situation. And you of all people know Chick

Corea had such a clarity of technique that it makes you think how clean can I play? McCoy Tyner is more like a palette. He's like a painter with all the colors in front of him. Playing with these guys means being careful as to which part of the painting you are looking at.

Richie: You had the rare opportunity to play with Chick when you were a kid in 1968–69 and later in the lofts. He loved you. And you went with him on a world tour in 1978. What would you say the main differences in his playing were between 1968 and 1978, and why?

Dave: Chick, as a member of the Pete La Roca group (with Steve Swallow on bass) did some of the best piano playing I've ever heard in my life. It was incredibly interesting rhythmically and harmonically.

Richie: Documented on one record called *Turkish Women At The Bath* from 1967.

Dave: More or less. During my time with Pete we had different piano players and bassists, George Cables, Joanne Brackeen, we even had Mike Garson for a minute. The difference with Chick and others is that you could tell he was a good drummer. The bar line was a "movable feast" because Chick was completely free within the beat ... he could do anything. He really is a time wizard.

Richie: Time and harmony.

Dave: He had everything down ... definitely the best musician I have ever known, let alone played with. Concerning how he changed, one could easily say "evolved." Everybody changes over time ... in some cases to the positive, in others you can't be academically sure, but you could feel the change in someone's playing. You are not sure if it is as good as it used to be.

Richie: What happened on that tour you played with Chick in 1978?

Dave: On that tour the music was written and I was the main soloist. Every night we played a duo, either "Lush Life" or "Crystal Silence" and of course I enjoyed playing with him very much. There were other things going on on that tour, personal dynamics that we don't have to mention here. But he is an amazing musician. You can't take that away from him. I never played with Keith Jarrett who obviously is another master and an amazing musician. And I never played with Herbie but I did play a few gigs with McCoy. And by that time McCoy was playing a bit different than he played in his heyday.

Richie: What would you say was the main difference between the harmonic content of Chick's music when he played with you and Pete La Roca in 1969?

Dave: A lot of elements of 20th century music sneaking in in time, like clusters and flat nine voicings in the middle of "There's No Greater Love." He would just throw stuff around harmonically. He definitely knew 20th century music. When we lived in the loft together he was practicing the Charles Ives and Alban Berg piano sonatas besides Monk and Bud. Chick was in my opinion the most informed of all the pianists you mentioned. And he even played trumpet. As far as him changing harmonically, *Light As A Feather* and *Return To Forever* were not quite the best harmonic vehicles around. But he still played his ass off no matter the content.

Our Approach to Preparing for Concerts and Recordings

Richie: How is Chick as an accompanist in a jazz situation?

Dave: He could be good, it's a matter of attitude. He could be as supportive as you are if he wanted to be ... setting up rhythmical hits but he usually has another agenda. Also he didn't play with those kind of horn players, though he did some records with Wayne Shorter in the 1970s ... one offs.

Richie: In the 1960s Wayne Shorter, Joe Henderson, Freddie Hubbard, McCoy Tyner, Herbie Hancock, Elvin Jones, Tony Williams, and many other used to play and record together on many records. But in the early '70s they all became leaders and started to hire younger musicians. It was kind of a loss, don't you think?

Dave: It was, when we all become leaders and want to get our names out there. I've been thinking about it lately.

Richie: I remember once we were in San Francisco playing at Todd Barkan's Keystone Korner club, staying at Arthur Baron's house. So we came in a couple days early and there was a superb band playing at the Keystone Korner—Sonny Rollins, McCoy Tyner, Ron Carter, and Elvin Jones. It was some of the worst music I ever heard. I couldn't believe it. These cats were fighting on stage! And I could see Todd Barkan thinking—I hired the most famous guys so I can charge $40 at the door and this is the result? It was really weird ... not happening.

Dave: It doesn't work unless everybody gives up their individual egos.

Richie: It was not organic. Maybe because they are all leaders with their own bands.

Dave: I just played a couple of weeks ago with Esperanza Spalding, Terri Lyne Carrington, and Kenny Werner who hired them. It was his group for a few nights in Boston. We didn't see the music until we had a short rehearsal before the gig. The concert was as smooth as it could be. Esperanza was great, I had never met her before. Terri Lyne was as cooperative as she could be. They were really great. NO EGOS! So when you come into a situation with people who are equal or on a higher level or more famous, it's about everybody loosening their egos up. That's not something everybody can do, and that's why sometimes the music doesn't work. I can't say this about Sonny Rollins or McCoy Tyner, They're not very egotistical from what I know about them, definitely not McCoy. But somehow, sometimes things just don't work because nobody wants to say anything or they don't want to step on somebody else's foot. It's personal ... it's human stuff. Just like in a corporation where one guy is not in accord with the leadership and you have to deal with it.

Richie: Jazz is a music of self-expression. If you don't have enough of a confident ego, you will never make it. Classical music is about the composer, Mozart, Beethoven ... all written. Interpretation? Yes, ten percent, five percent. Buy ten recordings of Chopin's "Preludes" by Vladimir Horowitz, Arthur Rubinstein, and others. The recordings are very much the same except for Glenn Gould, because he was different.

2016

Comping

Dave: Okay, now since we haven't been talking a lot about you and me, let me ask you a few things. What do you consider your specific role comping for me?

Richie: It is to provide an absolute creative, musical, harmonic, and rhythmic environment so that you can play whatever you want at any time and still feel comfortable. And not just comfortable but supported. Sometimes the most important thing I can do is not play and lay out. Then there are times when less is less. This may mean I have to wait and enter with something which is really needed and critical. It is such a delicate fabric, the balance between soloist and accompanist. Me, the chord guy, can easily destroy this relationship. If you are going in a certain direction and I don't pick it up harmonically and rhythmically with your placement, I can ruin your idea of the moment and throw you off. You are not going to get mad ... you will just say okay, because it's always choices in this music. There are very few choices in classical music. It is all written ... everyone knows what's coming. So I have to create the proper environment. Now, this is very difficult especially with time constraints. After all we don't have all day to make these decisions and moves.

The pianist is the helmsman of the rhythm section controlling them in a positive way when needed. This is what the great bands of Miles Davis always did, especially with Herbie Hancock. They supported Miles incredibly and interacted with him on occasion ... and for Wayne Shorter also. I have been thinking about this. In Miles Davis's third great quintet with Chick Corea, Dave Holland, Jack DeJohnette, and Wayne Shorter, they were supporting Miles, but they also played very free for themselves. For me the second great Miles quintet with Wayne, Herbie, Ron, and

Our Approach to Preparing for Concerts and Recordings

Tony was probably the greatest band in the history of contemporary jazz ... right? I'm not talking about Charlie Parker and Dizzy Gillespie and Thelonious Monk for example.

Dave: These bebop groups did not stay together ... they were not consistent. Rhythm section interaction is a 1960s innovation.

Richie: To answer your question going back to what you expect from your piano player, I am listening with every ounce of my attention to what I think your intention is and where you want to go. This is a very interesting game because it's never the same because you also keep your ears open to that situation. You make sure it's never the same. And that's what's so difficult about playing jazz on a night to night basis. We try to be different all the time. In other words, it has to have intrinsic value and hopefully it's different from the night before. It's very hard and we never win one hundred percent. But it's okay because if we play the same set, the same tunes, for six nights in a row at the Village Vanguard this is where the creativity enters.

That's what Miles did, that was his template. They played the same 20 tunes, "Stella By Starlight," "Walking," etc. They played all the same tunes, but it was different every night. And also the musicians had a chance to develop these same tunes keeping the repertoire fresh. This is very different than bebop which you play and don't worry about being different. You have a language and you are creative within it. But as a pianist when I play for you I have the most freedom because I do not know what will happen next. Jazz is the sound of surprise and that's the truth. I want to be surprised. You want to surprise me and yourself. So I, as your pianist, have a microsecond envelope in which to make a decision. And let me tell you, these musical decisions are not like should we go out to eat or should we stay in? No, these decisions happen in a nanosecond ... they are reflexive ... they're not intellectual. They don't come from the front of the brain. They are based on lots of experience, intuition, and thought from playing with you over years and years.

Dave: So how do you know when you are playing too much and you might be getting in the way?

Richie: When you stop playing for a long time. You are not pissed, it is not a value judgment. It's just like okay, Richie's got it. This "giving it up" point is very important. This is very critical. Let's say you are standing by a river and it is moving. You put your foot in the river. Where's the water that you put your foot in? The water has already gone. You can't get it back ... you can't make it stop. So there are no tracks to follow like there are in classical music. I'm always thinking in terms of classical music which I love. It is just a different function that we can't get back on an existing track. So my tendency even though it doesn't sound that way is to underplay. You and I have been playing together for over 50 years. Sometimes I listen with horror to our really early music. I mean, I listen to our first recording *First Visit*, 1972, recorded in Japan with Dave Holland and Jack DeJohnette. I am not happy with how I played, but the content was good.

Dave: And I played out of tune...

Richie: But it's ok ... we were young, in our 20s. That's the way it's supposed to be unless you are a genius. With one ear I am listening to Dave and then with the other ear, I'm listening to the drums and the bass ... I have to.

The Masters

Dave: You had some masters you played with, most notably Stan Getz and Chet Baker. And they are very much alike as artists coming from the same era and playing from a similar song book ... standards from Broadway, movies from Hollywood, plus a good helping of original compositions from present and former sidemen.

Richie: This was my beginning, like you had Elvin Jones and Miles Davis, I had Stan Getz and Chet Baker. Stan was my first important gig. I was not a baby. I was 25, but I was inexperienced in playing with young masters like Dave Holland on bass and Jack DeJohnette on drums. They both had just finished playing with Miles Davis for a couple of years with Chick Corea on piano. They certainly didn't need young Richie, they didn't need the little green kid.

Dave: But Stan wanted you, obviously that's why.

Richie: Chick Corea recommended me. He started Return to Forever so he told Stan to hire me. Getting hired or fired was the way band leaders put bands together in those days. It was very ad hoc ... no big deal except to me! He auditioned Ralph Towner and Hal Galper ... they were not hired. He liked me first of all because I have a certain kind of energy. Also like him, I am Russian Jewish. And I had chops. He liked that! He liked his piano players to be very fluent.

He loved Chick Corea but he actually liked Herbie Hancock the best because Herbie could really swing the most and had the best taste. Stan and Herbie played together on the recording *Bob Brookmeyer and Friends*, recorded in New York in 1964 which featured Bob, Stan, Herbie Hancock, Gary Burton, Elvin Jones, and Ron Carter ... quite a cast!

Dave: Did Stan ever say anything to you about comping?

Richie: Yes. The first thing he said, and he was trying to con me by saying, "You are going to be a big star, kid. I like the way you play, great and beautiful intros, but you are too active when you accompany me. I don't need that much ... leave me some space. The bottom range of my saxophone gets covered right away. My low notes need space. Don't comp ... just take your left hand away." That was his first advice. Then he said, "Be careful concerning the register of your chords in ballads which is not right. Move them up. This is a tenor sax. I don't play soprano." He was very cool. Then of course, I was comping too hard even when we were not burning. He loved the way Horace Silver rhythmically comped for him.

Dave: That was way back in the 1950s!

Richie: Yes. Horace had this very light rhythmic thing, like a guitar. He had great time and a solid groove which Stan loved.

Dave: Stan was such a natural with great time. He might have been one of the most talented of all jazz musicians ever.

Our Approach to Preparing for Concerts and Recordings

Richie: He was the Michael Brecker of his era, the way people look at Michael in this era.

Dave: But Michael Brecker practiced a lot. Stan Getz never practiced. He had a natural ear, natural time, and a natural technique ... the whole package.

Richie: A very important note, Stan had a small town nervous system. He was not ready for success. He was very much like Elvis in that respect. Stan was already famous as a kid when he was 16 with the Four Brothers in the Woody Herman Big Band. And then in 1963 he recorded "The Girl from Ipanema" and it became the number one song in the world. Not the number one jazz song, but number one on the pop charts. This song was in every jukebox, in every bar, in every city around the world. It was a complete accident, but he became the most famous saxophone player in the world. It was unbelievable.

Dave: He was the most famous jazz musician on a level with Louis Armstrong and Duke Ellington.

Richie: When I played with Stan in the 1970s his popularity was equal to Duke Ellington so when we played a club or concert it was always full. Tuesday night is usually a dead night in a jazz club. But when Stan played a club like the Colonial in Toronto it was packed every night.

Stan, bless his heart, was a complex person. He was probably bipolar. I'm sure he was schizophrenic and all the success and fame did not help him. It encouraged his mean nature and split personality. He was a total Dr. Jekyll and Mr. Hyde, but only off the band stand, it never showed in his playing. Musically he was also unique because he admitted that he did not know much about music. But he seemed infallible to me and told me, "I am all feeling, and all atmosphere, I just play off the last thing I heard."

This is another subject. Sometimes I would get lost listening to Jack because I was nervous and he was at times "taking no prisoners." When Jack played behind Stan he was very cool and more conservative than his norm with a lot of clear downbeats. But for the piano solos he just stopped playing those downbeats. Instead Jack played these brilliant mysterious accents that could be uncomfortable for me to play with at the time. But when you listen back they sounded like an orchestration ... like the percussion section in the Bartók Concerto For Orchestra. It's almost independent and Stan and Jack were similar in that they were so gifted that they did not have to rely on their intellect. So for me being a young, inexperienced, but talented guy, being in a band with Stan, Jack, and Dave Holland was the ultimate learning experience for a young musician.

Dave: Let's go back and talk about comping. What about Chet Baker?

Richie: Chet Baker was very different. Chet was not a split personality. He was a very sweet guy from Oklahoma. He was a stoned, committed junkie ... he lived to get high and he built his life around whatever was necessary for him to get high. He was such a great naturally gifted musician that somehow he was able to accommodate his addiction. He was not mean ... he did not drink ... he would just do his drugs. When he was in his element and all set up, meaning he was "feeling no pain." In those times he had his dope and was super kind to me. He didn't talk to me about specifics except once when he told me I was playing too loud. You know that story?

Chet comes back from spending time in jail in Italy. He was in for a couple of years. They knocked his teeth out around the same time he returned to New York. Now Chet is doing good. He is still getting high but it's under control, so he doesn't have to worry about finding drugs. We have a gig with Chet, Elliot Zigmund, Eddie Gomez, and me at the Jazz Gallery in Washington. I'm all excited. I've got the music ready and officially became the musical director. I had a great relationship with Chet. This is the first time we rehearsed my tune "Leaving," just Chet and me. I didn't know he couldn't read music. Here lies the collision between modern jazz and bebop, the old and the new world. A lot of the older guys could not read music, George Benson, no, Wes Montgomery, no, Errol Garner and Buddy Rich, no, Chet, nothing!

So I write out the chart for "Leaving" ... transposed ... (I'm a good boy!). He looks at the music and doesn't say anything because those guys don't talk much. He was high, so of course he's quiet, but relaxed. I am all excited. He goes, "Yeah Richie, play the tune for me once." Okay, so I play for him and then he goes, "Great tune, I love it, play it again." I wonder why he isn't playing with me, maybe I wrote it out wrong? I say okay, so I play it again. Then he plays it ... he has his eyes closed and he plays the melody better than I do. He plays on the changes better than I can at that time. "Leaving" is not an easy tune. It has some things that are not normal chord progressions. He has a smooth, beautiful sound, like right in your ear, like a whisper. You know, a trumpet can sound like matador shit, you think about Woody Shaw and Freddie Hubbard, those cats, right? Chet's playing is like a quiet whisper, beautiful. You can see why women loved him.

So he is playing my song "Leaving"—it's fantastic. We finish playing the tune and he opens his eyes and he says, "great tune." And I say, "Thanks Chet, but there is one thing, you missed the coda, it's on the paper, over here." He says, "Richie, I don't read music, didn't you know that?" I could not believe it, how did his ears find those chords and the melody after me playing it for him only twice? So Chet says again, "I don't read music ... I don't want to read music. I just want to live in my own world."

Chet did the same thing with my tune "Broken Wing," that is not an easy tune either. Comping for him was easy. Who knows what he was listening to? He might not be listening to anything ... just totally internal. But his time, his natural feeling for time was so great, and his sense of form was so solid and unconscious that he never got lost in the tune. Also his placement of his notes in the beat was remarkable. So he was totally self-contained.

Dave: One more thing about you and me. How do you look at me for direction in terms of dynamics, an almost forgotten quality in music today?

Richie: Dynamics are very important. Of course everyone says that but dynamics are very important within the tune, within the solo. Not just dynamics like soft in the beginning and then you build it up and you burn ... no. The most

Our Approach to Preparing for Concerts and Recordings

interesting music for me again comes from the second Miles Davis Quintet with Wayne Shorter, Herbie Hancock, Ron Carter, and Tony Williams. The rhythm section in that band made it possible for Miles to play solos with different levels or plateaus of energy and volume. In other words, Miles invented the idea to have multidimensional dynamics in one solo. Please check out the Miles Davis recording *My Funny Valentine*, recorded in 1964 live at Lincoln Center in New York.

In terms of dynamics I know you very well. I know the shape that your body takes when you want something. Also when you are reacting to what we play. Sometimes I just watch your left shoulder. If you drop your left shoulder it means you are listening for us and means you want us to play. This is like, okay, come on man, play. But if you are leaning a little bit back it means wait, you are playing too much. And then if your head turns left that means that something is wrong. That means mofo, who's solo is this anyway? If there is a rhythm section and you really like what is happening you will play a giant climax, look around, letting the rhythm section burn through while you are waiting for the next plateau. You probably learned that from playing with and listening to the Miles Davis groups.

Dynamics ... all the signs are really in the music. You can tell we want to drop in dynamics by playing just one note in a specific way. Those signs are very important because the end of a phrase will set you up for the next one. The answer to what's coming is in the end of what you are playing now in the present tense. And we must be awake...listening for that every second. In a good band everybody listens for these junctures all the time so there is a confluence of dynamics.

Dave: Done, man.

Richie: Nice.

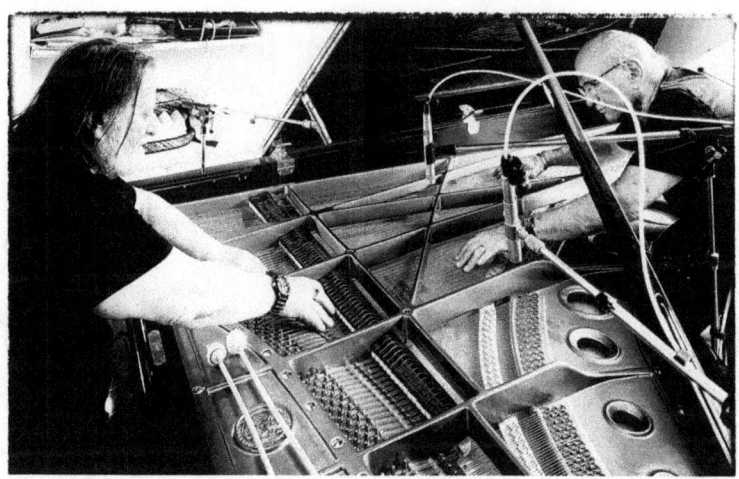

2019

A LISTENER'S GUIDE

A Short Introduction to a Band Called Quest

by Richie Beirach

Quest is a journey, not a destination. It has been an over 40 year long journey, starting in 1981 and going through several incarnations, but eventually leading up to the present line up for the last several decades with Lieb, Ron McClure, Billy Hart, and myself. Various live concerts that have been released in the past few years, whether from Hamburg, Paris, Stockholm, Detroit, or New York are all like chapters in a long never-ending book of what I think is an incredibly varied collection of contemporary small group improvised music. Simply put, great live jazz quartet music!

For this band, as for other musicians and many listeners, music is more than just music. It is a way of life, a similar view of the world, and a musical expression that delves deep into what is called the collective unconscious of humans all over the planet. There is music that surrounds us out in the world that is disposable, annoying, horrible, like audible poison. Remember, sound is all around us but *real music* is quite rare and must be nurtured, shared, and universally heard.

Quest is a band of very individual personalities, musically welded together into one of the most powerful and expressive bands in jazz history. I have seen the power of this music and of course felt it myself. Almost all the times we have played, each concert is a similar but a paradoxically different experience for the listeners, *and* for us. We have a rotating body of compositions, covering many varied moods and colors, but depending on how the band feels individually and as a group on a night to night basis, it can and does sound significantly different.

Live music, whatever the style or genre, if it is really good has a power to reach people in their heads, hearts, and bodies. The range of emotions felt by us in the group and in the audience is enormous, like holding up a kaleidoscope and turning it in the light of the sun. It can be earthshaking, delicately tender, whisperingly dark and frightening clouds of sound, or a wild group of uncaged beasts marauding about the big city at 4 a.m.

Those of us in the band feel like we are in the eye of the storm. It takes considerable mastery of so-called basic skills and lightening fast musical reflexes to survive playing nightly and yearly in Quest.

I for one am stretched to my limits of creativity to enlist the necessary sheer emotional and physical endurance needed to be part of this tsunami called Quest. It feels like a certain kind of relentless ongoing boot camp for the seriously elite special forces groups like the Navy Seals or Air Force recon which exist in the best of any military force.

A Listener's Guide

The mantra: you never know what your true limits are until you push them! This is not at all a macho mania boy's club. We use the years and years of individual practice and mastery of our instruments, combined with playing together in all the major cities of the world in front of different audiences, towards creating musical challenges and attempting to climb Mt. Everest, but each time we climb it we try a different route.

Ron McClure (we call him McJolt)

Ron is one of my oldest and dearest friends, a truly great jazz bass player and journeyman of countless nights playing with just about every great musician you could play with, including Miles Davis, Herbie Hancock, Tony Williams, Wynton Kelly, Wes Montgomery, Charles Lloyd, Keith Jarrett, Jack DeJohnette, Blood, Sweat and Tears, and more. In Quest he is the ultimate guide of the bedrock trail through which we traverse, revealing the often difficult and winding paths of the always unscripted map of our performances. McJolt offers great warm solos, an unerring sense of what to play when, and very importantly when *not* to play. He brings his enormous experience playing with the masters to us every night. Ron hears, then feels, then plays what's really needed, brilliantly, making what is happening a beautiful unexpected moment to remember.

"Jabali" (Swahili for wisdom) Billy Hart

What can I say in words to describe the audible cyclone that invaded and has permeated my musical life for over 30 years. He is for sure one of a kind. One of the most beautiful and important things that he does with Quest is that when we are tackling a well known tune or musical moment that a normal talented drummer would be satisfied with playing the standard accompaniment to, Jabali takes that normal moment or piece and by sometimes playing *against* the usual or expected, he plays something that seems completely *unrelated* musically to it, transforming it into something miraculous and unexpectedly beautiful. What the brother is doing is in fact *orchestrating* the music as it moves along and it is never the same.

Of course we all have our own vocabularies, replete with individual elements like the understood grammar of a wonderful but slightly secret language, only spoken by certain people at certain times. Jabali's genius is never doing it in the same place or same way twice. For example, he transforms a nice and simple eighth note ballad into a dramatic and almost symphonic musical screenplay of enormous power and depth. This is very helpful and a necessity if you are playing in a band that plays the same tunes every night in the great tradition of the Miles Davis quintets of the 1960s. Specifically it was the inspiration Jabali received from Miles's whiz-kid drummer, Tony Williams, to dissolve the molecules of sound and then resurrect them shortly thereafter—truly a legendary and innovative skill. Finally of course, he is *jabali* who brings his delightful, sometimes shy, sometimes African shaman multifaceted personality to the dance. Jabali has now risen to the level of a national treasure and deserves every award, accolade, and praise, which he earns every day with Quest, his own bands, and the dozens of other groups that are blessed to play with him.

And then there's Dave Liebman

"Lieb" to us in the fraternity of the music community. He is and has been for over 50 years my oldest and best friend. This is the cat who has actually changed the state of the jazz world's music and education scenarios. But his playing in Quest is in my opinion some of his best individual and group performances on record or live as you can easily hear on these concert releases. His ability to really lead the music in the most creative and structurally spontaneous direction is legendary and is especially noticeable and necessary in the wild rollercoaster ride that Quest displays when we are really rolling, which is almost all the time. I love his tenor and of course that cheap two dollar wooden flute that he probably bought on the side of the road in Morocco or India. No one can figure out how he is able to coax all those notes out of a true primitive little instrument. He can play real melodies in tune and amazingly chromatic lines on that little stick! It is a true wonder, especially on his signature piece for that flute, Ornette Coleman's "Lonely Woman."

But the soprano sax—let's just say that along with Wayne Shorter, he is at the highest level of excellence and creativity on that horn. He has transformed the soprano into an instrument capable of carrying the entire weight of a band with a personal view of the world and a singular contribution to the essence of the Quest sound. He has extended the range of the horn, up and down—not necessarily meaning higher or lower notes on the horn but I mean the *substance* of the sound he gets and the unusual and completely personal way he articulates those sounds. His phrasing,well, I could and probably will eventually write a book just on Lieb's innovative and plain mofo brilliant and hip phrasing. Lieb has reached great heights of instrumental virtuosity and group creativity revealing not only many moments of incredible intensity, but also warm and sometimes heartbreaking passages of tender and sweet expression. This is especially true in tunes like my "Elm" or his "Tender Mercies," and as well in his incredible solo soprano intros.

The bottom line is that his soprano is the group's sword! He is the guy you want leading the charge up the hill or covering your back. He is a great friend, a great musician, and a great bandleader.

Quest is not over. We love to play with each other and for the people. I never did understand just why the Taliban or other authoritarian groups ban music, but now I know as a result of listening to these powerful and extremely expressive live concerts. It's because the individual expression of each musician in the group comes across front and center. Fascists cannot stand individual *anything*. It goes against their stone-age brutally inhumane way of controlling people by fear and death. What really scares them is that it's not just an individual expression but truly group expression—remember that "group" means more than one person, like possibly four people playing together along with many people listening with their hearts and minds open. When honestly presented, music, is pure truth.

A Listener's Guide

Get four more people together and it's a small insurgent group. Then it's a quick leap to forty people with open minds and hearts demanding their basic human rights. Quest is the quintessential enemy of any kind of bullshit, oppression, or attempt to destroy the human spirit as evidenced in *any* good music. In this strange period of seemingly dwindling interest and support for truly new and powerful contemporary jazz, we hopefully can always count on people who love great music and continue to make Quest relevant and a great listening experience for years to come.

Quest: Ron McClure, Billy Hart, Dave, Richie

Richie's Tour of Our Favorite Recordings from 1970 to 2021

by Richie Beirach
Introduction by Dave Liebman

With over fifty recordings together, mostly as co-leaders, we decided to spotlight what we consider the essential Beirach/Liebman catalogue. We were very fortunate over the decades in the professional sense to be able to document our work during this period. (Please note, we are STILL recording together and probably will add more recording projects in due time.)

What makes this text come alive is Richie's inimitable writing style, whether it be about the technical aspects of the music itself (something his students know he executes at the highest level), or the more casual approach that he has taken here. Richie makes the reader *feel* the recording process as it unfolded, bringing the reader/listener into the eye of the hurricane. He is the absolute epitome of intellect and passion, whether playing or writing. You are reading a kind of novel featuring two musicians who admire and love each other deeply. The word "highlights" is exactly what the Code (Richie's nickname in the jazz world) offers here—fantastic insights into the hours spent in a recording studio—a process that takes no prisoners. Even if you are not familiar with these recordings you are invited to enter this highly emotional, and to be honest, nerve-wracking process that is documented by the published recording.

I am very grateful personally to Richie for his friendship and high artistic sensibility—one of a kind!

Dave Liebman

1970	David Liebman & Carvel Six *Night Scapes*
1973	Dave Liebman *First Visit*
1973	Dave Liebman *Lookout Farm*
1974	Dave Liebman *Drum Ode*
1975	Badal Roy *Passing Dreams*
1975	Lookout Farm *Live at New Jazz Festival Hamburg, Germany*
1975	Dave Liebman & Richie Beirach *Forgotten Fantasies*

1978	Dave Liebman *Pendulum*
1979	Dave Liebman *Dedications*
1981	Quest *Quest*
1985	Dave Liebman & Richie Beirach *The Duo Live*
1987	*Tribute to John Coltrane - Live Under The Sky*
1987/2005	Quest *Redemption: Live in Europe / Midpoint*
1988/1991	Quest *Live in Europe 1988 + 1991*
1990	Quest *Of One Mind*
2009	Dave Liebman & Richie Beirach *Quest For Freedom*
2009	Dave Liebman & Richie Beirach *Unspoken*
2010	Dave Liebman / Richard Beirach / Lee Konitz *KnowingLee*
2011	Quest *Circular Dreaming*
2015	Dave Liebman & Richie Beirach *Balladscapes*
2016	Dave Liebman & Richie Beirach *Eternal Voices*
2021	Dave Liebman & Richie Beirach *Empathy*

1970
David Liebman & Carvel Six
Night Scapes
CBS/Sony – SOPN 16

Night Scapes, recorded in 1970 at Upsurge Studios on 19th Street in Manhattan was my very first recording date ever. I was 23 and still going to Manhattan School of Music studying for a degree in music theory and composition. It was a very exciting time to be a young man living in Soho on Spring Street in Manhattan as a budding jazz pianist. The recording date was led by Dave Liebman, my best friend and close musical partner. It also involved a poet named Carvel Six, a beat generation wannabe who was on the scene then. He was nice to us and his poetry was very shall we say expressionistic. We also had Nancy Janoson on flute, Frank Tusa on bass and Armen Halburian on percussion.

There was no written music. Carvel would read one of his poems and we would all jump in with whatever we thought was appropriate musically, completely improvised and unscripted. The musical language was that of most so-called free playing at that time, usually atonal, often very dissonant, flurries of fast streams of notes. There was lots of intentional interplay, all either as an intro to, during, or after Carvel's recitation of his poetry. We were all young kids and excited to actually be recording an album of music together. We happened to be recording for one of the biggest record companies in Japan at that time, CBS Records. It was exhilarating fun and we were very proud that we were chosen to do this project.

The truth is the poetry was not very good and Carvel himself was of questionable character, kind of a lush and hanger on. He was actually living in the recording studio while we were doing the recording, in other words he was homeless. But we didn't care and were swept up in what was a very positive experience for myself and the others. We were inexperienced but willing, and as a first recording it stands up historically.

1. Prologue
2. Hello
3. Strangers Passing In The Night
4. Falling Star
5. Once Upon A Moon
6. Desert Air
7. Am I?
8. Epilogue

Carvel Six: Vocals
David Liebman: Tenor Saxophone, Flute, Clarinet
Richie Beirach: Piano
Nancy Janoson: Flute
Frank Tusa: Bass
Armen Halburian: Percussion

Recorded at Upsurge Studio New York City, February 1970
Producer, Engineer – Tom Di Pietro
1973

1973
Dave Liebman
First Visit
Philips – RJ-5101

First Visit was Dave Liebman's recording as a leader with myself on piano, Jack DeJohnette on drums, and Dave Holland on bass. This was a dream situation for us and the real beginning of our serious recording careers. The magical circumstances seemed to materialize by themselves when Dave's first tour of Japan with the Miles Davis band and my first tour of Japan with the Stan Getz quartet featuring Jack and Dave were miraculously booked at the same time. Dave and I were both very happy and proud to have gotten hired to play with these two world famous jazz icons. Miles was coming off his great success with *Bitches Brew*, which changed the course of jazz music and basically created a new genre called jazz rock or fusion. Stan Getz was still feeling the enormous success of his number one recording in the world, introducing and forever establishing bossa nova as a viable genre for jazz musicians, with the iconic album *The Girl from Ipanema*. So it was natural that King Records of Japan would ask Dave if he would record a quartet LP with me and the rhythm section from Stan's band. We all met in a recording studio at midnight after a Miles Davis and a Stan Getz concert. This was pure excitement and extreme levels of adrenaline coming from Dave and myself.

The material was simple but effective compositions from myself and Dave along with a duo version of "Round Midnight" of myself and Dave. It included the very first tune I ever wrote and my first recorded composition called "Man-Child." (It was written for Stan who was very much a man-child.) The atmosphere during the recording was electric and inspired. Dave and I both got the chance to make a real contemporary jazz record with Jack and Dave, two young masters of the music whom we loved. I remember an exhausted Jack grabbing some nods on three chairs in the studio while Dave and I played our duo. Then he woke up and we started recording the main burnout of the album, a tune appropriately titled "First Visit" by Dave, a short but brilliant combination of chromatic motives and rhythmic hits for a duo with Jack and Dave. It was a perfect springboard for some really heated and focused up-tempo blowing for the two of them. The session ended when a cymbal fell off the stand during Jack and Dave's duo. What a night!

1. Man-Child
2. Vedana
3. Round About Midnight
4. Tommy's Hut
5. Lonnie's Song
6. First Visit

David Liebman: Soprano Saxophone, Tenor Saxophone, Flute
Richie Beirach: Piano
Dave Holland: Bass
Jack DeJohnette: Drums

Recorded at Aoyama Victor Studio, Tokyo June 20,21 1973

1973
Dave Liebman
Lookout Farm
ECM Records – ECM 1039 ST

In 1973 I was 26. We recorded the first Lookout Farm recording for ECM in New York City at Generation Studios. It was an amazing experience and was central to the development of the group over the next few years. This was our first recording for ECM and it was *happening*. Manfred Eicher came to New York to produce it personally. It was a large undertaking because it ended up being Dave, me, Frank Tusa, and Jeff Williams plus John Abercrombie. On two tunes I played electric piano and acoustic on the other two. The atmosphere was totally electric. ECM was just getting going as a small but very hip European label. This was before the enormous success of Keith Jarrett's solo piano albums like the *Köln Concert*, and before Pat Metheny and John Abercrombie signed with ECM. They still did not have a good distributor in the states but the word on the street was that ECM was the new Blue Note Records.

We were on top of the soon to be exploding jazz world. We were young, not famous, and not yet totally ourselves musically and personally, but were enough of both to make a good statement that was well played, creative, and of course well produced and recorded. We got some great takes of our original tunes like Dave's "MD" written for Miles Davis and his iconic "Pablo's Story" for Pablo Picasso. For myself it was the beginning of my career and relationship with Manfred Eicher, the producer and major force behind the company. I will never forget, after I played a good solo piano introduction to Dave's tune "MD," he came right over to me in the studio, smiled his shy smile and said, "That was a beautiful intro. Would you like to make a trio recording sometime for ECM?" Hah! Yesssss! That was it, no auditions, no demos, no sending a tape around. I was a lucky mofo. I said yes, and about a year later I did my first record as a leader for ECM called *Eon*, a trio with Frank Tusa and Jeff Williams. But the *Lookout Farm* record was the beginning. Lookout Farm by the way was the name of an area in Napanoch, NY where a major inspiration for Dave and me lived, the artist Eugene Gregan.

The *Lookout Farm* recording went on to get great reviews and sold well, leading to Lookout Farm's tours around the world for the next few years. Dave was a good if young and inexperienced leader. His success with Miles Davis and ensuing visibility helped to launch the band. We were at the real beginning and it felt good!

1. Pablo's Story
2. Sam's Float
3. M. D. / Lookout Farm

Dave Liebman: Soprano Saxophone, Tenor Saxophone, Flute
Richie Beirach: Electric Piano, Piano
John Abercrombie: Acoustic Guitar, Electric Guitar
Frank Tusa: Bass

Jeff Williams: Drums
Badal Roy: Tabla
Don Alias: Congas, Bongos
Armen Halburian: Percussion
Steve Sattan: Tambourine, Cowbell
Eleana Steinberg: Voice

Recorded at Generation Sound Studios on October 10 and 11, 1973
Producer – Manfred Eicher

1974
Dave Liebman
Drum Ode
ECM Records – ECM 1046 ST

This was Dave's second recording as a leader for ECM with an expanded version of Lookout Farm, recording again in New York City. This was Dave's homage to drums and drummers. There were many drummers and percussionists on this recording from Badal Roy and Collin Walcott on tablas, Ray Armando and Patato Valdés on congas, etc. I played only electric piano, a special one made for me with an 88 keyboard, a Steinway Renner action, plus two heavy 12 inch Altec Lansing speakers in the bottom part of the piano. It weighed a ton but had an amazing full, round sound and was a dream to play, with a real deep feeling to the action rather than the shitty accordion-style actions on most Fender Rhodes. Harold Rhodes himself working with American Steinway designed it. Since I was a Steinway artist it was perfect for me. And Manfred Eicher loved the fat, rich sound. I used a phase shifter effect box and Mutron III device that gave an even broader and more colorful sound to this special Rhodes electric piano.

This was not a normal ECM record date! The atmosphere at most ECM studio dates, especially the ones recorded in Europe at either Bauer Studios in Ludwigsburg, Germany or at Rainbow Sound in Oslo are completely different than the two American productions from Lookout Farm and this Drum Ode record. In Europe a wonderful, peaceful, and orderly feeling pervades, because Manfred's basic personality is quiet with a strong intensity. The recording proceeds in that way. It's not a bad atmosphere, and is especially suitable for recording the beautiful pastel colors of many of his great ECM productions. The music is elegant, deep, and mostly slow with lots of gorgeous ballads and controlled free pieces. There is the special ECM sound and of course the acoustic piano is always magnificently recorded.

But here in the heart of Manhattan with the electric piano and electric bass and a million drummers, plus John Abercrombie on guitar, Gene Perla on electric bass, Bob Moses and Barry Altschul on percussion along with Jeff Williams on drums, and of course Lieb himself, it was a completely different story. Here were a few intense Latin brothers that have a whole other kind of recording sensibility shall we say. They are loud and excited, speaking Spanish with laughter and palpable camaraderie which we all got caught up in. The music was not ethereally quiet and ECMish! We burned the shit out of Dave's "Loft Dance" with tons of interlocking percussion making this track very alive and vibrant. Manfred was okay at the beginning but as we got more intense within the music he started to get unhappy. He knew the music was good but it certainly had veered off into something else that I don't think he bargained for. And then the real shit hit the fan. The control room in most record dates maintains some kind of order and concentrated working atmosphere, but here after a few tunes the cats got hungry and thirsty. So food was ordered, sushi, burgers, salads, and of course beers and cold drinks. Now in between takes there was not much room to sit and quietly listen. We were a whole bunch of wild cats that kind of took over the control room. There was food and beers on the mixing board and to be honest, some guys rolling and smoking things. The air was blue with all kinds of smoke. Manfred finally nutted and said in his quiet but forceful way, "I cannot werk like dis!" Poor Manfred, surrounded by drummers (not his favorite instrument anyway), and by a serious tribe of Latin cats mixed with gringos. Manfred started to come apart. Dave as leader came in and said to him, "Manfred, this is America, New York City, these are drummers, the record is called *Drum Ode*, what am I supposed to do? Don't worry, it will be cool." Then Eleana Steinberg, Dave's squeeze at the time sung on a nice tune from Dave called "Oasis." Well, after that Manfred was pretty silent. The record was a hit, and like the *Lookout Farm* record still has notoriety years later.

We broke the rules, the ECM rules, good! The force of Dave's personality and the honesty and intensity of the music still holds up today. But there were consequences from Manfred—it was the last ECM production that Dave did as a leader for ECM.

But what big fun we all had! Sadly, John Abercrombie has passed and also Collin Walcott. One way or another, Dave's *Drum Ode* became a classic among the ECM catalogue.

1. Goli Dance
2. Loft Dance
3. Oasis
4. The Call
5. Your Lady
6. The Iguana's Ritual
7. Satya Dhwani (True Sound)

Dave Liebman: Soprano Saxophone, Tenor Saxophone, Flute
Richie Beirach: Electric Piano
John Abercrombie: Electric Mandolin Guitar
Gene Perla: : Electric Bass
Jeff Williams: Drums
Bob Moses: Drums
Patato Valdés: Congas
Barry Altschul: Percussion
Steve Sattan: Percussion
Ray Armando: Bongos, Percussion
Badal Roy: Tabla
Collin Walcott: Tabla
Eleana Steinberg: Vocals

Recorded by Tony May at the Record Plant, New York City May 1974
Producer – Manfred Eicher

1975
Badal Roy
Passing Dreams
Geetika Records

In 1975, Lookout Farm, which at that time was Dave, myself, Frank Tusa, Jeff Williams, and tabla player Badal Roy, did a State Department tour of India supported by the United States Information Services (USIS). It was the first time any of us had been to India except Badal of course who actually came from Bangladesh. It was through him that the tour was organized for eight cities. Little did we know what kind of life changing experiences waited for us there collectively, both as a touring band and individually as human beings entering into the surrealistic time warp and awful beauty of India in 1975. This was India before its big economic boom, an immense country of shocking and disturbing contrasts.

I will never forget landing in Calcutta at 3 a.m. in the dead of night during the summer. We had just come from a tour of Japan and a night spent in Hong Kong—there couldn't have been more contrast. I can say without a doubt that I became an adult during that ride from the airport and the next day witnessing such crushing poverty in our faces.

We met many people who came to the concerts to hear us, deep friendships were made, and ultimately we made this astounding and very moving recording one night after a concert in Bombay. The concerts in many cities were generally greeted with wonderful applause and smiling faces shining with real love and a feeling of thankfulness that an American band came all the way from New York City to play for them. I think the last jazz they had was Benny Goodman, a decade earlier. They made us feel more than at home. This humanity acted as a balancing factor to the absolute horror we saw around us.

After a particularly good concert in Bombay we climbed five flights of rickety, darkly lit stairs up to a recording studio (TEAC reel to reel and some mics). Badal as the leader helped us put together the music for a recording between our band and these incredible Indian master musicians he found playing sitar, ghatam (clay pot), veena, and the most amazing player of the warangi, Mr. Sultan Khan, a true master of the incredibly deep classical music of India. Badal translated when needed, which wasn't much. Upon arrival in the studio by the way, we were met with a silent but smiling bunch of listeners already sitting in chairs to witness the event. The vibes were very good which was one of the astounding things about

India in 1975. The living scene for the people was abysmal, conditions beyond deplorable, but these people and the musicians kept their sense of balance and community, generating a gentle and loving atmosphere towards us and each other. To be appropriate Dave used his alto flute a bit, along with tenor and soprano sax while Jeff somehow had a passable drum set, and Badal had his tablas. There was a black upright piano in the corner. Nobody was talking, just gestures and smiles, Badal going around from one guy to us all smoothing the path.

Sultan Khan, a big fleshy man with the body of a wrestler suddenly started playing his sarangi, a violin-like instrument but with three times the raw projecting power. This sound caught my ear—it was unbelievably beautiful and heart wrenching. It was as if all of the horror, the beauty, the fear, the joy, and massive emotions of the Indian people were being expressed by this man's incredible sound, his heart and burning spirit in every note. I sat down at the upright piano and just started playing along with him. Accompanying him with my heart and my instinctual ear, my brain not necessary, not really wanted. It was sooooo beautiful! I remember it starting in a C minor kind of feeling. As I played things to support his wailing phrases he responded to me, all with ears and heart, without any paper or talking,- capturing the real primal pure stuff that if we are lucky comes a few times in a musical lifetime. It was truly a meeting of divergent musical elements. With a few duo sections, some group playing, even a rendition of Trane's "Equinox," it was a magic time, never to be forgotten.

Sultan with his sarangi brought the truth and sorrow as I was bringing western music and harmony, classical, Chopin, improvisation, my own style, etc. I must confess that I was internally crying while hearing Sultan and myself playing, luckily it was being recorded. We were eventually all creating this music as a large group, spontaneously, effortlessly, as if we were involved in some kind of group service or prayer.

I could say more about this amazing experience, but I think this captures the essence of a truly remarkable recording and musical experience. It was really like being in a passing dream!

1. Passing Dreams
2. Dadrain
3. Atma
4. Dhun
5. Equator
6. Vale Of Kashmir
7. Moti Mahal
8. Ajoy
9. Sultan Bhai

Badal Roy: Tabla, Tambura
David Liebman: Flute, Soprano Saxophone, Tenor Saxophone (tracks 1,2,5,7,8)
Richie Beirach: Piano tracks 1,5)
Ustad Sultan Khan: Sarangi (tracks 1,5,9)
Arjun Sehgal Sarod, Sitar (tracks 1,3,5,9)
Frank Tusa: Bass (tracks 1,3,5)
Jeff Williams: Drums (tracks 1,5)
Tracks 1,3,5,8,9 recorded in Bombay, India September 1975
Tracks 2,4,6,7 recorded at Badal Roy's home, East Brunswick, NJ May 1998

1975
Lookout Farm
Live at New Jazz Festival Hamburg, Germany
Jazzline Records D 77071

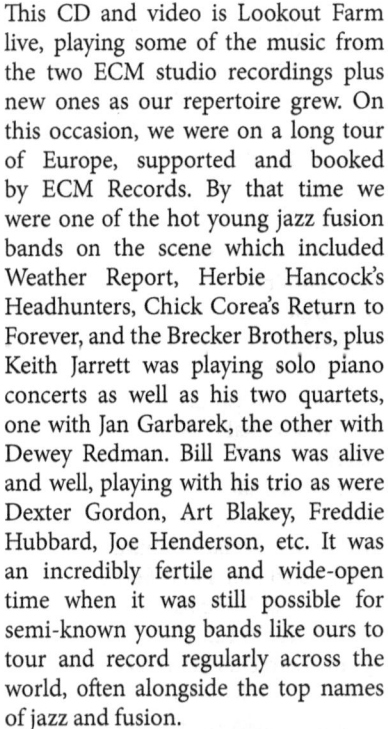

This CD and video is Lookout Farm live, playing some of the music from the two ECM studio recordings plus new ones as our repertoire grew. On this occasion, we were on a long tour of Europe, supported and booked by ECM Records. By that time we were one of the hot young jazz fusion bands on the scene which included Weather Report, Herbie Hancock's Headhunters, Chick Corea's Return to Forever, and the Brecker Brothers, plus Keith Jarrett was playing solo piano concerts as well as his two quartets, one with Jan Garbarek, the other with Dewey Redman. Bill Evans was alive and well, playing with his trio as were Dexter Gordon, Art Blakey, Freddie Hubbard, Joe Henderson, etc. It was an incredibly fertile and wide-open time when it was still possible for semi-known young bands like ours to tour and record regularly across the world, often alongside the top names of jazz and fusion.

The club Onkel Pö's Carnegie Hall in Hamburg already had a long and interesting history. With its enthusiastic young audience it was really a blessing for us to have the opportunity to play for such a cool and knowing bunch of people throughout the tour and this night in particular. The club had a special drink called Pineau which was a kind of French liqueur that tasted sweet but after a few knocked me on my ass, albeit in a mellow way. The NDR, which is the German radio and TV station in Hamburg, was there to film and record us as part of a New Jazz Festival.

We did our best to combine our version of contemporary straight ahead jazz using acoustic and electric bass and piano. We opened with Dave's "Napanoch," then on to the tune "The Iguanas Ritual," another by Dave that was all electric with me on that special 88 key souped up electric piano using the Mutron III and phase shifter. Frank on electric bass and Jeff on drums sounded like a category 5 hurricane, with Badal Roy coming in on his delicate but strong tablas, and finally Dave on the horns. Lieb was very influenced by Miles Davis in terms of his great playing and also his band-leading personality accompanied by a strong stage presence. (You don't play with the Chief without some things rubbing off on you!) We played the Coltrane tune "Your Lady" giving it a very different arrangement than Trane's. We were a truly energetic bunch of guys. I played a long solo piano intro on the old Sinatra-inspired standard "I'm A Fool to Want You." I think we did a good job combining the music we came from with the colors and instruments of the time we lived in. Eclecticism was the style of the day.

This was a memorable night for us and was made historic by the wonderful fact that it was documented by video as well as audio. Life on the road was organized chaos with many small and big problems of life happening that had to be solved and conquered along the way. There was the great joy and feeling of really getting out there and living in the moment, taking whatever comes, good and bad, making the most of it. Traveling by van, which we did mostly to save money, was a big adventure, interesting and fun at the same time. It did allow time for a lot of discussion of the music which would be reflected in the next performance, so change was a big thing that we loved—meeting new people, parties, girls, drugs, etc. Also the tough daily grind of sitting sometimes six or eight hours in the van, jumping out to lift and set up our shit, sound check, grab a sausage and a beer, play the gig, hang out after, then go to the hotel usually after the gig late at night. We were young and strong so all was possible. Then one or more of us might catch a cold or be hungover but we still had to do our jobs and function like a band with shared responsibilities.

Dave was a very good leader and sometimes because of a very demanding schedule of one nighters like Hamburg to Rome to Amsterdam, tempers flared and egos got bruised. But we were brothers and deep friends as well and it always blew over very soon. I was left with a wonderful sense of a shared group experience and the totally creative and ever-changing story of a living, breathing, and working jazz fusion band all over the world. I will never forget Lookout Farm live at Onkel Pö's Carnegie Hall in Hamburg!

1. Napanoch
2. The Iguana's Ritual
3. I'm A Fool To Want You
4. Your Lady
5. Fireflies

Dave Liebman: tenor & soprano saxophone, alto flute
Richie Beirach: electric & acoustic piano's
Frank Tusa: electric & acoustic basses
Jeff Williams: drums
Badal Roy: percussion

Recorded live at Onkel Pö's Carnegie Hall, Hamburg, Germany June 8, 1975 New Jazz Festival Hamburg, Germany

1975
Dave Liebman & Richie Beirach
Forgotten Fantasies
Horizon A&M Records – SP-709

This was our first duo recording and a pivotal release in our discography for many reasons. This recording signaled our sense of having arrived at a certain level of artistic and commercial success in our own country even though our records were released by ECM, a German-based company. Horizon Records was a subsidiary of A&M Records, a big corporation headed up by Herb Alpert and Jerry Moss with big American commercial acts like the Tijuana Brass, Peter Frampton, and others in the pop field.

Dave had signed with them and after a first recording (*Sweet Hands,* which celebrated Badal Roy's contributions as well as our Indian trip), this was next release, an acoustic duo recording with all original compositions representing our musical evolution, especially in the harmonic realm. We had their big promotion machine behind us and it was great. We picked the best new compositions we both had written for duo and worked hard on forging a new way to play in a duo context. We had to throw out some good possible pieces because they worked fine in a quartet with bass and drums, but not in a duo context. This was the true beginning of our more mature personal approach and it felt great to be in Electric Lady Studios in Manhattan, New York City, making a real record that would be heard, distributed, and yes, bought in 1975!

"October 10th" was my piece, a brooding requiem-like ballad with a pleading melody and descending bass line, surrounded by rich and unusual harmony. With Lieb on soprano the vibe was haunting and dark but set a beautiful mood that people immediately were drawn to. October 10th was a special date in my life where many important wonderful and awful things happened to me. Dave's great waltz and the title tune of the record, "Forgotten Fantasies" shows his mastery of one of the iconic formats in the jazz composition lexicon, the jazz ballad waltz, featuring a soaring melody with very creative and logical harmonic progressions. I love this duo. Solo piano playing for me is great and I have many recorded and released all over the world. But I am a collaborator at heart and I like to work with people rather than stand alone. I always said that when Dave stops it is after all, solo piano time!

My suite "Obsidian Mirrors" is an attempt at a longer compositional statement setting up Lieb with different springboards for improvisations that I know he likes. While at the same time the music must be challenging, because Dave does insist on that element being there. My piece "Eugene" is for our dear friend and mentor, the great painter Eugene Gregan. It's clear from the shape of the rubato melody and the following eighth note blowing form that we love Geno and hold him in high regard as an artist, a friend, and a creative brother in the pursuit of our dreams.

Duo with Dave is a privilege for me. This was the first of many to come and it was a great beginning.

Thanks Lieb!

1. October 10th
2. Repeat Performance
3. Eugene
4. Forgotten Fantasies
5. Troubled Peace
6. Obsidian Mirrors

Dave Liebman: Soprano Saxophone, Tenor Saxophone, Flute
Richie Beirach: Piano

Recorded at Electric Lady Studios, NYC November 18, 19 & 20, 1975 and mixed November 22 & 23, 1975.
Producer – John Snyder

1978
Dave Liebman
Pendulum
Original LP: Artists House – AH 8
Complete Recording: Download only

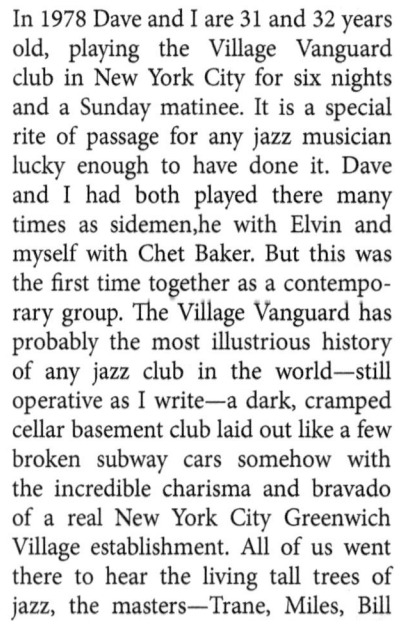

In 1978 Dave and I are 31 and 32 years old, playing the Village Vanguard club in New York City for six nights and a Sunday matinee. It is a special rite of passage for any jazz musician lucky enough to have done it. Dave and I had both played there many times as sidemen, he with Elvin and myself with Chet Baker. But this was the first time together as a contemporary group. The Village Vanguard has probably the most illustrious history of any jazz club in the world—still operative as I write—a dark, cramped cellar basement club laid out like a few broken subway cars somehow with the incredible charisma and bravado of a real New York City Greenwich Village establishment. All of us went there to hear the living tall trees of jazz, the masters—Trane, Miles, Bill Evans, Mingus, etc. When we were just underage kids, we snuck in here and the other iconic jazz heaven, the original Birdland club on 52nd Street. So, Dave and I decided to hire our good friends and great peers Randy Brecker, Frank Tusa, and Al Foster. Then it came about that Artists House Records under the direction of John Snyder agreed to record us live. This was big news, great news, scary consequential news. We weren't kids in our twenties but neither were we mature yet. The bottom line is that when you are asked to make a live recording at the Vanguard, to be considered along with the other great and iconic live recordings such as Coltrane live, Bill Evans live, Sonny Rollins live, etc. you just say yes and take on the challenge.

David Baker, our great ingenious engineer friend set up his equipment in the kitchen of the Vanguard. An amazing bunch of wires ran from the microphones to the kitchen in the back of the club, taped down along the long twisting way to the stage (which by the way was not a real stage). The piano sat on the extreme left with that cool but intimidating picture of Bill Evans behind it. This was a band of peers as I said earlier. We loved playing together and it was always fun. But more than fun now, because with the recording it became forever documented.

The material was simple. During the week we played the standard jazz repertoire, plus a few selected originals: "Solar," "There Is No Greater Love," "Footprints," "Blue In Green," "Softly as In Morning Sunrise," etc. plus my "Pendulum" and Dave's

"Picadilly Lilly." "Pendulum," the title tune of the record and one of my so-called hits began as a request from Dave. Coming from the Miles Davis academy he doesn't like to talk as much as I do but he took on some of the qualities of Miles. He says to me one night why don't you write something new for us to play off a pedal point? Okay, I went home and wrote "Pendulum." It popped out pretty easily. I found a pedal note, F sharp which I liked because there were almost no other tunes written in that key. It's kind of a tough key for the sax and trumpet, and the piano too, but I loved F sharp just for that reason—the road less travelled stuff. Also on the piano F sharp is a very resonant and vibrant key with a lot of tension, colorful overtones, and just plain kick ass tonality. (One other F sharp classic is Clare Fischer's "Pensativa.")

So, I find the pedal tone I like. Then I come upon the simple 2-bar rhythmic vamp figure. I am rolling—a chromatic phrase comes into my ear—a 6 note intervallic motive that works well with the vamp. I start developing it and follow the contour of the descending phrases leading smoothly to a 16-bar phrase that ends with a cadence-like turn, even suggesting a kind of faux cadence. Cool. Dave sight reads it in the concert key—he likes it, we play it, it works, it flies! We try it with the band, Randy reading it down perfectly. Nothing is hard for these cats! Frank digs into the rhythmic vamp, then Al, who loves these kinds of rhythmic hits—his playing is full of them. Al and I have a serious deep connection underpinning the whole band in terms of how we develop and distribute these powerful rhythmic hits through the solos.

Since it is a pedal point there are no chord changes like a normal tune. The pedal point is a wonderful way to give the band a tonal center without the cadential imperatives of chord changes. Because when you change chords the bass must move, a movement which creates expectations and sometime phrasing pressures. In the end a sophisticated player can play anything he or she wants over the pedal point, even creating temporary superimposed chord changes over the pedal. A good contemporary improvisor will use free chromatic ideas, suggested chord changes, and a time-no-changes technique to vary the interest in his solos. These are all musical choices to pursue when playing over a pedal point. Randy solos first. It is a textbook lesson on how to play a burning, balanced, and beautifully motivicly driven trumpet solo. I am on him like a mofo, trying to support his cool dissonant out notes against that F sharp pedal. Then I play what I think is one of my best recorded solos. Dave comes in on his tenor and with great sweeping lyrical waves taking us back to the head and out for a very smoking version of my tune!

Al and Frank are constantly pumping the music forward. Frank is a strong and subtle bass player, his time on this track is really happening while loosely locked into my comping. Al is like the guy who stokes the engine in an old locomotive, shoveling that coal into the engine. We are fucking rolling. There is a kind of joy that a great rhythm section feels when loosely locked in, not stiff, but independently together. The soloists love this kind of support, trusting the rhythm section, leading to taking the kinds of musical, improvised risks we've come to expect. No risk, no rewards, right?

Adam Nussbaum, a brother and colleague drummer was very young in 1978. He came almost every night and sat in the seats right behind Al. You can hear him screaming and cheering Al on—it was a cool catalyst.

I must thank my brothers Al, Frank, Randy, and Dave for an amazing musical experience, forever documented by our late and loved brother David Baker. And thanks to John Snyder for making the whole thing happen for us.

1. Pendulum
2. Picadilly Lilly
3. Footprints
4. No Greater Love
5. Solar
6. Picadilly Lilly
7. Impressions
8. Night and Day
9. Well You Needn't
10. Bonnie's Blue
11. Blue Bossa

Dave Liebman: Soprano Saxophone, Tenor Saxophone
Richie Beirach: Piano
Randy Brecker: Trumpet
Frank Tusa: Bass
Al Foster: Drums

Recorded at the Village Vanguard, New York City, February 4th and 5th, 1978
Producer – John Snyder

1979
Dave Liebman
Dedications
CMP Records – CMP 9 ST

This is a whole different kind of project, a string quartet plus Dave, me, and Eddie Gomez on bass. The compositions feature Lieb's arrangements of three pieces for that instrumentation, one written by me, arranged by the conductor of the date and master teacher, David Baker, produced by a young man with whom we would and still do have a lot of contact with, Kurt Renker, for his new company, CMP. No drums, no burn outs, just very intense concentrated original music leaning towards contemporary classical style but with a jazz awareness in terms of harmony, melody, and for sure rhythm.

Improvisation is the one consistent element that must be present in my opinion for something to be considered jazz music.

"The Delicacy of Youth," written and arranged by Dave, is self-explanatory in its inspiration, a beautiful essay on the freshness and innocence of being young. "The Codes Secret Code" was also written by Dave for me, alluding to my nickname in jazz circles—the Code. This is a deep expansive composition that really captures the way Dave and I play together. The addition of the bass player Eddie Gomez was a master stroke, because the bass acts as a bridge between the string quartet, Dave, and me. Gomez is one of the world's greatest bass players and overall musicians. His amazing intonation, creative and powerful rhythmic force, and above all, his heartfelt emotion in his solos are a wonder to hear and adds much to the emotive power of this extraordinary music. My own composition (arranged by Baker), "Treblinka," was hard to write and harder to perform and record. The subject matter is horrifying and inspiring at the same time. It is about the Treblinka concentration camp in Poland during WW II. I got the story from Terence Des Pre's brilliant book about the Treblinka concentration camp where towards the end of the war 600 Jewish prisoners somehow made a plan to escape. They banded together and by sheer force of will and phenomenal courage they managed to overpower the armed Nazi camp guards and killed all of them, burned down the camp, and escaped into the woods. I read this story and it affected me deeply. Being Jewish and having a grandmother who lost her whole family in Buchenwald stunned me, inspiring the writing of this piece.

We owe an enormous debt to David Baker for arrangements and general help during the recording. Dave's uncommon knowledge of both genres made him a natural for this job and gave us a fantastic platform from which we were able to create our improvisations.

I must say a few words about what it feels like to play with a string quartet and to have the wonderful and rare opportunity to improvise with one. The piano is a string instrument that can become percussive, but the inherent singing nature of the piano is supported and enhanced greatly by the musical cushion and vibrant stimulation of a great string quartet. And believe me, this was one mofo string quartet! Young, smart, and open minded with a great joyful spirit of its own. No old men in suits with beards and closed judgmental faces!

To hear and play with Dave's beautiful and brilliant soprano sax, with the rich deep tones of Eddie's bass, with the perfect Steinway grand combined with the gorgeous sound of a real string quartet playing was a pleasure and honor. And the great acoustics in the legendary Nola Studio, located in the Steinway building in New York helped to make this record very special.

A record date for the ages! Thanks Lieb, and thanks Kurt.

1. The Delicacy Of Youth
2. Mother / Father
3. The Code's Secret Code
4. Treblinka

Dave Liebman: Soprano Saxophone, Tenor Saxophone, Flute
Richie Beirach: Piano
Eddie Gomez: Bass
Charles Veal: Violin
Susan Ornstein: Violin
Judy Geist: Viola
Clay Ruede: Cello
David Baker: Arranger

Recorded by David Baker at Nola Studio, New York City Sept. 1979, Producer – Kurt Renker

1981
Dave Liebman, Richie Beirach, George Mraz, Al Foster
Quest
Absord Music Japan Co. Ltd. – ABCJ-509

This was the first incarnation of the band called Quest with Dave, me, George Mraz on bass, and Al Foster on drums. Quest would evolve into other combinations of bass players and drummers, but this was the first. A special feeling of discovery permeates this recording. Dave and Al had played with Miles Davis for a period; Dave and I were old bros together for years; I played with George in the John Abercrombie Quartet. I had a working trio that had just finished a recording the week before called *Elegy for Bill Evans* with George and Al, plus we recorded *Pendulum*, our live recording at the Village Vanguard in 1979 on Artists House so we had deep and very strong connections and cross connections which all contributed to the unusual, sometimes telepathic moments of collective creativity. It is my belief that the best small group jazz music comes from steady working groups that are mostly peer oriented, meaning similar levels of experience, talent, and the will to want to play the best stuff capable of the group. Think of John Coltrane's classic quartet, Miles Davis quintets, the Bill Evans Trio, etc.

Well, this Quest band was that for sure. The material included "Dr. Jekyll And Mr. Hyde," an original tune from Al; "Wisteria," a beautiful waltz from George; "Napanoch" from Dave, and a tune from me, "Elm," plus two standards with extreme recompositional treatments, "Softly, As In Morning Sunrise" and "Lonely Woman" from Ornette Coleman. "Softly, As In Morning Sunrise" was transformed by me into a burnout pedal point tune with a reharmonized bridge and a special intro vamp that also worked as a background for the melody. The band was somehow on fire from the first note. Everything seemed to fall into place, with a very intense concentrated heat, yet a sense of relaxation. I know that sounds like polar opposites but it's not. Dave's solo on "Softly, As In Morning Sunrise" is one of those amazing textbook examples of how to play a totally cohesive, motivically driven, compositionally unified solo that really unfolds and does not sound premeditated or stiff at all. Under it all is this collective agreement on many things in the rhythm section, which results in a deeply swinging and flowing wave of sound.

Everybody is doing their job, the functions of the instruments are incredibly well articulated and meld together.

The rhythm section is as of one mind, supporting Dave. Al is killing with his deep groove and subtle but powerful interactive comments all along and in between Dave's phrases. Dave's solo is so good that it has been transcribed completely and appears with my comping in his great book on chromaticism, *A Chromatic Approach to Jazz Harmony and Melody*. We answer the perennial question we are asked all the time, "Can you please tell us how to play chromatically on a standard tune playing in and out of the changes?"

"Elm" is close to my heart and this was one of my absolute favorite versions. I play a long romantic solo piano intro before the melody, which is played beautifully by Dave's soprano sax, mournful but somehow lifting. His soprano sound is stunning and is instantly recognizable to the world by now. He carries the humanity of a universal lament in his tone and notes. George, surely one of the world's finest bass players, plays a fantastic solo that combines perfect intonation with exceptional singing and lyrical phrases that are not usually playable on the bass. But George is an artist of rare stature. Dave's solo is played off of an E minor vamp found in the last 4 bars of the melody. We move into another gear and it evolves into a massive powerful vamp, building to a shattering climax, then back to the plaintive melody with a short coda in the major key.

"Lonely Woman," a classic tune from Ornette, is given a radically different interpretation than Ornette's great recorded version. Here it is all spacious rubato, strings of the piano, and George's bass tuned down to a low D for the symphonic bottom we wanted. This frames the amazing melody by Dave's alto flute in washes of shimmering color and delicate but explosive question and answers, causing a powerful orchestral sound to pervade the jazz quartet. Many people from our audiences are always moved and touched by our arrangement of this great piece from Ornette.

This record I must say was a very high point in Dave's and my career, and our personal musical development. While recording a jazz album, we sometimes don't really know whether it will stand up to our own hard scrutiny and very high standards but I felt that this was a mofo from the first note. It has everything you want in a well-balanced contemporary jazz small group recording. I am very proud to have been involved with this first Quest recording. There would be many more to come but there is only one first time.

1. Dr. Jekyll And Mr. Hyde
2. Wisteria
3. Softly, As In A Morning Sunrise
4. Elm
5. Napanoch
6. Lonely Woman

Dave Liebman: Soprano Saxophone, Tenor Saxophone, Flute
Richie Beirach: Piano
George Mraz: Bass
Al Foster: Drums

Recorded by David Baker at Vanguard Studio, New York on December 28th & 29th, 1981

1985
Dave Liebman & Richie Beirach
The Duo Live
Advance Music – 86102CD
CD and transcription book

This particular recording is very important to our duo discography for many reasons. It shows a great deal of progress from the first duo LP, the studio recording called *Forgotten Fantasies*. The setting here was a live concert and recording in a concert hall in Rottenburg, Germany, sponsored by our dear friend who has sadly passed, Hans Gruber.. It was the kind of close personal production that Dave and I are lucky to have where dear friendships and professional relationships happily coincide. A gigantic Bösendorfer Imperial concert grand piano added to my anticipation and excitement to both perform with Lieb, combined with a feeling that it was going to be, hopefully someday, a real recording out in the world. The pressure of the deep, psychological awareness that what you are playing will be permanently documented is like a strong tonic for Dave and myself. It is difficult to describe in words this complex feeling of excitement, humility, nervousness, adrenalin, and pure old-fashioned ego/bravado to face both the pressures of a live audience and a document for posterity. It is a good thing we were not aware of the transcription and book element before the recording. Actually, it was an idea that Hans put on the table after the concert and executed by one of the great master teachers in jazz, Bill Dobbins. Hans and his wife Veronika were just beginning their publishing company, Advance Music. So, it was a business deal that was spontaneously created at this concert.

The four long pieces recorded and eventually transcribed were my "Gargoyles" and "Elm," and Dave's "Tender Mercies" and "Third Visit." Happily, we were both very on the case that night, inspired and accurate, dancing on that precarious razor edge of taking creative risks while balancing the absolute need for technical accuracy. Dave is a great, generous, and powerful partner, as a main stay of my life for nearly 50 years and counting. He somehow leads without directing, shows movement without forcing the development and reacts consistently to my ideas with great taste and very quick reactions. That allow us to really be inventive in the instant of creation on stage in front of the audience under the glaring presence of the microphone. To me a live recording is the most difficult way to document your music. Difficult because you must satisfy the live audience sitting in front of you as well as satisfying the musical requirements. We must remember that listeners will be checking the music out in all kinds of situations, probably in the calm and quiet atmosphere of their own homes. This duality can lead to challenges which I recognized personally on other occasions.

The monster Bösendorfer Grand Imperial has extra keys, an octave more than the Steinway. This extra octave is below the lowest note on the standard 88-key piano and can be transformed into a percussive role. These notes have enormous power and massive percussive capabilities that I used on Dave's hip call-like tune, "Third Visit." The piece is a very up tempo, all out burn that we usually play as a closer to balance out the more reflective and balladic pieces in our repertoire. In my piano solo I really get down in that sub-basement register, using it very percussively to punch out a long series of lines and rhythmic phrases that builds to a powerful and virtuosic climax that I don't often do. The amazing piano lead me right into it!

A word about the book and the true genius of Bill Dobbins who transcribed the whole deal. Without slowing the playback speed down for transcription purposes, not only is it an accurate rendition of exactly what we both played, but Bill had to invent a whole new vocabulary of notational devices to communicate our quite often unusual ways of improvising, like Dave using extreme registers, along with a very personal and often rubato rhythmic sense of phrasing that is notated in stunningly creative ways. Bill also came up with great ways of notating my playing in the piano strings. Bill has a knack for clarity and fresh ideas about notation. My above-mentioned percussive solo on Dave's "Third Visit" is brilliantly printed for all to see and marvel at. I can hardly describe both Dave's and my reaction when we first saw the transcriptions. Holy shit!

Good thing we didn't know while we were recording that our every note would not only be recorded but printed! Hah!

I want to thank my brother Dave for his great playing and general high-level approach to our musical life for 50 years. Also, thanks to Veronika and Hans Gruber for their generous support over the years.

1985 doesn't seem so long ago, just 34 years at this writing, but considering the way the world has become in these last years this project seems to gain in its own rich musical life.

1. Gargoyles
2. Tender Mercies
3. Elm
4. Third Visit
5. Lonely Woman
6. The Code's Secret Code

Dave Liebman: Soprano Saxophone, Flute
Richie Beirach: Piano

Recorded at the Advance Music Jazz Workshops on April 11th, 1985, Tübingen

1987
Tribute to John Coltrane – Live Under The Sky
Wayne Shorter, Dave Liebman, Richie Beirach, Eddie Gomez, Jack DeJohnette
Columbia – FC 45136, CD + DVD

This was one of the high points of both Dave's and my musical lives featuring a quintet with Wayne Shorter, Dave, Jack DeJohnette, Eddie Gomez, and myself—a dream band for a dream occasion. It was the 20th anniversary of the death of John Coltrane, our musical and spiritual master and a truly inspiring icon for the entire world of music and beyond. Everything about this once in a lifetime concert was like a movie. Dramatic, moving, that feeling you rarely have when the musical planets all line up to create a new but ancient moment in musical history. I had never before played a note with Wayne. I had followed and admired him from the audience and from recordings of course, but never stepped on a bandstand or entered a recording studio with him, so this was an amazing opportunity for me to play and record with one of our modern masters and tall trees. I had played my whole life with Dave, Eddie, and Jack before of course. We were brothers, but Wayne was special for me. He was very kind but quiet, and a bit removed as he always was.

We played a program of all Coltrane compositions, "Mr. PC," "India," and "Impressions" plus a duo with Dave and me playing "After The Rain" and "Naima." No real rehearsal needed, a short sound check and that was it. Plus a great Yamaha concert grand piano, incredibly loud but smooth sounding monitors, and an almost invisible video recording set up. I asked Dave where were the cameras? The vibe was relaxed but for me electric. I had always dreamed of playing with Wayne someday and now it was here. I had to get my nervous excitement under control. Fortunately, as soon as we started playing "Mr. PC" I relaxed into the music and was fine, able to enjoy playing as though I was listening from the audience.

Some background—Lieb had broken his leg just a few weeks before the concert, trying to change a painting standing on a damn ladder alone in his house in Long Island! If you look, you can see in the video that Lieb is sitting on a stool with crutches on the floor. In those days he never sat, but there was no choice for this hit. He was and is such a warrior that he just refused to miss this gig of gigs. Through his incredible strength of character, he not only pulled it off but played some of his most inspired music ever. We started at 10 p.m. for the final act of the festival which was and has become known as Live Under the Sky. It was extremely hot and humid but there were 22,000 Japanese jazz fans waiting and ready to love it!

You can hear me counting off the first tune with my loud snapping fingers and we were off! "Mr. PC," played up tempo, burning from the get go with applause like a rock concert from the people. Lieb, who hadn't played a note for the last month because of the accident, completely burns on soprano with an urgency that was palpable. At one point he brings down the volume but not the intensity. I lay out and he builds it back up to a giant climax. Then Wayne enters with some amazing lyrical and memorable melodies. You hear contrasting free and double time sweeping lines of cascading notes with the rhythm section responding to every nuance. Wayne is the interactive improvisor of his generation. He plays a phrase, then leaves a space. He actually listens to the rhythm section. For me, I am feeding him comping chords. At one point he picked up a direct musical suggestion from me where I played a F sharp octave as a fill for him. He heard it and instantly included it in his next phrase—total connection. Then after a staggering solo from Wayne, I played my solo.

Now a word about Jack. Playing with Jack is like playing with an African drum group. He was loud but clear in the sophisticated monitor system. I could hear everything he played, sometimes like thunder or artillery, overwhelming and swamping the band, but somehow right and commensurate with the entire intense burning spirit of all our energy. I could feel Jack reacting to playing these tunes from Trane. He was living his own powerful memories of his private connections to Trane as we all were. But as I maintain in my teaching, the essence of jazz is the absolute and essential gestalt found in the drums, not only as an instrument, but also spiritually. Of course you can hear wonderful improvised music without drums. I have had trios with bass and violin, and duos without drums, but I do believe that the very heart of contemporary jazz has to do with the vibrant power and enormous energy of the drums, and who more than Jack to represent that and honor Trane, Elvin, etc.

So now I am soloing and it's going well. It feels good and the ideas are flowing. I am not forcing and I can hear everything. Eddie's playing is a gift allowing me massive freedom of phrasing, of reharmonization, of bending the time. Eddie is strong like a horse but can turn on a dime and is totally sensitive to my playing. We were bros when I was playing with Chet and Stan, while he was with Bill Evans and the Steve Gadd band. Yes, we are playing "Mr. PC" but we are going wherever the music takes us. I am free in the form and changes. We play the head out and with two soprano saxes it ends with a monster screaming minor second held by Dave and Wayne. Jack finishes, implying that he is the drummer and should have the last word. Enormous applause—the audience is behind us. These are 22,000 fans, not just people.

Dave gives a short but beautiful speech from the heart about Trane and the vast, far reaching effects of his music, especially the spiritual aspects. More cheers.

Then Dave and I play a duo medley of two beautiful Trane compositions, "After The Rain" and the classic "Naima," both with our own arrangements. Magic—22,000 silent and reverent mofos in the steamy night out of doors. There is a giant picture of Trane behind my best friend Lieb and we are playing two of John's most lyrical pieces for a loving audience—this is the top of the mountain!

Then "India" with a beautiful heartfelt solo bass intro from Eddie. He is in general a quiet cat with a big heart and a lot to say, especially in 1987. In his intro he plays a lovely quote from the bridge of that classic ballad "My One and Only Love,"Eddie's subtle personal dedication to Trane. We burn "Impressions" down with a short drum transition solo from Jack. He sets the table and we are in. I am flying—I feel great, calm, excited but in that creative zone some call the alpha state. I am one with the piano, with Eddie, with Dave, Jack, and the audience, with my heart full and open to Trane and his clear presence in our music and lives.

I don't remember much after that. There was a party where Miles, Scofield, and all of us hung out but for me the music we played on that stage remains etched in my mind, body, and soul. To this day I can still feel that special magic. I am so grateful to CBS Sony and the late George Butler for recording and video taping this truly night of nights.

Thanks brothers Dave, Wayne, Jack, Eddie, and of course John Coltrane. His spirit lives in us.

1. Mr. P.C.
2. After The Rain / Naima
3. India
4. Impressions

Wayne Shorter: Soprano Saxophone
Dave Liebman: Soprano Saxophone
Richie Beirach: Piano
Eddie Gomez: Bass
Jack DeJohnette: Drums

Recorded live Tokyo, Japan on July 26, 1987

1987 + 2005
Quest
Redemption: Live in Europe (2005)
hatOLOGY 642
Midpoint (1987)
Storyville – STCD 4121

The recording *Redemption* from 2005 and the earlier recording *Midpoint* from 1987 capture the band Quest in the whirlwind of playing on tour, on the road in a club before a hot live audience. *Redemption* was recorded at the Sunset Club in Paris and in Switzerland, while *Midpoint* was recorded live at the Montmartre Club in Copenhagen. Listening now to "Dark Eyes" from the *Redemption* CD I am walking around my house filled with fire and yelling at the speakers like a crazy fan in our audience. I admit it, I love this music. It is so on fire, so burning, so together in terms of its fine attention to dynamic tension and release, pure swinging joy, and serious deep reflection. It's really a band, a working living breathing group of peers and brothers with an attitude of being all in the center of a storm! We put it all out on the bandstand with no holding back, but still somehow not overplaying. "Dark Eyes," that old Russian folk song, sung at many weddings and funerals, is dreaded by some, but adapted by Lieb. Dave's amazing arrangement and simple but effective reharm transforms this war horse,

universal folk song into a brilliant vehicle for Quest to do its thing to the max. Dave puts the melody chorus and his entire solo into a deep medium slow 6/4 rhythm; with his dark but lyrical tenor we begin inside a cocoon of familiarity and freshness. While the tune itself is known worldwide, the reharm and the 6/4 feel is foreign and a bit unusual. This quickly becomes totally comfortable and right. We must mention the great creative work of our drummer Jabali Billy Hart. His ultimate mastery of this kind of feel and his enormous accumulated experience allows him to flow through this track with amazing fire, swing, and an uncanny ability to anticipate and complement what each soloist is trying to do. Just listen to Jabali's storm-chasing ability to whip up unbelievable intensity driving towards multi-leveled climaxes, over and over, spilling on top of each new one like a big 60 foot wave, crashing on to the shore only to begin another wave of musical intensity breaking over the rocks.

McJolt (Ron McClure) is fundamental in these situations. Ron's monster list of playing experiences does indeed show up in his highly intuitive ability to play the right note at the right time, when to break up the time, when to walk, when to lay out, and when to jump in for a split second musical decision. McJolt and Jabali are a team, like Ron Carter and Tony Williams, like Jack DeJohnette and Dave Holland, like Elvin Jones and Jimmy Garrison, and like Scott LaFaro and Paul Motian. And I am the lucky mofo that gets the fruits of their combined massive experiences, with the three of us playing like one mind and heart, working for Dave under his solo. We are supporting, shaping, suggesting, waiting, and basically launching Dave's ideas from his tenor. This tune "Dark Eyes" is like a textbook sonic lesson for all interested in learning about the dynamic workings of a contemporary small group jazz ensemble in free flight, all done in front of a live, enthusiastic French, Swiss, and Danish audience.

Some thoughts about the extramusical things that are not usually spoken about. On the road with four bros, friends, colleagues, etc., you appreciate the small things that make traveling easer. We did many one nighters, but also sometimes three, four, or even five nights in one club, like the Montmartre in Copenhagen, with the cool Kong Arthur Hotel around the corner. This is not a luxury hotel by any means but the rooms are clean and serviceable, if a bit small, but with everything you need. The people that run the hotel know and like the musicians that stay there. This hotel accommodates all the bands that work at the Montmartre so they are familiar with jazz musicians and their needs and desires. For example, we like a late breakfast if possible, and they do it for us with breakfast untill 11 o'clock instead of 10 or earlier in most places. And after the gig, after we hang out, we are hungry! The little guy at the front desk at the Kong always has some sandwiches for us, and DVDs! Sometimes it is hard to sleep after a burning night of music and drinks and friends, etc. So you can't sleep? Go to the front desk, grease the guy with the green jacket and bingo! He will find a cool action movie for you to fall asleep with.

The club too can help create good vibes for the band. We appreciate a nice dressing room with bathrooms inside, fresh towels, a big refrigerator filled with beer, soft drinks, water, etc., and sometimes even fresh fruit for us. Add some big chairs and couches to relax with friends between and after sets and it's heaven. Nils from the Montmartre actually rented a 9 foot Hamburg Steinway for the Quest gig that week of recording. It made a big difference in the sound of the group and most importantly showed his great respect for us and the music.

The Sunset Club in Paris where *Redemption* was recorded is also a cool place, not as expansive as in Copenhagen but still good. A much smaller venue with a packed audience literally sitting almost on top of you, it nevertheless creates a wonderful atmosphere to play in. The piano was tuned every night and the audience was one of the best in Europe.

These are two truly interesting and in my opinion very relevant CDs recorded eight years apart. In comparing the composition "Redemption" written by Billy Hart and performed by the same band, with both versions recorded live, but differently arranged from the Montmartre in Copenhagen in 1987 and the Sunset in Paris in 2005, we can hear the development of the band—especially on this iconic tune from Billy.

The Copenhagen Montmartre version from 1987 is a much simpler arrangement. It is also three times shorter than the 19 minute version from Paris in 2005. We have a straightforward statement of Billy Hart's great melody from Dave's soprano. Then there is a long soprano solo from Dave only playing off of the D pedal which is the general tonality of the melody. We have simplified the entire harmonic chord progression of the head melody to just this D pedal for improvisation and it's a great idea. Why? Because the simplicity of the blowing format allows for great freedom of expression, especially for Dave. And in turn this affects the way the rhythm develops too. Dave at the outset of his solo starts floating his phrases over the bar line without suggesting the normal 4/4 feel of the head melody. We instantly understand what he is playing and the entire rhythm section shifts into a much freer sense of the beat. We arrive at a floating rubato swirling flow that was first heard in John Coltrane's language in 1965 and especially in '66, after five years of the more or less of the same repertoire played by his classic Quartet during the early '60s. This way of playing is like a door we opened to use for our own personal expression. Dave's solo is a great example of just how melodically lyrical a soloist can be without a steady time feel and still by his extreme creativity and total mastery of motivic development he is able to create a very convincing and unified musical statement. The D pedal serves as a foundation, but Lieb utilizes the entire chromatic universe as an enormous palette for the vocabulary of his solo. After the soprano solo, there is no piano solo but the head melody out, an intentionally concise but powerful statement.

The 2005 live version from the Sunset Club in Paris is very different. This track is over 19 minutes long and it has now grown into a kind of extended composition with many parts to it. It starts with a drum introduction. This is, after all, Billy Hart's composition so from the start he puts his classic, iconic personal drum style on the piece. Then we have a new written melodic intro composed from the D minor pedal with the pulse established by the rhythm section. Now the melody is played but with some new rhythmic hits and rephrasing from Dave. The head is stated strongly with a clear eight bar A pedal in between the melody and the first solo. This time the piano solo is first, but now Dave has written an interesting set of changes specifically for the blowing for both of us, the piano solo and the following sax solo. This new set of changes captures the essence of the head melody but extends and broadens it, giving the soloist a wider template to choose from for the improvisations. The piano solo is on fire and very intense. I must admit it took me a while to feel free on this new format but it was worth it. Dave comes in and plays a great solo on the chord change form aspect of the tune. With the rhythm section behind him he can soar to new heights of intensity, followed by a full drum solo from Billy, a truly great statement. We play the head out and we are done—there is only the echo of the cymbals and the sound of a distant chord drifting after.

Hearing it all now in the comfort of my own home sure brings back those stirring nights of music and friends.

Redemption: Live in Europe (2005)
1. Round Midnight
2. Ogunde
3. WTC/Steel Prayers
4. Dark Eyes
5. Lonely Woman
6. Redemption

David Liebman: soprano sax, tenor saxophone, wooden flute
Richard Beirach: piano
Ron McClure: bass
Billy Hart: drums

Track 1 to 3 recorded live at Kantonsschule, Baden/Switzerland on November 3, 2005

Track 4 to 6 recorded live at Sunset Club/Paris by Radio France, on November 2, 2005.

Midpoint - Live At The Montmartre Copenhagen Denmark
1. The Code's Secret Code
2. The Snow Leopard
3. The 4th. Wall / Rectilinear
4. Midpoint
5. Pablo's Story
6. The Hollow Men
7. Redemption

David Liebman: soprano sax
Richard Beirach: piano
Ron McClure: bass
Billy Hart: drums

Recorded at the Montmartre, Copenhagen, Denmark, April 21 and 22, 1987

1987

1988 + 1991
Quest
Live 1988 + 1991
(Download)

So what is inspiration? Is it a perfect Hamburg 9-foot Steinway? A great sold out concert with 3,000 rabid fans? Ten-thousand dollars each?and Perfect monitors? A great meal before the concert? Amazing hotel suites for each member of the Quest quartet? Private planes? Ten roadies to carry everything?

Well, those things can be inspiring, but more often than not inspiration in our music comes directly from the music itself and the enormous empathy from each member to the others. This version of my tune "Pendulum," comes exactly 10 years after the original live version of this tune on a record called *Pendulum* recorded live at the Village Vanguard in New York. It makes for an interesting comparison. Ten years later with a different bass player, Ron McClure, and a different drummer, Billy Hart, but without Randy Brecker who was on the Vanguard recording which also had Frank Tusa on bass and Al Foster on drums.

Quest on tour was and is like a living, breathing entity all is own. Every band is in the end a collection of different personalities, different needs, and different types of interacting. Quest with Dave as the leader is a wonderfully disparate but extremely unified ensemble. We are united by very similar unspoken agreements about who are the real masters and important icons in our music's history, and the rich but relatively short legacy of contemporary small group improvisation. The Miles Davis Quintets, the John Coltrane Quartet, and the original Bill Evans Trios were our touchstones and our musical and spiritual inspirations.

I am sitting here in my house in Hessheim, Germany listening to this unbelievable Quest version of "Pendulum" from around 1988, recorded live in Europe. We were on a long tough tour with Quest, booked by Saudades, who were former ECM people. We had a big red tour bus with beds, TV, bathroom—funky but serviceable. Most importantly we had a great vibe with a cool, calm, tall driver named Stephen who drove us all over Europe. We had just flown in from someplace on Yugoslavian Airlines, which had an annoying little theme song, da, duh da da da duh, playing incessantly in the plane and the airport.

An awful little fucking earworm which we all laughed at, and then somehow wormed its way into the piano solo of the first tune of this concert,

"Pendulum." So here I am listening to this recording, 34 years later and I am up yelling and saying yeah to this remarkable band in free flight! The energy is amazing! We were all in our 40s but sound like much younger men. I hear not just energy but real power and enormous sensitivity to each other's playing and of course to the music as it unfolds in front of us, by us. Dave is a great leader, he learned from his years standing next to Elvin Jones and Miles Davis. He knows how to suggest things, not instruct. He can with one note followed by a short silence, inflect the subtle changes of dynamics necessary to keep a performance from just being one burnout after another. His very generous nature gives the band in "Pendulum" a kind of formless spontaneous form by instigating an asymmetrical kind of trading with himself and my piano soloing in unusual but fascinating back and forth long trades of ideas. This trading acts as a catalyst to keep giving Ron and Billy new impetus, driving the momentum forward. Always forward, back and forth from a deep throbbing 4/4 feel anchored by our great bass player, Ron McClure, picked up and exploded by Jabali Billy Hart. I feel like there is a fucking volcano erupting under my feet! It picks me up and rolls me, cascades me down a mountain, like a controlled avalanche, controlled because we don't fall or get covered up and killed by the snow!

Listen to the truly awesome power and deep swing of Billy himself driving us ahead with his uncanny ability to know exactly in the multitude of phrases where to put his accents and cymbal crashes, and especially the important big ones that come up in tandem with myself and Ron. It is a fucking boiling red hot cauldron of fire and ice, but under it all is a total respect for the time, for the individual phrases, and importantly where does each phrase go and what does it need to make its best showing as an entity of music. The rhythm section has great flexibility and can and does turn on a dime. The dime being Dave's notes and my accompaniment.

There is the feeling while playing and listening again now that everything seems possible. Straight ahead swinging shit, broken time, freer feeling of rubato time, open rubato ballad at the beginning of the piano solo. The time breaks down and there is an acknowledgement that there has been enough straight ahead 4/4 walking from the long trading with Dave and myself. This happens automatically, with strong but unspoken results, the music tells us what to do. Here Ron and myself are freely associating with interactive ideas that move far away from the mostly F sharp pedal tone of the first long trading section. Ron has the ears of a human fucking radar machine! Billy goes to brushes and completes the new landscape for the beginning of the piano solo. Soon we build it up and go back to the energy vibe, but at a slower more swinging tempo. Why not? It felt right and we did it. Why must we keep the whole 16 minute plus performance at one tempo? I finish my solo at a great burning point and then Ron takes a great lyrical bass solo.

Back to the quartet and instead of a normal unaccompanied dramatic drum solo Dave has decided wisely to keep the feeling of uneven bar length trades with the quartet and Billy alternately. It is great showcase for the power and brilliance of Jabali. He sounds like a combination of Mt. St. Helens erupting while the soft ethereal sounds of his brushes resemble a Japanese calligrapher at work. Dave brings back the melody of "Pendulum" but with a very creative spontaneous radical unison phrasing suggested to me, which I immediately pick up and continue. We finish, the audience explodes, they love it. What started as a recalcitrant audience standing in the cold transformed after one long tune into a warm enthusiastic response.

So what inspired us in the end? Actually, it was the music and each other's great contributions.

The party after didn't hurt either.

Big fun! The next morning we all piled back into the big red bus and traveled to the next gig, next town, next hotel, next club, or concert.

What a great life!

Quest Live 1988
1. Pendulum
2. The Code's Secret Code
3. The Hollow Men / Third Visit
4. Elm

Quest Live 1991 - Standards
1. On Green Dolphin Street
2. Softly, As In A Morning Sunrise
3. After The Rain
4. Footprints
5. Green Dolphin Street

Quest Live 1991 - Originals
1. Gargoyles
2. Carissima
3. Napanoch
4. The Hollow Men
5. Redemption
6. Pendulum
7. Constellation / Rectilinear
8. Pablo's Story
9. Tender Mercies
10. Redemption

David Liebman: soprano sax
Richard Beirach: piano
Ron McClure: bass
Billy Hart: drums

Produced for release by Kurt Renker

1990

Quest

Of One Mind

CMP Records – CMP CD 47

This CD was a very special experience. It is a perfect example of what I like to call *minimum structure = maximum creativity*. But this could only happen in a band of serious, seasoned, empathetic, and experienced creative musicians, preferably a working band. Well, those elements were certainly met with our band Quest. Dave, Jabali Billy Hart, Ron McClure, and myself have pretty much been there and done that for many years. So it was in 1990 that Kurt Renker, the owner and producer of CMP Records invited Quest to his great studio in the forest of Zerkall, Germany, for a recording.

Originally we were going to just go in and play, without any preconceived ideas. But the morning of the first day of recording Dave and I had a short but intense discussion about the session. He felt, and I agreed after a while, that we would get better results if we had a very basic and simple program rather than just jumping in and going for it. These were not even sketches on paper but just some simple verbal instructions. Like starting with bowed rubato bass accompanied by light cymbals. Then the piano comes in with some kind of harmonic idea, a pedal point possibly, followed by Lieb entering on soprano sax, still rubato, finding a melody, and then developing it. All accomplished with lots of interaction and group sharing of ideas. This procedure is certainly not new in jazz history but it was the first for us with Quest, since previously many of our recordings centered upon originals supplied by all of us mixed with personally arranged standards.

The whole CD eventually involved this minimum structure = maximum creativity approach. In the first piece that we called "Commonality," there is a wonderful melodic opening from Dave, really like a small flower opening rapidly in front of you. Then I have a long lyrically based improvised free duo with Ron. His amazing ears and deep sensitivity are really on display here as he follows my every twist and turn harmonically, most importantly in the emotional arena. Jabali joins us for a gathering of strength and with a more insistent flow, while Dave returns and gives us a final closing statement.

The second long piece is called "Of One Mind" and it certainly is! I begin with some broken intervallic ideas in a kind of loose pulse, staying "broken" and with lots of space for interaction from Dave and rhythmic interpolations from master drummer Jabali Billy Hart. Ron joins in the fray, then we are exchanging phrases and collectively using with short burning ideas, from which it evolves into a straight ahead 4/4 time feeling but without chord changes. We let the need for a chord progression go. The forward motion of the time and a few broken angular phrases are enough to generate a killing long track.

Track three features Billy on a song he called "Changuito Tapestry." It is about a special beat that Billy knows from master percussionist Changuito, from which we built a whole track just around that cool beat! A great vamp develops and is thrown around the various instruments in the band.

This recording is extremely dear to me because it shows our vulnerability, taking big risks in a recording situation that I am very proud of. It is a true axiom that in science the simpler the structure the more it can support. This is the principle here, but this way of communicating can only occur with the right cats of peer/equal experience and total agreement about the essential elements of what it is that results in a great spontaneous jazz ensemble recording!

1. Commonality
2. Of One Mind
3. Changuito Tapestry
4. Passages

David Liebman: soprano sax
Richie Beirach: piano
Ron McClure: bass
Billy Hart: drums

Producer – Kurt Renker
Recorded By Walter Quintus at Ztudio Zerkall, Germany, July 1990

Quest 1990

2009
Dave Liebman & Richie Beirach
Quest For Freedom
Sunnyside – SSC 1266

Imagine my extreme surprise when I first heard big Jim McNeely's amazing arrangements of Dave and my compositions for big band, played by the Hessischer Rundfunk Radio Big Band in Frankfurt! They were truly one of a kind. My tune "Pendulum" got a fantastic creative and totally contemporary arrangement that brought out many new sides of the duo with myself and Dave. Jim's great arrangements showed us never before conceived creative techniques which were unusual but totally logical extensions and new directions for our kind of chromaticism that we had been playing in small groups and duo for years. The essence of the project was that big Jim knew our music. He knew me, my tunes, my harmony, my rhythmic comping approach, etc. And being a piano player himself with major figures like Stan Getz and Chet Baker, Jim has his own wonderful personal creative vocabulary that he brought to this project.

This original arrangement of "Pendulum" was like a tapestry of supporting material completely composed by Jim. But it was as if he had transcribed some of my own comping patterns from our long recorded history yet with his own individual stamp. He made the big band sound at times like a big enormous Steinway with all the instruments in the big band! His backgrounds and comping acted as a real catalyst to the three solos. First Tony Lakatos on tenor sax with a great big tone and wonderful sweep on these interesting changes that Jim wrote to enhance the F sharp pedal. These original chord changes gave us a boost and a platform to launch our solos. After Tony there is a long burning piano solo that I still enjoy hearing right now. By the way, this track is from the live concert in a big hall in Frankfurt. You can hear the intensity of the band and the reaction of the enthusiastic audience.

So now comes Dave with his soprano solo and its a tour de force! At times with just me comping and then with the band trading crazy four bar phrases with him, it is a solo for the ages. Big Jim pulls out all the traditional and non traditional big band setups. The harmony sounds cool and contemporary, the rhythmic shit swinging but not corny, and the drums killing. This is all of us reading the difficult and not usual rhythmic hits with precision, grace, and I must say a great degree of power, balls, and intensity.

The other tunes from Dave show many other moods and colors. We played a great piece composed by Jim called "The Sky Is The Limit" that ends the CD with amazing flights of creative writing and playing.

Big thanks to the Hessische Rundfunk Big Band cats for their great playing, to Jim for his unbelievable arrangements, and to my brother Lieb for his iconic and consistent great playing.

Big band, big fun!

1. Pendulum
2. Jung
3. Vendetta
4. WTC (David Liebman)
5. Port Ligat
6. Enfin
7. The Sky Is The Limit

David Liebman: Soprano Sax, Wooden Flute
Richie Beirach: Piano
Julian Arguelles, Tony Lakatos: Tenor Saxophone
Heinz-Dieter Sauerborn, Oliver Leicht: Alto Saxophone
Rainer Heute: Baritone Saxophone
Axel Schlosser, Bijon Watson, Martin Auer, Thomas Vogel: Trumpet
Christian Jaksjö, Günter Bollmann, Peter Feil: Trombone
Manfred Honetschläger: Bass Trombone
Martin Scales: Guitar
Peter Reiter: Piano
Thomas Heidepriem: Bass
Paul Höchstädter: Drums
Jim McNeely: Conductor, Arranger

Tracks 1 and 7 recorded live in concert HR Sendesaal, Hessischer Rundfunk Frankfurt/Main June 20, 2009
Tracks 2 to 6 recorded at Hörfunkstudio II, Hessischer Rundfunk Frankfurt/Main June 18 & 19, 2009

2009
Dave Liebman & Richie Beirach
Unspoken
Outnote Records – OTN 011

This duo recording from 2009 has a feeling all its own among the many CDs recorded by Dave and myself. It includes a collection of originals, standards, and a classical piece with improvisation. With such diversity of material it somehow holds together because of the musical and spiritual thread woven by us throughout. After so many years making music together there is a common heart, a common purpose, and of course a common goal to make the most beautiful, interesting, and intense music we can.

The first piece is called "Invention" which has a very unusual history and uncommon path to our door. Written by Aram Khachaturian, the great Armenian composer for his ballet called *Gayaneh* it is truly a one of a kind composition. I had heard it when I was a child studying with my great classical teacher and first mentor James Palmieri in the 1950s. It had been adapted into a short piano piece; interestingly it was without any chords until the final phrases. This miracle of two part counterpoint somehow felt incredibly complete. Even though we play only line against line, it gives the feeling of extreme harmonic and melodic richness, and of course beauty. Khachaturian's genius as a composer, in this case using only two lines, implies a world of harmonic tapestry and variety. Very influenced by the greatness of Bach's many pieces, especially the "Goldberg Variations" and the two part inventions, this deceptively simple writing held enormous riches and turned out to be a perfect vehicle for improvisation for Dave and myself.

My arrangement involved Dave playing the melodic line written in the treble clef of the piano score, with me doubling his line in unison, playing the complimentary lower melodic line in the bass clef of the piano score. At certain points I let Dave play his part without my unison doubling because I wanted more of a sense of independent counterpoint and this created a question and answer feeling which I wanted to keep for the piece. Now, how to use this composition as a springboard for improvisations? Each written composition has within it a hidden or obvious improvising format. It must be discovered, created, and brought into being. It is not always easy or obvious. Should it be a set of chord changes drawn from the essence of the harmonic structure of the piece? Should it stay linear,a two part linear adventure in weaving a new variation on what is given? Well, this took some time and much thought by me in preparing the piece for our recording. Finally the answer emerged magically and unintentionally. I looked at the key signature—hmmmm, it had a strong B flat minor feeling—yes!

So I checked the harmonic implications going through the piece like a detective looking for clues! Yes, B flat minor, but what else? Okay, D flat major, G flat major, C diminished, A flat Mixolydian. I suddenly saw a blueprint through the piece, not in every bar of course but a kind of template that could provide a loose but clear basis for improvisation. It was the B flat Aeolian scale! Pure and simple! In other words, a simple D flat major scale but from B flat, C, D flat, E flat, F, G flat, A flat, and finally back to B flat. A modal B flat Aeolian scale that implied a chord built on each note of the scale. Man, it worked! I was able to tell Dave my idea, from which he could move freely around that particular scale, while at the piano I was able to use each note in the scale as a possible root for a chord built on it, but still staying within the confines of the Aeolian notes in the scale. It worked and allowed us to have a clear harmonic framework while not restricting us to a set of fixed chord changes in time with exact bars and a closed structure. Wow!

So after we play the written head we begin a duo improvisation on that scale with the implied roots, etc. With Dave's stunning and elegant soprano sound and beautiful expressive melodic ideas using this kind of mournful scale, our interaction keeps the natural flow of the original writing and also allows our own style of duo playing to come through.

This CD also has my very creative and radical reharmonization of the standard "All The Things You Are," which redefines the possibilities of this old warhorse tune.

And finally we play a piece by John Coltrane called "Transition," a relatively simple and short line Coltrane recorded with his classic quartet in 1965 in an amazing version for the ages. Here is our duo version of it, freely interpreting Trane's deep and compelling piece in a tour de force for our duo.

1. Invention
2. All The Things You Are
3. Ballad 1
4. Awk Dance
5. New Life
6. Walz For Lenny
7. Tender Mercies
8. Transition
9. Hymn For Mom / Prayer For Michael

Dave Liebman: Tenor Saxophone, Soprano Saxophone, Wooden Flute
Richie Beirach: Piano
Producer – Kurt Renker

Recorded by Walter Quintus at CMP Studio, Zerkall, Germany December 2009

2010
Dave Liebman & Richard Beirach with Lee Konitz
KnowingLee
Outnote Records – OTN 006

This CD began with me and Dave sitting around somewhere talking about guys we would like to record with. Soon enough Lee Konitz's name came up, envisioning a trio presentation. He still sounded great but was getting older, 82 at the time. Our producer and great friend Kurt Renker agreed and the idea was confirmed. Calls were made, dates and other details established allowing Dave and myself to move into the next gear, the "What should we record" mode. We came up with what we thought would be a varied, yet challenging tune list that Lee would like and be comfortable with, and also kick his ass a bit. We both knew Lee was very flexible musically and had played in many different styles including free improvisations which we especially wanted to capture with him.

We three were connected in some interesting ways. Lee studied with Lennie Tristano and played a lot with him. Dave and I also both studied with Lenny. Meaningful or not, we were all Jewish! Lee was always himself wherever and with whomever he played with, something which both Dave and I aspire to over our careers.

The recording had many wonderful heartfelt musical moments, with generous amounts of spontaneous and free undetermined tracks, along with some real chestnut standards like "Alone Together," "What Is This Thing Called Love," and "In Your Own Sweet Way." An original written in tandem with Lieb called "KnowingLee" was specially written for our guest. The music sounds very relaxed and smooth; the recorded sound excellent from Kurt's great studio in the forest of Zerkall near Cologne; the amazing 9 foot Bechstein piano; and the great, late recording engineer Walter Quintus. We were very happy with the results.

There were crazy unsettling things going on behind the scenes that were really not anticipated and not welcome at all. There is a time for truth telling and not just ignoring or focusing on the end result. Dave and I are always involved and also enjoy very much the process of recording, but not this time! To be honest and blunt Lee was a drag personally which only slightly improved over the two days of recording. We tried to keep this tension and strange vibe out of the music and I think we did well, but it was a fight, to tell the unpleasant truth! Lee, being the senior guy with two younger bros (even though Dave and I were well into our 60s), seemed to want to put us and especially me in my place.

Maybe we made him nervous, although I find that hard to believe. Actually we bent over backwards trying to make him feel comfortable in every way. The choice of the material was built around putting Lee in an ideal place where he didn't have to learn much of our music, deferring to him constantly. But I felt that he talked down to me, in general disrespecting me in ways that I hadn't encountered in 40 years since I was a very young cat coming up in New York City! For example, he said to me while in the studio, "Hey Richie, do you know 'Stella By Starlight'?" I couldn't believe it! That's like asking a surgeon if he knows what a scalpel is. But I swallowed my anger and pride and said, "Sure Lee…in B flat?" Which is the key the tune is always played in. Then, to add insult to injury, my question of the key freaked the brother out. Lee said, "Shit! Now why did you have to say that? Why are you jamming me up? Maybe I want another key!" I should have gotten up and walked over to him and said something like, hey mofo, who you think you're talking to? I'm not some damn student you can try to humiliate. Stop that abusive bullying shit or get the hell out of here!

But I didn't, for the sake of the music. And I am glad I didn't cause that would have been fatally disruptive and the end of the recording. But that was just one of several examples of Lee's shitty and unnecessary behavior. Okay, maybe I was too sensitive, but Dave was there and he was shocked too!

Maybe Lee felt that we needed that old bebop hard-ass combination of tough love, and by being overbearing and testing some macho shit he was trying to train us for some future situation. But that made no sense for a variety of reasons.

Anyway, the music is really good and even great in spots. An amazing duo improvisation with just Dave and Lee on soprano saxes, one on "Body And Soul," and one completely free improvisation called "Migration" were fantastic. Then a beautiful moving improvised duo with Lee and myself named "Universal Lament" which Lieb particularly loved, with Lee sounding stunningly beautiful on soprano sax.

No one ever promised you a rose garden!

1. In Your Own Sweet Way
2. Don't Tell Me What Key
3. Universal Lament
4. Alone Together
5. KnowingLee
6. Solar
7. Migration
8. Thingin' / All The Things That …
9. Trinity
10. Body And Soul
11. Hi Beck
12. What Is This Thing Called Love

Dave Liebman: Tenor Saxophone, Soprano Saxophone
Richie Beirach: Piano
Lee Konitz : Alto Saxophone, Soprano Saxophone
Recorded and mixed by Walter Quintus at CMP Studio, Zerkall, Germany 2010
Producer – Kurt Renker

Richie, Lee Konitz, Dave 2010

2011
Quest
Circular Dreaming
Enja Records – ENJ-9594 2

I have been talking a lot about inspiration in these notes looking back over 50 years of recordings with Dave. That is as it should be because it is not a topic often discussed in general. But for this recording I would like to speak about the nuts and bolts of putting together the music, specifically for recording purposes. The responsibilities of the leader(s) involves several aspects: an overall concept of the CD beforehand, choosing material, rehearsals, and finally recording. Then post production which means listening, choosing best takes, editing, mixing;,mastering, and finally the possibility of writing liner notes as well as cover design. There is quite a lot of stuff to do!

For these notes concerning the *Circular Dreaming* CD, and in fact referring to the general procedure described above, the interesting thing is the idea to record a body of music in the first place. This is where Dave and myself go into our partnership/duo colleague mode. We have been doing these pre-production activities seemingly forever, having collaborated on nearly 60 CDs where we are co-leaders or featured sidemen together. Quest was a collaborative style band but most of the musical decisions and composition choices were made by Dave and me.

This CD was unusual in that we usually record our own compositions, as well as featuring a few highly personalized standard tunes. But in this case, because of the great influence along with enormous love and respect we have for Miles Davis and his groups, we devoted an entire CD to covering some of the tunes he recorded in the 1960s, mostly written by Wayne Shorter. Also we decided to record one original tune each to round out the album. We had a long list of possible choices of tunes because the Miles groups had an extensive repertoire. We chose the Miles tunes together and created some very interesting and natural arrangements of "Prince Of Darkness," "Hand Jive," "Vonetta," and of course Dave's own "MD," a tune he wrote for Miles years ago that we recorded on our first ECM record, *Lookout Farm* in 1973. I did the arrangements for "Footprints," "Nefertiti," "Paraphernalia," and my own waltz called "Circular Dreaming" which is dedicated to Miles and his great groups.

About six months before securing the record date, Dave and I started our work towards the project. There were many phone calls and e-mails going back and forth as I was living and teaching in a professorship position in Leipzig at the time (2011), while Lieb lived in Pennsylvania. Luckily we met quite a few times for a few gigs so we did have face to face encounters and duo rehearsals. Actually we both love this part of the creative process. Starting with a feeling, we take the material apart with both of us throwing out ideas until we come up with a rough working plan. In this case it was the concept—Quest plays the music of Miles Davis Quintets of the 1960s. Then the lists start—we keep all of our ideas fluid—there is nothing fixed or set in stone at this point. We have both learned to be open and flexible at this stage of the process, actually trying to keep that open attitude right to the end. Dave is a great organizer. He knows how to take an idea and come up with possibilities for arrangements and various treatments of someone else's tunes. He enjoys adding specific rhythmic hits and rephrasing the melody for a more personal interpretation of the piece. I like to simplify the written parts and blowing forms as much as possible to allow for the most freedom in the actual recording and performing process.

The truth is that Lookout Farm and Quest both developed primarily out of our duo. We first started playing as a duo in 1968 in Dave's loft on West 19th Street in New York over 50 years ago. Since then we still follow the process just described when putting music together, whether for the duo or quartet. Of course, we don't ignore our bass players and drummers! Jeff Williams and Frank Tusa were young but very creative mofos, giving us good input with Lookout Farm in the 1970s. Ron McClure and Jabali Billy Hart are great musicians, leaders, and composers in their own right who contributed a great deal to the many recordings of Quest we have done together over the years.

In the case of this CD, we had the opportunity to play a week at Birdland in New York City prior to this recording session and this was a great warmup. The vibe in the recording studio was very cool! Relaxed intensity is the best way to describe it. We did just a few takes of each tune, two to three at the most, capturing the essence of the music. We always try to be accurate, with intonation and a smooth rhythmic feel as an imperative. But we are old hands at this and we usually get what we want pretty quickly. It helps to have two good days in the studio, no cheap one day of rushing a recording which we have done on more than one occasion.

The magic was present at this one for sure. Listening back briefly there was a lot of "wow!!" moments, with big smiles and head nods all around.

This was a fun recording to do and definitely some music you could listen to in the future and be proud of. Along with our producer, Kurt Renker, we had the chance to meet and work with Florian Van Volxem who mixed this recording, and with whom we have a wonderful relationship to this day, all beginning with *Circular Dreaming*.

1. Pinocchio
2. Prince Of Darkness
3. Footprints
4. M.D.
5. Hand Jive
6. Vonetta
7. Nefertiti
8. Circular Dreaming
9. Paraphernalia

Dave Liebman: Tenor Saxophone, Soprano Saxophone
Richie Beirach: Piano
Ron McClure : Bass
Billy Hart: Drums

Recorded at Tedesco Studios, New Jersey February 2011
Mixed by Florian Van Volxem at CMP Studio, Zerkall, Germany
Producer – Kurt Renker

Quest 2011

2015
Dave Liebman & Richie Beirach
Balladscapes
Intuition Records – INT 3444 2

When Dave and I were kids living in New York City, him in his loft on 19th Street and me on Spring Street in Soho, we often listened to records together. From 1968 through the early seventies we were listening of course to John Coltrane and Miles Davis daily, the really burning stuff. We were young and learning our craft. But after hours of listening and playing duo we would get some energy by eating together in Chinatown or other low cost places like Ratner's on the Lower East Side where the bread was enough to keep you going!

Then we would go back to his loft and chill, listening to ballad albums like Coltrane's of course, or Bill Evans *Sunday at the Village Vanguard*, sprinkled with some beautiful classical stuff like Debussy, Ravel, or contemporary folks like Schoenberg, Scriabin, etc., all slow movements, or Charles Ives's "Central Park in the Dark," and of course great Bach compositions like "Air on a G String" and the "B minor Mass," etc.

We always wanted to make an all-ballad CD and here it is.

Beginning with my arrangement and reharm of Bach's amazing piece, "Sicilana," we explore this universal gem of a composition. Dave's warm soprano sax sound is both very elegant and sensuous at the same time. Besides the Bach piece, this recording features a few originals from both of us, selected jazz standards, and show tune standards, all extremely reharmonized and recomposed but still keeping the original feeling of whatever the tune being explored might be. There is an amazing tune from Wayne Shorter called "Sweet Pea," a stunning ballad dedication to Billy Strayhorn, while John Coltrane is well represented by Dave's great arrangement of "Welcome" and "Expression" as a medley. In my opinion, "Expression" is Trane's greatest composition, reaching the absolute top of jazz ballads.

We wrote "Kurtland" together which is one of my favorite co-written pieces with Dave, something that we have done more of in recent years, meaning co-composition with my harmony and Lieb's melodies. It is written for Kurt Renker, our long time friend, patron and producer who without his great consistent support for over 40 years we would not be anywhere near the musicians we have become.

Here's the way it happened: Dave calls me from Budapest late one night and says, "I got a melody...okay!" He is sitting on his bed in a hotel room where he takes out his soprano and plays me this beautiful lyrical melody. I am totally stunned. It's great—long and multi-faceted with incredible development. So he sends it to me asking if I would write chords to it. Yes, of course! I go over to the piano and everything is flowing along beautifully. The melody is so well written that within the notes are already suggestions of chords supporting it. I can hardly keep up with my ideas, working like a mofo for hours... my neck hurts... my back is killing me, but fuck that, I just keep going. I don't want to stop for fear of losing it. Finally after hours I get a rough sketch. The next day it still sounds good but I instantly hear a few things I must fix. The bottom line is that I got it! I am excited. This does not happen every day even for us. I call Dave and play it for him. He says yeah and we agree to continue to work on it together.

I love this tune, dedicated to Kurt. It is contemporary but not dissonant, permeated by complex chord formations. The content of the harmony is not simple for sure but I wanted to highlight the absolute beauty of the melody and I think I did.

I love this *Balladscapes* CD! Thanks Lieb! Thanks Kurt!

1. Siciliana
2. For all we know
3. This is new
4. Quest
5. Master of the Obvious
6. Zingaro
7. Sweet Pea
8. Kurtland
9. Moonlight in Vermont
10. Lazy Afternoon
11. Welcome / Expression
12. DL
13. Day Dream

Dave Liebman: Tenor Saxophone, Soprano Saxophone, Wooden Flute
Richie Beirach: Piano

Recorded by Florian Van Volxem at CMP Studio, Zerkall, Germany April 2015
Producer – Kurt Renker

Richie and Dave 2015

2017
Dave Liebman & Richie Beirach
Eternal Voices
Jazzline Records N 77067

This release celebrates the 50th year anniversary of Lieb and I meeting, playing, and recording our music together. It has been an amazing run and happily is still ongoing, stronger than ever. This recording called *Eternal Voices* is very special even for us. We chose to use short but very powerful masterpieces of classical music from Bach to Schoenberg as a format for our improvisations. We have both played this kind of music before but this is the first time that we concentrated on a complete repertoire of these great compositions by the masters.

Rather than outline a tune by tune analysis of the music I prefer to speak about the atmosphere of the recording and its preparation. I have always studied and loved classical music. Starting at five years old, I studied for thirteen years with a great old Italian master teacher, James Palmieri. This was before I became interested in jazz piano playing. I was a good student but there always seemed to be something missing. In my foolish young and uninformed mind I thought I would somehow, someday, improve these short pieces that I used to play, some of which we have recorded here. Little did I know that years later, and after thousands of hours of work I would be in a position to actually use these pieces as a springboard for improvisation!

Jazz improvisation at the level that we aspire to is really about mutual trust, unconscious skill level, collective feelings, and the unknown. The risk is real, we are sometimes hanging out there on the precipice of disaster. Which direction to go in the instant? No time, no possibility of rehearsing or directing, no forcing the duo music into a preconceived notion—we are sometimes one inch from kitsch! Especially in the limited diatonic but elevated language of Bach, Mozart, and Beethoven. Like all the great masterworks, difficulty and personal satisfaction go hand in hand. The wonderful pressure of making a recording that will live in digital information forever certainly focuses the mind and spirit. We are not afraid but alert to the opportunities of the moment. The challenge is to honor iconic composers from 400 years ago and still create something fresh and relevant to our time that will hopefully last eternally.

We need to say a few words about the Bartók recordings of this project which was really a mysterious process and outcome. Talk about going back to our roots! From 1968 to 1972 I studied theory and composition at the Manhattan School of Music with Ludmila Ulehla. One of the greatest series of works that we analyzed were the six Bartók string quartets. I still have the pocket scores I used in school to understand and absorb these great iconic works of contemporary music for the ages. Dave and I spent hours looking and listening with these scores. It was Dave's great idea to arrange just the slow movements for this recording of classical pieces.

So much of my own jazz vocabulary comes from Bartók. The incredible intervallic ideas that are super developed in extraordinary ways, not just in the string quartets but in his "Music for Strings, Percussion and Celeste," the "Concerto for Orchestra," and the "14 Bagatelles for Solo Piano." This was the wealth of musical ideas from which Dave and I drew from. Like a great giant reservoir, we drank from it over and over. The content of the six String Quartet's slow movements were especially important to our development as young jazz improvisors. As well, I must say the great spirit and powerful energy of Bartók's statements moved us and inspired our imaginations. There is a connection between Bartók and Coltrane which connects us to much of the source of the chromatic universe. That universe and the all-embracing humanity of both Coltrane and Bartók's music surrounded and supported our journey through these interpretations offered here.

A fascinating revelation came after our recording of the more contemporary pieces like the Scriabin, Schoenberg, and of course Bartók. The harmonic and melodic language that Dave and I used to improvise on these pieces was actually derived from the essence of the exact melodies from these masters! So when recording we had a strong feeling of returning to the actual sources of what had become our personal language over the years. This was something unpredictable but very comforting and life giving. In summary, our own personal ways of improvising are in some ways directly related source-wise to these iconic pieces. Combined with the various styles of bebop and the impressionistic voices of Fauré, Debussy, and Ravel, the well we drank from ran deep. Add to this wealth of sources the ever-present references made to the John Coltrane Quartet (especially the incredible modal chromaticism of McCoy Tyner) and we had a large, colorful palette from which to paint our improvisations.

The rough history of classical music can be generally understood to be from Bach to Ligeti. That does not mean there aren't many other composers before, during, and after that we love and that are important, but just as loose bookends, Bach to Ligeti offers the general parameters and historical scope of what musicians have to deal with when referencing the classical repertoire.

The two tunes from Dave and myself for Ernst Bucher and Walter Quintus are basically written off a very old and preset form called the passacaglia. The structure is derived from a repeated, revolving, and ascending or descending bass line figure with simple chords, harmonized along the way, highlighted by a yearning and soulful crying melody with a suggestion of a blues feeling. Ernst and Walter were our close friends and brothers that we lost in the last few years. Here they are memorialized in song.

These recordings, like many of our duo projects, are all done in a very special place in the forest of Zerkall, Germany, with our old and dear friend and patron Kurt Renker. An old house functions as a recording studio with an incredible older Bechstein piano and a youngish genius engineer named Florian Van Volxem. It is intimate and very relaxed but totally focused and creative. In this atmosphere we are free to create our duo music—no time limits, no other musicians in other studios, no distractions. We are blessed with Kurt and Florian. The other critical component of the success of these projects is the piano tuner, Egon Zähringer. To have a tuner of such great skill who knows me and the instrument is the perennial dream scenario of most pianists and saxophonists because (especially in a duo) intonation is critical. The piano must be *perfectly* in tune all the time. The luxury of having Egon be there during the recording is wonderful insurance against any intonation problems. Dave's intonation is really great so we can go with the flow of the music and not waste precious creative energy time with fixing mechanics.

Dave is an ideal partner, I describe his approach as relaxed intensity. We love this intense focus on the continuous challenge of collective creativity. We rehearse very little but after our lifetime of playing, thinking, and recording music together we get to the essence of the music immediately.

Dave Liebman has contributed much to giving our music longevity and consistent greatness. He is still full of surprises— a quality that is the essence of jazz in all its marvelous and varied forms and colors.

This sound of surprise still enthralls us and brings life and light to the world of music and beyond.

CD 1

1. W.A. Mozart - Piano Concerto No. 23, K, 488, 2nd Movement, Adagio in F sharp minor
2. L.v. Beethoven - Piano Sonata No. 30 opus 109 in E major, 3rd Movement, Adagio
3. J.S. Bach - Little Prelude No. 4 in D major, BWV 936, Andante
4. F. Mompou - Impressiones Intimas
5. G. Faure - Pavanne
6. For Ernst (Beirach)
7. For Walter (Liebman)
8. A. Khatchaturian - Childrens Song No. 1, Andantino
9. A. Scriabin - Prelude, Op. 74, No. 2
10. B. Bartók - Bagatelles, Op.6, No. 6, Lento
11. A. Schoenberg - Colors, from 5 Pieces for Orchestra, Op.16, piano reduction by Richie Beirach

CD 2

1. Bartók String Quartet No. 1, Sz. 40 (Op. 7) _ I. Lento
2. Bartók String Quartet No. 2, Sz. 67 (Op. 17) _ III. Lento
3. Bartók String Quartet No. 3, Sz. 85 _ I. Prima parte_ Moderato
4. Bartók String Quartet No. 4, Sz. 91 _ III. Non troppo lento
5. Bartók String Quartet No. 5, Sz. 102 _ II. Adagio molto
6. Bartók String Quartet No. 6, Sz. 114 _ IV. Mesto

CD 1, Track 1,2, 3,4,5,10 arranged by Richie Beirach
CD 1, Track 6,7,9,11 arranged by Richie Beirach and Dave Liebman
CD 2 arranged by Dave Liebman with help from Richie Beirach

Dave Liebman: Soprano Sax, Tenor Sax, C-Flute
Richie Beirach: Piano

Recorded by Florian Van Volxem at CMP Studio, Zerkall, Germany December 2016 and August 2017 Producer – Kurt Renker

2021
Dave Liebman & Richie Beirach
Empathy: Five Improvised Soundscapes 2016-2020
Jazzline Records N 77094

Between 2017 and 2020 Dave and I recorded five different independent projects with producer Kurt Renker and engineer Florian Van Volxem: a saxophone and piano duo; a trio with saxophone, piano, and iconic drummer Jack DeJohnette; a solo saxophone CD; a solo piano CD; and a 55 minute CD of a piece with Dave and I overdubbing on a prepared soundtrack created by Kurt and Florian.

Dave and I have improvised a lot in our 50 years of playing together but never with such laser-like focus. The intense feelings of discovery, joy, and pure freedom one gets from just sitting down and playing are a special gift that we surely worked for for our whole musical lives.

In the fall of 2020 during the Covid-19 pandemic, I was stuck in my house in Hessheim, Germany with all concerts and tours canceled. It was a difficult situation for an active, performing jazz musician and with so much free unstructured time I found myself trying to focus on some positive things that could be done.

One of those positive things for us was listening back to these recordings. What connects them is that all the music is improvised, no compositions, and no preconceptions. Talking with Dave and Kurt on the phone during this lockdown the idea emerged that these five recordings should be released together because they are all really a part of the same whole. This was a crazy, wonderful, and pretty unrealistic idea for any time, but during a world pandemic? Forget about it!

So the big question was, can we find a record label that would be interested in releasing these five very different recordings?

But there are times when extraordinary ideas converge during unusual times. This was one of them for sure in our musical lifetimes. With the vision and persistence of Kurt Renker and the totally heroic and massive artistic support of Joachim Becker from Jazzline Records, it is now a reality. Instead of being counterintuitive to release a five-CD box of improvised music during a monster pandemic, it was absolutely the right thing to do. We hope it will give hope and inspire all the listeners and creative musicians suffering from the loss of their collective artistic outlets.

CD 1
Dave Liebman - Richie Beirach

Empathy

All the music on this CD was completely improvised. Non-linear, spontaneously formed structures which just unfolded in front of our ears.

When playing this music I have a feeling, an emotion, a wordless thought originating from my heart or an instinctive part of me. This feeling or emotion then runs from my heart to my ear in a nanosecond. The feeling becomes a melodic idea or a sound leading to a chord or a whole phrase.

And because of over sixty years of involvement with music, ear training, and experiences accumulated over this time, the notes, phrases, chords, and ideas literally flash from my ear to my fingers on to the piano.

There is no hesitation, no insecurity, and it completely bypasses my brain, heart, ear and hands. The brain is way too slow and unfortunately too judgmental to be a part of this almost reflexive series of interlocking acts. That's how I play in this situation.

Now imagine me and Dave doing this esoteric, slightly magical operation together, in tandem so to speak! Sounds like a magic trick, right? But happily it is not a trick, just the wonderful result of each of us having a lifetime of experience and opportunity to exercise these extremely sophisticated and hard-won skills.

We started this recording session with nothing planned, just to play together and see what happens. There was very little talking before the recording or between takes. Just maybe something like "Code, let me start this one with the soprano" or "Lieb, how about I begin this one and then you come in on tenor?" That was basically it!

After we finished the recording we didn't really know what we had on tape, the way we usually do when we play tunes. After taking the music home and listening, I was astonished at the cohesion, the natural flow of ideas, the inherent and instinctual logic, and especially the transcendent beauty of the duo music we improvised together. It was an amazing, inspiring, and truly hopeful experience shared by us all.

1. Instinct   **Dave:** Beyond technique; what is most natural and undefinable in ones music
   Reverence **Richie:** For all life and the life of our improvised music

2. Wisdom   **Dave:** An offering to the listener
   Grace   **Richie:** Our humble but strong attitude while playing this music

3. Truth   **Dave:** Especially obvious when improvising
   Ephemeral **Richie:** That which is fleeting and the permanent state of mind involved in creating this music

4. Beauty   **Dave:** Hopefully one of the elements the listener feels and takes with him or her
   Intuition **Richie:** That which is felt rather than thought or learned

5. Integrity **Dave:** Like truth but adheres to universal values beyond the music
   Humanity **Richie:** The collective unconscious embedded in all of us if we choose to listen

6. Telepathy **Dave:** Cannot be planned but obvious when it is happening
   Joy **Richie:** One of the essential elements of musical expression, sometimes easily forgotten

7. Empathy **Dave:** What this is all about
   Richie: The essence of our shared state of musical and emotional being ... the foundational condition for creating this music

Music by Dave Liebman
& Richie Beirach

Dave Liebman: soprano sax, tenor sax
Richie Beirach: piano

Recorded by Florian Van Volxem at CMP Studio, Zerkall, Germany October 2018

Produced by Kurt Renker

CD 2
Dave Liebman - Richie Beirach - Jack DeJohnette

Lifelines

Imagine a recording date with three very old friends and colleagues who have played and recorded together for fifty years. Dave on saxes, Jack on drums, myself on piano—we came together one afternoon in September, 2019, in upstate New York for an unusual recording date, just piano, sax and drums. That's right, no bass. And the music to be recorded? That is what lead to the uniqueness of this special meeting. There were no predetermined tunes to be recorded. We agreed to meet, say hello, sit down, and improvise the entire recording, trusting the outcome of the meeting completely to our individual and collective imaginations. No easy feat! Free improvisation has been around in jazz famously since Lennie Tristano recorded some short, free pieces in the late 1940s. The artistic challenge is, did the essential quality and sustained interest of the music pass the test? Especially considering the pressures of coming up with truly spontaneous compositions.

It was a very relaxed but intensely focused experience for the three of us. We have deep musical connections with each other that gave us a wonderful reservoir of collective and individual musical vocabularies. This enabled us to access and draw upon these factors instead of relying on predetermined tunes that make up the more familiar and usual kind of springboards for jazz improvisations.

| felt a very deep and magical atmosphere pervading the entire session. There was not much talking about the music before or after.

When we finally listened back to the tracks we, as well as the few folks in the studio, were surprised and elated how the eight tracks covered many different moods, colors, tempos, and textures. We left feeling very good, imbued with a kind of mysterious new feeling of connection.

Words are difficult to describe music under the best of conditions. I will just say that the true spirit of jazz improvisation is alive and well on this recording.

1. Lifelines
2. Firestorm
3. Nowness
4. In The Wind
5. Landslide
6. Synchronicity
7. Tightrope
8. Lamentation

Music by Dave Liebman, Richie Beirach and Jack DeJohnette

Dave Liebman: tenor and soprano saxes
Richie Beirach: piano
Jack DeJohnette: drums

Recorded by Scott Petito at NRS Recording Studio, Catskill NY September 2019
Mixed by Florian Van Volxem at CMP Studio, Zerkall, Germany
Produced by Kurt Renker

CD 3
Dave Liebman

Aural Landscapes

It is true that this solo sax CD is built from combinations of intervals, and yes, intervals are the basic building blocks of all music. But what needs to be said is this—the way Dave puts his intervals together creates so much more than any words can describe this music. It speaks volumes to me about life, love, integrity, tragedy, joy, redemption, acceptance, and the triumph of the human spirit through sound, through Dave's saxes, and flute and piano.

This CD is a beautiful and fascinating personal musical trip through Dave's kaleidoscopic vision!

1. - 15. Aural Landscape 1 - 15

Music by Dave Liebman

Dave Liebman: Tenor Sax, Soprano Sax, Piano, Wooden Flute
Recorded by Florian Van Volxem at CMP Studio, Zerkall, Germany August 2019
Produced by Kurt Renker

CD 4
Richie Beirach

Heart Of Darkness (Improvised Dedications)

My first solo piano recording, *Hubris*, was done in 1977 and released on ECM Records. During the last 43 years I have recorded many more solo CDs but this new recording stands out to me in many ways. It's not easy to describe why, but iIwill try.

I wanted to set up a challenging musical situation in order to stimulate my creativity. I wanted to do something new, something dramatic, to take risks, and reach for the unknown.

So after discussions with Kurt Renker, my old friend and producer of many of my recordings for the last 35 years, we came to this idea—I would go in to the solo piano recording date with no compositions! No preconceived notions of what to record, in other words no preparation except to try and empty my musical mind so at the moment of actual recording, I would be forced to start from zero and play what I hear and therefore create a whole CDs worth of piano music that would still be interesting to listen to.

Keith Jarrett began his long career with many improvised solo piano recordings and I always admired him for his courage and his wonderful imagination. He was a big inspiration for me especially in the 1970s and '80s.

This process of recording totally improvised piano music is very different than recording my compositions or standard tunes. I enjoy both of course, but the challenge and risk regarding totally spontaneous recording was just the stimulation I needed. The result has exceeded my expectations and proves an old but true saying, no risk no reward!!

The last piece called "Tschernobyl Diary" was the one piece loosely conceived before recording it. But it was just a mental sketch with again nothing at all on paper.

Curiously we didn't listen to anything during the entire recording process, which is highly unusual. Days after the recording while listening for the first time to the rough tracks I was very surprised and happy about the results. Jotting down ideas about titles for the tracks, I looked at my page of notes and it read like a list of my mentors, heroes, and inspirations, not only in music but in painting, poetry, playwriting, contemporary classical composers, and of course my essential group of great jazz musicians including pianists, drummers, sax players and trumpeters. This gave me the idea to dedicate this music to my mentors and heroes.

I must say I do feel proud of this new fresh piano music and hope you will find interest and pleasure in listening.

1. Long Days Journey Into Night
   (For John Coltrane, Miles Davis and Bill Evans)

2. Ancient Sound
   (For Paul Klee, Wayne Shorter and Rainer Maria Rilke)

3. Footsteps In The Air
   (For Claude Debussy, Maurice Ravel and Frederico Mompou)

4. Black Paintings
   (For Mark Rothko and Alexander Nikolayevich Scriabin)

5. Stillpoint

   (For Morton Feldman)

6. Drone Spirit
   (For Zbigniew Seifert and Béla Bartók)

7. Quantum Jazz
   (For Elvin Jones, Tony Williams and Jack DeJohnette)

8. In The Dark Park
   (For Charles Ives)

9. In My End Is My Beginning
   (For Tōru Takemitsu)

10. Heart Of Darkness / Tschernobyl Diary
    (For György Ligeti and McCoy Tyner) / (For The People of Tschernobyl)

Music by Richie Beirach
Richie Beirach: piano

Recorded by Florian Van Volxem at CMP Studio, Zerkall, Germany July 2020
Produced by Kurt Renker

CD 5
Dave Liebman, Richie Beirach, Florian Van Volxem

Aftermath

Listening once again to this music it still sounds like a dazed walk through the aftermath of a gigantic apocalypse. Or waking up from a 100 year sleep and remembering this music as if a dream, or nightmare. It is pretty dark and menacingly forbidding. It's scary and bleak in spots which is what

I think we are coming to sooner or later, especially considering the way the world is moving and with the characters that are supposedly running it. Things are definitely not cool in the world these days and seem to be getting worse every day. This music is a kind of commentary from myself,

Dave, Florian, and Kurt about the grim and fearful realities pervading the scene, but it also has moments of beauty, calm, and even love weaving in and out. We never sound angry, for which I am glad, and for us to be able to express intensity with power, force, and volume without any unnecessary harshness is a goal we have had for years.

But this recording is mind-blowing for me personally as Florian, Dave, Kurt, and myself were totally in this project together. The moods are intense and sustained with many strands of over-dubbed improvisation entering and exiting like streams of water coming down from a mountain, all eventually pouring into a lake. It is very dark in general but the bright colors of the prepared piano and the wooden flute keep it from being overly depressing and monotoned out.

The music is powerful and sensuous at the same time. The tenor sax, soprano sax, and flutes are like the protagonists in a play, carrying the messages and commenting on the incredibly rich backgrounds with great calmness at times, but also a sense of crazy frenzy. I like the acoustic piano sound against the prepared piano along with the electric piano. There are vast horizons suggested by playing inside the piano strings of the massive nine foot Bechstein concert grand piano in Kurt's studio, residing for years in the forest of Zerkall. I must say that Kurt and especially Florian, whose whole idea was the instigating catalyst for this project, have hit it out of the park! It's not easy to make the necessary choices as to which strands to bring in and out and discover exactly where in the overall tapestry of sound does this music become whole.

1. Aftermath

Dave Liebman: Tenor Sax, Soprano Sax, Wooden Flute, C-Flute
Richie Beirach: Piano, Prepared Piano, Electric Piano
Florian Van Volxem: Buchla Synthesizer

Basic Track:
Leo Henrichs: Modified Tympani and Gong Constructed by Kurt Renker

Recorded by Florian Van Volxem at CMP Studio, Zerkall, Germany 2016/2017
Producer – Kurt Renker

The Complete Liebman-Beirach Discography

1970	Dave Liebman & Carvel Six - *Night Scapes* (CBS/Sony Records)
1973	Dave Liebman - *First Visit* (Philips Really Records, Japan)
	Dave Liebman - *Lookout Farm* (ECM Records)
1974	Dave Liebman - *Drum Ode* (ECM Records)
1975	Lookout Farm - *New Jazz Festival Hamburg '75* (Sampler) (Polydor Records)
	Lookout Farm - *At Onkel Pö's Carnegie Hall 1975* (Jazzline Records)
	Lookout Farm - (Jugoton Records) *Jazz Na Koncertnom Podiju* Vol. 1 (Sampler)
	Frank Tusa - *Father Time* (Enja Records)
	Dave Liebman - *Sweet Hands* (A&M Horizon Records)
	Badal Roy - *Passing Dreams* (Geetika Records)
	Dave Liebman + Richie Beirach - *Forgotten Fantasies* (A&M Horizon)
1976	Lookout Farm *Live 1976* (Mosaic Records)
	Dave Liebman + Richie Beirach - *Live 1976* (Mosaic Records)
	Dave Liebman + Richie Beirach - *The Duo Live 1976 + 1990* (Vaju Prod.)
	Dave Liebman + Pee Wee Ellis - *Light'n Up Please!* (A&M Horizon)
1978	Dave Liebman Quintet - *Pendulum* (Artists House Records)
	Dave Liebman Quintet - *Pendulum* Complete Recordings (Mosaic Records)
	Dave Liebman + Richie Beirach - *Omerta* (Trio Records Japan)

1979	**John McNeil** - *Faun* (SteepleChase Records)
	Dave Liebman - *Dedications* (CMP Records)
1981	**Quest** - *Quest* (Trio Records Japan)
1985	**Dave Liebman + Richie Beirach** - *The Duo Live* (Advance Music)
	Dave Liebman + Richie Beirach - *Double Edge* (Storyville Records)
1986	**Quest** - *Quest II* (Storyville Records)
1987	**Quest** - *Midpoint : Live In The Montmartre* (Storyville Records)
	Dave Liebman/Wayne Shorter/Richie Beirach - *Tribute To John Coltrane - Live Under The Sky* (Columbia Records)
1988	**Quest** - *Live* (Mosaic Records)
	Quest - *Live 1988 + 1991* (Vaju Prod.)
	Quest - *N.Y. Nites - Standards* (Pan Music)
	Quest - *Natural Selection* (Pathfinder Records)
1989	**Dave Liebman + Richie Beirach** - *Chant* (CMP Records)
1990	**Dave Liebman + Richie Beirach** - *Live 1990* (Mosaic Records)
	Quest - *Of One Mind* (CMP Records)
1991	**Quest** - *Live 1991* (Mosaic Records)
1996	**Conrad Herwig** - *New York Breed* (Double-Time Records)
1997	**Frank Tusa** - *Reunion Of Old Spirits* (Frank Tusa Records)
2005	**Quest** - *Redemption: Quest Live in Europe* (hatOLOGY Records)
2007	**Quest** - *Re-Dial (Live in Hamburg)* (Outnote Records)
2008	**Quest** - *Live 2008* (Vaju Prod.)

The Complete Liebman-Beirach Discography

2009 **Dave Liebman + Richie Beirach** + Frankfurt Radio Bigband - *Quest For Freedom* (Sunnyside Records)

Dave Liebman + Richie Beirach - *New Life: Live in Cologne* (Vaju Prod.)

Dave Liebman + Richie Beirach - *Unspoken* (Outnote Records)

2010 **Dave Liebman + Richie Beirach + Lee Konitz** - *Knowinglee* (Outnote Records)

Quest - *Live in Paris* (Vaju Prod.)

2011 **Quest** - *Circular Dreaming* (Enja Records)

Dave Liebman + Steve Dalachinsky - *The Fallout Of Dreams* (Rogue Art)

Dave Liebman + Richie Beirach - *Beyond Words: Live in Poland* (Vaju Prod.)

2013 **Quest** - *Live in New York* (Vaju Prod.)

Quest - *Live at the Detroit Jazz Festival 2013* (Vaju Prod.)

2015 **Dave Liebman + Richie Beirach** - *Balladscapes* (Intuition Records)

Fred Farrell - *Distant Song - Fred Farrell Sings The Music Of Dave Liebman + Richie Beirach* (Whaling City Sound)

2017 **Dave Liebman + Richie Beirach** - *Eternal Voices* (Jazzline Records)

2021 **Dave Liebman + Richie Beirach** - *Empathy* (Jazzline Records)

Our List of Essential Jazz and Classical Recordings

Jazz

Art Blakey
A Night at Birdland (1954)

Paul Bley
Footloose (1962/63)
Open, to Love (1972)

John Coltrane
Giant Steps (1960)
Ballads (1961/62)
Impressions (1963)
Live at Birdland (1963
Crescent (1964)
Transition (1965)
Expression (1967)

Miles Davis
Round About Midnight (1957)
Milestones (1958)
Kind of Blue (1959)
Sketches of Spain (1960)
My Funny Valentine (1964)
Four and More (1964)
E.S.P. (1965)
Sorcerer (1967)
Nefertiti (1967)

Bill Evans
Portrait in Jazz (1959)
Sunday at the Village Vanguard (1961)
Conversations with Myself (1963)

Gil Evans
The Individualism of Gil Evans (1963/64)

Herbie Hancock
Maiden Voyage (1965)
Speak Like A Child (1968)

Joe Henderson
Inner Urge (1964)

Charlie Parker, Dizzy Gillespie, Bud Powell, Charles Mingus, Max Roach
Jazz at Massey Hall (1953)

Bud Powell
The Amazing Bud Powell
Vol. 1 and 2 (1952/1954)

Sonny Rollins
A Night at the Village Vanguard (1958)

George Russell
Jazz in the Space Age (1960)

Wayne Shorter
Speak No Evil (1964)
The All Seeing Eye (1965)

McCoy Tyner
The Real McCoy (1967)

Classical

Johann Sebastian Bach (1685 - 1750)
Goldberg Variations
1980 version
Glenn Gould: piano

The Well-Tempered
Clavier, Book 1 + 2
Swjatoslaw Teofilow-
itsch Richter: piano

Wolfgang Amadeus Mozart
(1756 - 1791)
Complete Piano Concertos
Arthur Rubinstein: piano

Mozart Requiem
Leonard Bernstein: conductor

Frederic Chopin (1810 - 1849)
Etudes and Balades
Maurizio Pollini: piano

Franz Liszt (1811 - 1886)
Piano Sonata in B minor
Vladimir Horowitz: piano

Sergei Vasilyevich Rachmaninoff
(1873 - 1943)
Piano Concerto No. 2

Claude Debussy (1862 - 1918)
Préludes, Volume 1 & 2
Arturo Benedetti Michelangeli: piano

Alexander Scriabin (1872 - 1915)
Preludes For Piano
Ruth Laredo: piano

Piano Sonatas 1–10
Vladimir Ashkenazy: piano

Arnold Schoenberg (1874 - 1951)
The Piano Music
Maurizio Pollini: piano

5 Pieces for Orchestra
Pierre Boulez: conductor

Charles Ives (1874 - 1954)
Central Park in the Dark
Leonard Bernstein: conductor

The Unanswered Question
Leonard Bernstein: conductor

Maurice Ravel (1875 - 1937)
Piano Concerto in G major
Arturo Benedetti Michelangeli: piano,
Sergiu Celibidache: conductor

Béla Bartók (1881 - 1945)
Concerto For Orchestra
Leonard Bernstein: conductor

Music For Strings, Percussion And Celesta
Leonard Bernstein: conductor

The Six String Quartets
Guarneri String Quartet

14 Bagatelles for piano Op. 6
Ruth Laredo: piano

Igor Stravinsky (1882 - 1971)
The Rite of Spring
Leonard Bernstein: conductor

Alban Berg (1885 - 1935)
Concerto For Violin And Orchestra
'To The Memory Of An Angel
Isaac Stern: violin, Leonard
Bernstein: conductor

Piano Sonata in B Minor, Op. 1
Glenn Gould: piano

Sergei Sergeyevich Prokofiev
(1891 - 1953)
Piano Concerto No. 2 in
G Minor, Op. 16
Yuja Wang: piano
Gustavo Dudamel: conductor

Federico Mompou (1893 - 1987)
Música Callada
Alicia de Larrocha: piano

Dmitri Shostakovich (1906 - 1975)
Symphony No. 5 in D Minor op. 47
Waleri Abissalowitsch
Gergijew: conductor

Olivier Messiaen (1908 - 1992)
Vingt Regards sur l'Enfant-Jésus
Peter Serkin: piano

Quartet for the End of Time
Tashi Ensemble

György Ligeti (1923 - 2006)
Atmosphères for Orchestra
Pierre Boulez

Lux aeterna
Pierre Boulez: conductor

Requiem
Pierre Boulez: conductor

Pierre Boulez (1925 - 2016)
sur Incises
Pierre Boulez: conductor

Tōru Takemitsu (1930 - 1996)
Requiem for String Orchestra
Seiji Ozawa: conductor

Waterscape / Water-Ways
Tashi Ensemble

Piano Distance
Peter Serkin: piano

Addresses in New York

These are some of the places in Brooklyn and Manhattan that played an important role in our lives. It lists the places were we grew up, our schools, apartments and lofts where we lived, jazz clubs where we played and hung out, and restaurants that we frequented. Some places are still around but unfortunately many have disappeared.

Dave

First Home
1328 East Fifth Street, Brooklyn, NY 11230

Public School 99 Isaac Asimov
1120 East 10th Street, Brooklyn, NY 11230

Other Homes
138 West 19th Street, New York, NY 10011
83 Warren Street, New York, NY 10007
114 Lexington Ave, New York, NY 10016
800 Sixth Avenue, New York, NY 10001

Richie

First Home
1649 East Second Street, Brooklyn, NY 11230

Public School 177
346 Avenue P, Brooklyn, NY 11204

Other Homes
305 Spring Street, New York, NY 10013

Stores

Gem Spa
131 Second Avenue, New York, NY 10003

Bleecker Bob's Records
118 West Third Street, New York, NY 10012

Music Inn - World Instruments
169 West Fourth Street, New York, NY 10014

Restaurants and Bars

Wo Hop Chinese restaurant
17 Mott Street, New York, NY 10013

Buffalo Roadhouse Grill
57 Seventh Avenue South, New York, NY 10014

Pink Tea Cup
88 Seventh Avenue South, New York, NY 10014

Katz's Delicatessen
205 East Houston Street, New York, NY 10002

Ratner's Restaurant
138 Delancey Street, New York, NY 10002

Stromboli Pizza
83 St Marks Place, New York, NY
10003

McSorley's Old Ale House
15 East Seventh Street, New York, NY
10003

Music Venues
Village Vanguard
178 Seventh Avenue South, New York,
NY 10014

Sweet Basil
88 Seventh Avenue South, New York,
NY 10014

Seventh Avenue South
21 Seventh Avenue South, New York,
NY 10014

St. James Infirmary
22 Seventh Avenue South, New York,
NY 10014

The Half Note
296 Spring Street, New York, NY
10013

George Braith's Musart
149 Spring Street, New York, NY
10012

Pookie's Pub
282 Hudson Street, New York, NY
10013

The Village Gate
160 Bleecker Street, New York, NY
10012

Boomer's
340 Bleecker Street, New York, NY
10014

The Bitter End
147 Bleecker Street, Brooklyn, NY
11221

Cafe Au Go Go
152 Bleecker Street, New York, NY
10012

Lush Life
184 Thompson Street, New York, NY
10012

Five Spot Café
2 St. Marks Place, New York, NY
10003

The Bottom Line
15 West Fourth Street, New York, NY
10014

Bradley's
70 University Place, New York, NY
10003

Fillmore East
105 Second Avenue, New York, NY
10003

Fat Tuesdays
190 Third Avenue, New York, NY
10003

Glossary

Bird – Charlie Parker's nickname among jazz musicians. He was called Bird because his fast saxophone solos sounded like a bird in flight.

Blowing – Jazz musicians term for improvisation.

Burn – Jazz musicians term for usually uptempo, intense, and energetic improvisation or a tune.

Chromaticism – A way of improvising and composing that involves the free use of the chromatic notes in the scale that accompany a chord.

Comping – Accompaniment. Either for a soloist or for the pianist using his left hand to accompany his right hand.

Corny – Jazz musicians use this word to define music that sounds out of date, schmaltzy, and kitschy.

Head – Usually the melody chorus of a tune.

Mofo – An abbreviation for "motherfucker" used by jazz musicians to show respect and admiration for the brilliance of a great solo or a tune. As in "your solo was a mofo."

Newk – Sonny Rollins nickname among jazz musicians. Newk because he resembled the great baseball pitcher Don Newcombe.

Pedal point – A pedal point is a fixed note that allows for improvisation over it. This greatly simplifies and opens up the possibilities of improvisation over the pedal point rather than the chord progression.

Pentatonics – Melodic phrases based on the intervals of major 2nd, perfect 4th, and perfect 5th. A pentatonic scale means a five-tone scale.

Polychord – A structure made up of more than one chord, superimposed together.

Reharm / Reharmonization – When a simple or traditional chord progression is re-imagined with more interesting chord changes and chord voicings.

Superimposed – When one triad is layered over another triad or a bass note.

Standards – For a jazz player it means tunes from the 1930s, '40s, and '50s from Broadway shows or movie themes. Jazz standards are classic jazz tunes like "Take the A Train" by Billy Strayhorn, "Round Midnight" by Thelonious Monk, and "Night In Tunisia" by Dizzy Gillespie.

Tessitura – Register

Tonguing – One way a saxophone player uses his tongue to articulate his notes.

Trane – John Coltrane. His nickname among jazz musicians.

Voicing – A particular way of arraigning the notes in a chord in a personal and creative way.

Caris, Dave, and Richie Jerusalem 1980s

Dedications

Dave: I would like to express my gratitude to my wife Caris ...for her support and deep musical judgment through the years.

Richie: I want to dedicate the book to the memory of Chris Scheuber.

Image Credits

Dave Liebman Collection
Page 12, 17, 19, 24, 26, 28, 76, 159, 161, 163, 222, 253, 258, 294

Richie Beirach Collection
Page 175

Tara Enke
Page 1

All other photos by Kurt Renker

Record icon by Made from NounProject.com

Dave & Richie 2019

About the Authors

Dave Liebman

NEA Jazz Master (2011) David Liebman's career has spanned nearly five decades, beginning in the early 1970s as the saxophone/flautist in both the Elvin Jones and Miles Davis Groups, continuing as a bandleader since. He has played on over five hundred recordings with nearly two hundred under his leadership and co-leadership. In jazz education he is a renowned lecturer and author of several milestone books: *Self Portrait Of A Jazz Artist*, *A Chromatic Approach To Jazz Harmony And Melody*, *Developing A Personal Saxophone Sound* (translated into multiple languages), in addition to teaching DVDs, journalistic contributions to periodicals, and published chamber music. The current group Expansions features some of the best of the younger generation. Lieb is the Founder and Artistic Director of the International Association of Schools of Jazz (IASJ) existing since 1989, which is a worldwide network of schools from nearly 40 countries. Liebman's awards, besides the NEA honor include the Jazz Educators Network (JEN) Legends of Jazz (2013); the Order of Arts and Letters (France 2009); Jazz Journalist's award for Soprano Saxophone (2007); Grammy nomination for Best Jazz Solo (1998); Honorary Doctorate from the Sibelius Academy (Finland-1997). He is currently teaching at the Manhattan School of Music and a guest lecturer at Berklee College of Music. Dave has consistently placed in the top positions for Soprano Saxophone in the *Downbeat*, *Jazz Times* and *JazzEd* polls since 1973.

Richie Beirach

Richie Beirach was born in Brooklyn and started playing the piano at the age of five. In the mid-1960s, Beirach entered the New York club scene, playing with, among others, Freddie Hubbard and Lee Konitz while at the same time occasionally working as a longshoreman at the docks of New York. After studying at Berklee College Of Music, he returned to New York in 1968 and graduated from the Manhattan School Of Music in 1972 with a Master Of Music.

In 1973, he joined the group Lookout Farm with saxophone player Dave Liebman. Lookout Farm became one of the most outstanding groups of the fusion movement and the natural collaboration between Beirach and Liebman developed into a lifelong musical partnership.

In the 1980s, Richie Beirach focused increasingly on the solo piano and co-founded the band Quest with Dave Liebman, touring Europe, Asia and South and North America.

Richie has been retired from his professorship teaching in Leipzig and since 2015 and is living in Hessheim, Germany.

Index

Symbols

9/11 memories 140
12-tone 44, 45, 46, 73
100 Club 144, 152

A

A & M Records 27, 29, 30, 234, 281
AACM 12
Abercrombie, John 15, 16, 20, 21, 27, 29, 31, 37, 138, 149, 170, 204, 226, 227, 228, 229, 241
Absord Music 241
ACT Records 201
Adams, Pepper 63
Adderley, Cannonball 135
Advance Music 51, 243, 244, 282
Ali, Rashied 83, 144, 150, 174, 175
Alias, Don 18, 20, 27, 29, 140, 143, 227
Ali's Alley (club) 35, 152
Allard, Joe 60
Allen, Steve 116
Allen, Woody 132, 144
Alpert, Herb 27, 234
Altschul, Barry 9, 73, 228, 229
Angry Squire (club) 141
Armando, Ray 20, 228, 229
Armstrong, Louis 49, 50, 81, 82, 180, 181, 192, 211
Artists House Records 33, 236, 241, 281
Avey, Bobby 202, 205
Ayler, Albert 45
Ayler, Donald 144

B

Bach, Johann Sebastian 43, 44, 46, 48, 50, 52, 182, 193, 259, 267, 269, 270, 289
The Back Fence (club) 144
Baker, Chet 13, 27, 31, 32, 35, 38, 58, 62, 67, 93, 165, 167–169, 189, 210, 211–212, 236, 246, 257
Baker, David 32, 236, 238, 239, 240, 242
Baker, Ginger 144
Barkan, Todd 207
Baron, Arthur 207
Bartók, Béla 6, 46, 47, 52, 75, 211, 269, 270, 289
Basie, Count 134
Becker, Joachim 273
Beethoven, Ludwig van 44, 47, 52, 77, 180, 182, 193, 207, 269
Belushi, John 140
Benson, George 27, 212
Berg, Alban 6, 45, 46, 73, 126, 188, 206, 289
Berg, Bob 12, 138
Berklee College of Music 59, 120
Bernstein, Leonard 180, 289
The Bill Evans Trio 6, 241, 252
Bill Haley and the Comets 108
Birdland (club) 35, 102, 118, 134, 156, 174, 236, 265, 288
Bishop, Walter Jr. 144
The Bitter End (club) 144, 292
Blade, Brian 87
Blakey, Art 58, 81, 87, 93, 98, 189, 232, 288
Bley, Paul 6, 17, 53, 55, 98, 151, 288

307

Blue Coronet Club 8
Blue Note (club) 35, 82, 152
Blue Note Records 73, 94, 147
Booker, Walter 149
Boomer's (club) 37, 140, 142, 152, 292
Bostic, Earl 175
Bottom Line (club) 144, 152, 292
Boulez, Pierre 11, 46, 61, 289, 290
Brackeen, Joanne 155, 206
Bradley's (club) 35, 37, 38, 39, 108, 147, 148, 149, 152, 292
Brahms, Johannes 44, 180
Braxton, Anthony 9, 12, 73
Brechtlein. Tom 76
Brecker, Michael 9, 16, 35, 82, 108, 142, 147, 185, 211
Brecker, Randy 9, 16, 31, 35, 74, 114, 137, 142, 147, 170, 236, 238, 252
Brookmeyer, Bob 210
Brown, Cameron 8
Brown, Clifford 168
Brown, James 10, 29, 71, 162
Brubeck, Dave 27, 93
Bruce, Jack 144
Bucher, Ernst 270
Burns, Ken 131
Burton, Gary 210
Butler, George 94, 247
Byrd, Donald 63, 137

C

Cables, George 155, 206
Cafe Au Go Go (club) 35, 152, 292
Cafe Bohemia 152
Calderazzo, Joey 70
Campbell, John 202
Canterino, Sonny and Mike 139
Cantor, Goldie 118
Carrington, Terri Lyne 207
Carter, Ron 73, 87, 134, 149, 168, 170, 201, 207, 210, 213, 249
CBS Sony Records 54, 247
The Cellar (club) 144
Chaikin, Joe 13

Chambers, Paul 172
Changuito 256
Charles, Ray 162, 168
Chopin, Frédéric 44, 45, 52, 180, 182, 193, 207, 231, 289
Christensen, Jon 15
Citron, Warren 5
Clapton, Eric 144
Clarke, Stanley 74
Cleopatra's Needle (club) 35
CMP Records 53, 239, 255, 282
CMP Studio 51, 260, 262, 266, 268, 272, 275, 276, 277, 278, 279
Cobb, Jimmy 65
Coleman, George 140
Coleman, Ornette 27, 98, 145
Coltrane, John 6, 10, 11, 14, 18, 22, 31, 32, 33, 35, 39, 45, 47, 49, 50, 59, 64, 69, 70, 73, 75, 77, 79–81, 83, 87–89, 93, 94, 102, 131, 134, 135, 137, 139, 140, 145, 156, 158, 160, 163, 168, 170, 174–176, 181, 185, 187, 192, 193, 198, 222, 232, 236, 245, 246, 247, 250, 260, 267, 270, 282, 288, 293
Coltrane, Naima 80
Columbia Records 94, 108, 245, 282
Cooper, Bob 140
Copland, Marc 138, 202, 205
Corea, Chick 8, 14, 15, 16, 17, 21, 22, 35, 46, 58, 65, 67, 70, 71, 73–78, 81, 83, 98, 151, 155, 156, 166, 170, 201, 205–207, 208, 210, 232
Coryell, Larry 5, 15
Cream 144, 204
Cummings, E.E. 142
Cunningham, Bradley 147, 148
Cunningham, Wendy 148
Curtis, King 108
Cuscuna, Michael 33

D

Dailey, Albert 37
Dalachinsky, Steve 283

Index

Davidovsky, Mario 47
Davis, Art 174
Davis, Bob 127
Davis, Clive 74
Davis, Miles 6, 8, 11, 13, 14, 15, 16, 18, 19, 27, 29, 31, 32, 33, 35, 47, 49, 50, 58, 59, 65–67, 72, 73, 74, 79, 83, 87, 88, 93, 94, 97, 102, 134–135, 136, 144, 151, 155, 160–162, 165, 166, 168, 170–171, 172, 175, 181, 185, 189, 190, 191, 192, 193, 195, 204–205, 208, 209, 210, 213, 218, 224, 226, 232, 236, 237, 241, 247, 264, 267, 288
Davis, Steve 175
Debussy, Claude 65, 71, 194, 267, 270, 289
DeJohnette, Jack 14, 21, 73, 74, 83–86, 88, 89, 94, 131, 137, 145, 165, 170, 208, 209, 210, 211, 218, 224, 225, 245, 246, 247, 249, 273, 275, 276
DeMicheal, Don 93
Desmond, Paul 49
Dobbins, Bill 51, 243, 244
Dolphy, Eric 88, 93, 134
The Dom (club) 145
Dorian, Pat 61
DownBeat magazine 30, 57, 93
Dreams 16

E

Ear Inn 139
East Village Inn 152
ECM Records 15–22, 30, 55, 67, 74, 77, 94, 226, 228, 229, 232, 234, 252, 264, 277, 281
The Ed Sullivan Show 129
Egger, Karl 17
Eicher, Manfred 15, 17–18, 20–22, 74, 94, 226, 227, 228, 229
Electric Lady Studios 28, 234, 235
Eleventh House (band) 15
Ellington, Duke 23, 35, 38, 49, 50, 69, 93, 181, 211
Ellis, Pee Wee 29, 30, 281
Emperor Jones. See Jones, Elvin
Energy Free Jazz 11
Enja Records 264, 281, 283
Evans, Bill (piano) 31, 32, 33, 35, 59, 64, 65–68, 71, 94, 98, 134, 147, 165, 168, 170, 172–173, 181, 194, 205, 232, 236, 246, 267, 288
Evans, Bill (sax) 151, 204
Evans, Gil 35, 65, 288
Evans, Harry 68
Expansions (band) 58

F

Farmer, Art 58, 189
Farrell, Fred 283
Farrell, Joe 74, 76, 140
Fat Tuesdays (club) 35, 114, 152, 292
Fauré, Gabriel 270
Fields, Lanny 11, 129
Fillmore East (club) 145, 292
The Five Spot (club) 79, 144, 145, 152, 292
Flanagan, Tommy 37, 38, 67, 69, 70, 187
Foster, Al 31, 85, 114, 144, 161, 203, 236, 237, 238, 241, 242, 252
Frampton, Peter 234
Free Life Communication 11–12, 13

G

Galper, Hal 210
Galprin, Luba 132
Garbarek, Jan 15, 18, 21, 232
Garland, Red 67, 172
Garner, Errol 212
Garrison, Jimmy 79, 135, 155, 174, 175, 249
Garson, Mike 118, 120, 134, 206
Gates. See Perla, Gene
Geetika Records 230, 281
Gem Spa 145, 146, 291

Getz, Stan 13, 28, 58, 83, 93, 94,
    165–166, 189, 210–211, 224, 246,
    257
Gillespie, Dizzy 49, 63, 70, 168, 209,
    288, 293
Gleason, Jackie 116
Golson, Benny 58, 63
Gomez, Eddie 88, 89, 172, 201, 212,
    239, 240, 245, 247
Gonzalez, Jerry 141
Goodman, Benny 23, 93, 230
Goodrick, Mick 204
Gordon, Max 31, 32, 33, 142
Gotti, John 118
Gould, Glenn 207, 289
Gravatt, Eric 29
Gregan, Eugene 20, 21, 226, 235
Grossman, Steve 9, 10, 14, 65, 138,
    147, 158, 204
Gruber, Hans and Veronika 51, 243,
    244

H

Haden, Charlie 27
Haig, Al 70, 148
Halburian, Armen 13, 223, 227
The Half Note (club) 62, 79, 139–140,
    152, 292
Hammer, Jan 143, 205
Hammond, John 94
Hancock, Herbie 6, 14, 17, 19, 35, 47,
    58, 59, 63, 67, 70, 71–72, 73, 81, 85,
    87, 97, 109, 134, 136, 137, 149, 155,
    170, 171, 201, 205, 206, 207, 208,
    210, 213, 218, 232, 288
Händel, Georg Friedrich 44
Hardman, Bill 137
Hart, Billy "Jabali" 32, 51, 85, 97, 203,
    217, 218, 248, 249, 250, 251, 252,
    253, 254, 255, 256, 265, 266
hatOLOGY (record label) 248, 282
Hauer, Josef 45
Hawes, Hampton 27

Hawkins, Coleman 35
Hayden, Tom 107
Haynes, Roy 73
Held, Pablo 54
Henderson, Joe 87, 93, 137, 189, 199,
    207, 232, 288
Hendricks, Jon 58
Hendrix, Jimi 6, 12, 28, 204
Herman, Woody 211
Herwig, Conrad 282
Hessischer Rundfunk Radio Big Band
    257, 258
Higgins, Billy 140
Hill, Calvin 147
Hillcrest Club 98
Hines, Earl 69
Hino, Terumasa 147, 150, 204
Holland, Claire and Louise 8
Holland, Dave 7–9, 12, 14, 53, 65, 73,
    83–84, 86, 94, 136, 165, 170, 208,
    209, 210, 211, 224, 225, 249
The Honeymooners 116
Horizon Records 22, 27, 29, 234, 281
Horowitz, Vladimir 135, 168, 207, 289
Hubbard, Freddie 58, 61, 67, 71, 93,
    168, 207, 212, 232
Huebner, Gregor 52, 201

I

Impulse Records 147, 175
Intuition Records 267, 283
Ives, Charles 6, 46, 73, 75, 206, 267,
    289

J

Jackson, Michael 184
Jacobs, Naomi 119
Janoson, Nancy 13, 223
Jarrett, Keith 14, 15, 17, 21, 22, 65, 71,
    72, 75, 98, 131, 201, 206, 218, 226,
    232, 277
Jazzline Records 232, 269, 273, 281,
    283

Index

Jenkins, Leroy 12
John Coltrane Quartet 6, 135, 241, 250, 252, 270
Johnson, David Earle 143
Johnson, J.J. 61
Jones, Elvin 10, 13, 15, 27, 31, 35, 58, 63, 71, 79, 80, 83, 93, 135, 138, 140, 158–159, 160, 174, 175, 185, 189, 204, 207, 210, 236, 246, 249
Jones, Hank 38, 187
Jones, Philly Joe 65, 66, 172, 205
Jones, Sam 140
Jones, Thad 35
Juris, Vic 204

K

Kaper, Bronisław 193
Katz's Delicatessen 114, 147, 291
Keane, Helen 147
Keepnews, Orin 94
Kelly, Wynton 65, 67, 71, 187, 218
Kern, Jerome 193, 194
Kerper, Mitch 14, 118
Keystone Korner (club) 207
Khachaturian, Aram 259
Khan, Sultan 25, 230, 231
King Records 94, 224
Kirkland, Kenny 70, 81, 82, 150, 204
Knickerbockers (club) 35, 148, 152
Kogan, Greg 150
Kong Arthur Hotel 249
Konitz, Lee 65, 222, 261–263, 283
Kramer, Eddie 28
Kubrick, Stanley 22
Kuhn, Steve 17, 69, 127, 175

L

La Roca, Pete 31, 32, 76, 155–157, 175, 206
La Boheme (club) 155
Lacy, Steve 101, 184
LaFaro, Scott 66, 249
Laird, Rick 76, 141

Lakatos, Tony 257, 258
LaSpina, Steve 148
Ledgerwood, LeeAnn 37, 141, 148
Lewis, Mel 35
Lieberman, Saul 7–9
Liebman, Caris 141, 149, 160, 294
Ligeti, György 11, 22, 43, 44, 46–48, 50, 182, 188, 270, 290
Lightsey, Kirk 37
Lincoln, Abbey 10
Lincoln Center 81, 82, 213
Lipman, Steve 120
Little, Wilbur 140
Lloyd, Charles 131, 218
Lone Star Cafe 152
Lookout Farm (band) 15–22, 23–26, 27, 30, 48, 127, 145, 221, 226, 230, 232, 233, 265, 281
  origin of name 20
Lovano, Joe 82, 141, 185
Lundval, Bruce 94
Lush Life (club) 35, 142, 144, 152, 292
Lutoslawski, Witold 46

M

Mahavishnu Orchestra 16, 17, 205
Mandel, Johnny 193
Mangelsdorf, Albert 184
Manhattan School of Music 6, 10, 52, 59, 60, 94, 140, 223, 270
Marino, Tony 129
Markowitz, Phil 202, 205
Marsalis, Branford 81, 82
Marsalis, Ellis 82
Marsalis, Jason 82
Marsalis, Wynton 65, 67, 81–82, 94
Matthews, Ronnie 37
Maupin, Benny 74
May, Tony 20, 229
McBee, Cecil 131
McClure, Ron 37, 51, 65, 114, 150, 197, 204, 217, 218, 248, 251, 252, 253, 254, 255, 256, 265, 266
McGovern's Bar 139

McJolt. See McClure, Ron
McLaughlin, John 16, 27, 137, 204, 205
McNeely, Jim 51, 52, 257, 258
McNeil, John 282
McSorley's Old Ale House 147, 292
Meadows, Audrey 116
Metheny, Pat 21, 204, 226
The Miles Davis Quintet 6, 87, 135, 201, 208, 213, 241, 252, 265
Milkowski, Bill 108
Miller, Mulgrew 37
Mingus, Charles 98, 236, 288
Mintz, Billy 129
Mitchell, Joni 140
Mitchell, Red 37, 38
Mompou, Frederic 52, 290
Moncur, Grachan III 144
Monet, Claude 75
Monk, Thelonious 75, 93, 145, 151, 175, 206, 209, 293
Monteverdi, Claudio 43
Montgomery, Wes 61, 63, 212, 218
Montmartre Club 248, 249, 250, 251
Moody, James 63
Moran, Gayle 76
Moreira, Airto 74
Morell, Marty 172
Morgan, Lee 137, 168
Mosaic Records 33, 281, 282
Moses, Bob 5, 10, 12, 13, 20, 142, 147, 155, 228, 229
Moss, Jerry 27, 234
Motian, Paul 249
Mouzon, Alphonse 29
Mozart, Wolfgang Amadeus 38, 44, 52, 71, 72, 77, 182, 193, 207, 269, 289
Mraz, George 37, 43, 149, 201, 241, 242
Mulligan, Gerry 134
Murray Louis Dance Company 13

Musart (club) 35, 152, 292
Musica Elettronica Viva 11

N

Newk. See Rollins, Sonny
Nola Studio 240
Nono, Luigi 11, 47
NRS Recording Studio 276
Nussbaum, Adam 32, 150, 204, 238

O

One Fifth Avenue 148, 152
Onkel Pö's Carnegie Hall (club) 232, 233
Outnote Records 259, 261, 282, 283

P

Palmieri, James 259, 269
Parker, Charlie "Bird" 6, 35, 49, 50, 69, 70, 87, 98, 162, 181, 192, 193, 209, 288, 293
Parker, Maceo 100
Pastorius, Jaco 108
Patitucci, John 87
Paul, Les 35
Penderecki, Krzysztof 46
Pepper, Jim 155
Perez, Danilo 87
Perla, Gene 20, 138, 142, 143, 158, 228, 229
Picasso, Pablo 77, 226
Pink Tea Cup (restaurant) 143, 291
Polydor Records 15, 76, 281
Pookie's Pub 140, 152, 292
Porter, Cole 193
Powell, Bud 49, 70, 73, 75, 206, 288
Presley, Elvis 129, 132, 211
Prez. See Young, Lester
Prokofiev, Sergei Sergeyevich 6, 46, 290
Purim, Flora 74

Index

Q

Quest (band) 13, 31, 37, 51, 65, 99, 128, 141, 161, 198, 217–220, 222, 241–242, 248–251, 252–254, 255–256, 264–266, 282, 283
Quintus, Walter 51, 64, 256, 260, 261, 262, 270

R

Ratner's (restaurant) 143, 267, 291
Ravel 71, 194, 267, 270, 289
Rehak, Frank 63
Reich, Steve 47
Renker, Kurt 1, 51, 53, 105, 239, 240, 254, 255, 256, 260, 261, 262, 265, 266, 267, 268, 271, 272, 273, 275, 276, 277, 278, 279
Return to Forever (band) 210, 232
Revolutionary Ensemble (band) 27
Rhinoceros (club) 140
Rhodes, Harold 18, 228
Rich, Buddy 212
Riverside Records 94
Rivers, Sam 53
Roach, Max 158, 160, 192, 288
Rodriguez, Bobby 141
Rogers, Richard 194
Roitman, David 5, 129
Rollins, Sonny "Newk" 31, 33, 35, 79, 87, 156, 181, 185, 192, 193, 194, 207, 236, 288, 293
Ronnie Scott's Jazz Club 8
Rowles, Jimmy 38, 187
Roy, Badal 18, 19, 20, 21, 23, 24, 25, 27, 221, 227, 228, 229, 230, 231, 232, 233, 234, 281
Rubin, Samuel 13
Rubinstein, Arthur 135, 168, 207, 289
Russell, George 98, 288
Rypdal, Terje 15, 18
Rzewski, Frederic 11

S

Samuel Rubin Foundation 13
Sanders, Pharoah 144, 174
Savio, Mario 107
Sawbuck (band) 30
Saxophone Summit (band) 185
Schildkraut, Dave 65
Schindelheimer (piano teacher) 121
Schoenberg, Arnold 6, 44–48, 49, 50, 52, 69, 73, 75, 126, 182, 267, 269, 270, 289
Schumann, Robert 193
Scientology 73, 74, 75, 76, 77, 81
Scofield, John 150, 170, 204, 205, 247
Scott, Tony 145
Scriabin, Alexander Nikolayevich 44, 46, 47, 52, 71, 267, 270, 289
Seventh Avenue South (club) 35, 142, 152, 204, 292
Shankar, Ravi 6, 10
Sharpe, Clarence "C" 144
Shaw, Woody 32, 63, 74, 212
Shepp, Archie 174
Shorter, Wayne 6, 8, 11, 14, 72, 87–89, 109, 134, 160, 165, 166, 170, 193, 201, 207, 208, 213, 219, 245, 247, 264, 267, 282, 288
Shostakovich, Dmitri 6, 46, 290
Silver, Horace 70, 210
Sims, Zoot 151
Six, Carvel 14, 221, 223, 281
Skidmore, Alan 8
Slug's Saloon 152
Smith, Cliff 134, 172
Smith, Eugene 151
Snyder, John 22, 27, 33, 95, 235, 236, 238
S.O.B. (club) 152
Sony Records 54, 94, 223, 247, 281
Spalding, Esperanza 207
Spielberg, Steven 114
Steig, Jeremy 29

Steinbeck, Alan 130
Steinberg, Eleana 20, 138, 227, 229
Stenson, Bobo 15, 205
The Steve Allen Show 88, 129, 170
Stitt, Sonny 84, 93
St. James Infirmary (club) 35, 142, 152, 292
Stockhausen, Karlheinz 11, 47, 48, 73, 182
Stone, Sly 71
Storyville Records 248, 282
Stöwsand, Thomas 20, 21
Stravinsky, Igor 6, 45, 46, 61
Strayhorn, Billy 38, 267, 293
Strykers (club) 144
Studio Rivbea (club) 152
Sunnyside Records 257, 283
Sunset Club 248, 249, 250, 251
Surf Maid Bar 152
Surman, John 8
Swallow, Steve 137, 155, 206
Sweet Basil (club) 35, 140, 142, 152, 292

T

Takemitsu, Tōru 46, 47, 48, 188, 290
Tatum, Art 69, 70, 181
Taylor, Cecil 37, 145, 180
Taylor, Creed 27
Ten Wheel Drive (band) 144
Thiele, Bob 175
Timmons, Bobby 71
Top of the Gate (club) 35, 152
Towner, Ralph 21, 210
Trane. See Coltrane, John
Tristano, Lennie 6, 261, 275
Troupe, Quincy 171
Tusa, Frank 13, 15, 18, 19, 31, 127, 223, 226, 227, 230, 231, 233, 236, 237, 238, 252, 265, 281, 282
Tyner, McCoy 6, 8, 10, 14, 67, 69–70, 71, 79, 135, 150, 174, 175, 205–207, 270, 288

U

Ulehla, Ludmila 52, 270

V

Valdés, Carlos "Patato" 20, 228, 229
Valente, Frank 122–124
van Gelder, Rudy 147
van Gogh, Vincent 75
Vanguard Studio 242
Van Volxem, Florian 53, 265, 266, 268, 271, 272, 273, 275, 276, 277, 278, 279
Veal, Charles 76, 240
Ventura, Charlie 108
Village Gate (club) 35, 62, 102, 142, 144, 152, 170, 292
Village Vanguard (club) 12, 31–33, 35, 39, 67, 72, 74, 75, 102, 134, 140, 141, 142, 152, 155, 168, 170, 171, 172, 174, 185, 190, 209, 236, 238, 241, 252, 288, 292
Visiones (club) 152
Vitous, Miroslav 29, 73, 74, 136

W

Wagner, Richard 44, 45
Walcott, Collin 20, 21, 228, 229
Walker, Junior 108
Walton, Cedar 69, 80, 140
Ware, Willbur 64
Washington, Dinah 66
Watts, Jeff 81
Weather Report 16, 17, 29, 109, 232
Webern, Anton 6, 45, 126
Wein, George 71
Werner, Kenny 61, 86, 202, 205, 207
White, Lenny 128
Williams, Jeff 15, 18, 19, 20, 21, 226, 227, 228, 229, 230, 231, 233, 265
Williams, Tony 8, 35, 73, 87, 134, 160, 168, 170, 171, 201, 207, 213, 218, 249

Willis, Larry 148
Wilson, Joe Lee 143
Wilson, Teddy 69
Wo Hop (restaurant) 9, 143, 291
Wonder, Stevie 89, 168
Woods, Phil 61
Workman, Reggie 80, 144

Y

Young, Lester 35, 38

Z

Zähringer, Egon 271
Zawinul, Joe 109, 136
Zemlinsky, Alexander von 44
Zigmund, Elliot 212
Zinno's (club) 148, 149, 152
Zwerin, Mike 135

Also from Cymbal Press

cymbalpress.com

CYMBAL
PRESS

Life in E Flat – The Autobiography of Phil Woods
Book of the Year - Jazz Journalists Association

Life in E Flat – The Autobiography of Phil Woods is the life story of the legendary saxophonist, composer, band leader, and National Endowment for the Arts Jazz Master. Look for it in paperback, hardcover, and e-book at cymbalpress.com.

Praise for Life in E Flat

"*Life in E-Flat* is a gift, a compelling and entertaining memoir by one of the leading alto saxophonists in jazz for 60 years. Phil Woods was a star soloist, influential lead alto player, savvy bandleader, underrated composer-arranger, and consummate studio musician. He was also a charismatic storyteller with a typewriter—literate, funny, insightful, self-aware, with a keen eye and ear for details that reveal character, including his own personal failings. Heroes and colleagues like Charlie Parker, Dizzy Gillespie, Quincy Jones, Benny Carter, and Ben Webster are drawn in quick, astute sketches. Observations about the music business, jazz education, and the vagaries of the jazz life are laced with wisdom and sardonic wit. The book is also an invaluable portrait of world that has vanished: Juilliard at midcentury, the band bus, the bustling post-war bebop academy of the streets, the New York studios of the '60s, the European jazz scene of the early '70s, and the energy and excitement of a remarkable life lived among some of the greatest giants in jazz history."

—Mark Stryker, author of *Jazz From Detroit*

"Phil Woods's voice on the page is as raw and lyrical and unmistakable as the sound of his alto. If you want to really know about The Life—the true day-to-day of a working jazz musician, with all its agonies and ecstasies and tedium and the ever-exciting challenge of getting paid something like what you're worth for playing your heart out—look no further. *Life in E Flat* pulls no punches and tells no lies."

—James Kaplan, author of *Sinatra: The Chairman, Frank: The Voice* and *Irving Berlin: New York Genius*

Jazz Dialogues with Jon Gordon

Backstage, on the bus, or in the studio, saxophonist Jon Gordon, winner of the prestigious Thelonious Monk International Jazz Saxophone competition, chats with several generations of great musicians. From Jay McShann to Renee Rosnes, *Jazz Dialogues* lets the reader hang out with dozens of jazz artists to learn about their careers, influences, and the dues they've paid. These candid, poignant, and often hilarious conversations paint a first-person portrait of jazz history.

Artists include: Jay McShann, Eddie Locke, Cab Calloway, Maria Schneider, Jan Garbarek, Ken Peplowski, Tim Hagans, Mark Turner, Hank Mobley, Bill Easley, Doc Cheatham, Scott Robinson, Eddie Bert, Phil Woods, Danny Bank, Billy Drummond, Ben Monder, Charles McPherson, Milt Hinton, Ben Riley, Bill Stewart, Art Blakey, Jon-Erik Kellso, Eddie Chamblee, Jimmy Lewis, Chuck Redd, Bill Charlap, McCoy Tyner, Melissa Aldana, Ronnie Mathews, Kevin Hays, Jim McNeely, Steve Wilson, Red Holloway, Barney Kessel, Joe Williams, Quincy Davis, Bob Mintzer, Dick Hyman, Lee Konitz, Leroy Jones, Renee Rosnes, David Sanborn, Gil Evans, Don Sickler, Sean Smith, Sarah Vaughn, Derrick Gardner, Sylvia Cuenca, Harold Mabern, Gene Bertoncini, Mike LeDonne, Essiet Okon Essiet, Bill Mays, and Joe Magnarelli.

Praise for Jazz Dialogues

"Jazz Dialogues is a rarity among books about jazz: It's a book about people—the individual creators who devote their lives to the making of this profoundly individualistic art. It took a writer who's a first-call musician himself to capture the way jazz artists think and feel, on the bandstand and off. From Cab Calloway and Doc Cheatham to Maria Schneider and Steve Wilson, Jon Gordon brings us face to face, mind to mind, heart to heart, with dozens of fascinating musicians. Like a great player in a jazz band, Gordon knows not only how to play, but how to listen."

—David Hajdu, author of *Lush Life: A Biography of Billy Strayhorn*

www.ingramcontent.com/pod-product-compliance
Lightning Source LLC
Chambersburg PA
CBHW070607170426
43200CB00012B/2616